DUBCEK

DUBCEK

WILLIAM SHAWCROSS

WEIDENFELD AND NICOLSON
5 Winsley Street London W1

SBN 297 00147 7

Printed in Great Britain by
Willmer Brothers Limited, Birkenhead

'That they should have done this to me, after I have dedicated my whole life to cooperation with the Soviet Union, is the great tragedy of my life.'

Alexander Dubcek at approximately 1.00 a.m. on 21 August 1968, on hearing that troops of his Warsaw Pact allies had illegally entered Czechoslovakia.

CONTENTS

ILLUSTRATIONS

DRAMATIS PERSONAE

STEFAN DUBCEK Slovak carpenter, born 1892; wandered the world. Joined Czechoslovak Communist Party, 1921; in Mauthausen Concentration Camp, 1943-5; died 1969.

ALEXANDER DUBCEK Born 27 November 1921.

KLEMENT GOTTWALD Czech carpenter and self-taught Marxist. Became Chairman of Czechoslovak Communist Party, 1929; exiled in Moscow, 1939-45; returned to Prague, 1945; became Premier of the National Front Coalition Government in which the Communists were the largest party. Asserted that 'Sneering at the Communists is not punishable by law, but will be one day!' Cleverly exploited crisis occasioned by resignation of bourgeois ministers and pressured Benes into accepting Communist Government, February 1948; President of the Republic, June 1948; died 14 March 1953. Succeeded as President by Antonin Zapotocky and as First Secretary of Party by Antonin Novotny.

ANTONIN NOVOTNY Born 1904; joined Czechoslovak Communist Party, 1917; leading official in Karlin, an industrial suburb of Prague, 1930; in Mauthausen, 1941-5. Excellent administrator, brilliant bureaucrat with no imagination. Notable for unquestioning acceptance of Moscow's orders and clichés and for dislike of Slovakia. Played an important part in the 1948 takeover of power. First Secretary of Party, 1953; President of the Republic, 1957; made himself President of the National Front, April 1959; liked personal power; position severely shaken by shock-waves of de-Stalinization, 1963; increasingly under attack from enemies within the Party, 1963-7; forced to resign as First Secretary, 5 January 1968; forced out of the Presidency and replaced by Ludvik

Svoboda, 22 March 1968; drummed out of the Central Committee and Party, 30 May 1968.

VILIAM SIROKY Slovak Communist who worked in Slovakia in the 1930s. Spent most of war in Bratislava prison. Chairman of Slovak Communist Party, 1945-55; loyal spokesman of Prague Centralism; Premier of Czechoslovakia, 1953-63; forced to resign in de-Stalinization of 1963. Hated in Slovakia.

KAROL BACILEK Czech Communist who worked all his life in Slovakia. Close associate of Siroky and disciple of Novotny. Minister of State Control, 1950-1; Minister of State Security, 1952-3; these two jobs gave him a leading role in the Stalinist purges. First Secretary of the Slovak Communist Party, 1953-63; replaced by Dubcek, 1963. Despised by most Slovaks.

JAN MASARYK Son of President Masaryk, Foreign Minister in postwar coalition. Fell to his death from his bathroom window, March 1948; officially he committed suicide – thousands of Czechs believe that he was murdered. (See Claire Sterling, *The Masaryk Case,* Andre Deutsch, London, 1970).

VLADOMIR CLEMENTIS Slovak Communist and ardent Nationalist, Masaryk's successor at Foreign Ministry; tried for 'bourgeois-nationalism' and executed, 1951.

GUSTAV HUSAK Slovak intellectual, born 1913; studied law at Charles University, Prague; led Slovak Communist Party during the war and organized the Slovak Revolt against the Germans. Became Vice-President and then President of the Slovak Board of Commissioners which ruled Slovakia 1945-8, Premier of Slovakia, 1948; dismissed from Board and Premiership, 1950; tried for 'bourgeois-nationalism' and sentenced to life imprisonment, April 1954; released, 1960; partially rehabilitated, 1963. During 1963-7 not allowed to re-enter political life; worked at Slovak Academy of Sciences; allowed space in Slovak press by Dubcek. Well-loved in

Slovakia; brought back into political life by popular demand, January 1968; at once appeared as a most radical reformer. Became Slovak First Secretary after Vasil Bilak's alleged complicity with the invaders, August 1968; spent next eight months in trying to please Moscow; succeeded Dubcek as First Secretary of Czechoslovak Communist Party, 17 April 1969. Has since systematically destroyed the reforms he helped to build.

LACO NOVOMESKY First-rate Slovak poet; Communist; Husak's best friend.

KAROL SMIDKE Czech Communist sent from Moscow to control Husak, 1943; failed; worked with Husak and became great Slovak hero; accused of 'bourgeois-nationalism' and died in disgrace, 1950.

OTA SIK Czech Communist, born Pilzen 1919. Imprisoned in Mauthausen with Novotny and Stefan Dubcek. Taught economics at various Czech universities, 1945-60; elected to Central Committee of Czechoslovak Communist Party and became Director of Economic Institute of Prague's Academy of Sciences, 1962; began to draw up plans for New Economic Model, 1965; put into effect January 1967; total failure because of emasculation by the government. During Prague Spring one of the most ardent and radical reformers. Hated by the Russians. Since the invasion has taught at Basle University.

JOSEF SMRKOVSKY Czech Communist; helped lead Prague Uprising against Nazis, May 1945; refused to allow General Patton, already at Pilzen, to relieve Prague: he wanted the Red Army to arrive first. Fighting in the city therefore lasted fifteen hours longer than otherwise, but the Russians got the glory. Worked on collectivization of agriculture, 1946-50; tried and found guilty of being a Gestapo agent, 1951; imprisoned for life; released 1954. Novotny's Minister of Forestry and Water Economy, became one of the most outspoken and popular of the reformers; Dubcek's right-hand man. His speech on 29 August 1968 was remarkable for its frankness and mirrored exactly the fears and despairs of millions of Czechoslovaks.

LUDVIK SVOBODA Born 1896; a soldier who fought in Russia in both world wars, with the Czech Brigade in the first, as Commander of the Czech Army Corps in the second. Benes made him Minister of Defence, April 1945; joined the Communist Party, 1948; forced on Stalin's orders to leave the army, 1950; in charge of State Sports Organization, 1950-1; then disappeared, was imprisoned and on release found a job as an accountant in a Moravian bee-keeping enterprise. Lived in obscurity till Khrushchev asked, on one of his visits to Prague, where his old friend was. It took some time to find him but after that he began to reappear in public life as a writer of military articles. Was made a Hero of the Soviet Union and of the Czechoslovak Socialist Republic, November 1965; succeeded Antonin Novotny as President of that Republic, 28 April 1968. A wise choice by Dubcek: Svoboda was a stubborn old man, well respected by the Russians.

SHORT CHRONOLOGY
1918-1970

1918	28 Oct.	Foundation of the State of Czechoslovakia.
1921	27 Nov.	Alexander Dubcek born in Uhrovec, West Slovakia.
1925		Dubcek family go to Interhelpo, Kirghizia.
1933		They move to Gorkiy: Alexander attends secondary school.
1938	Summer	Alexander Dubcek returns to Slovakia. Chamberlain meets Hitler at Munich.
1939	March	Hitler occupies the Czech lands and Slovakia becomes an autonomous but puppet state. Dubcek joins the new, illegal Communist Party of Slovakia and goes to work as a locksmith in Dubnica-nad-Vahom.
1944	28 August	Beginning of the Slovak National Revolt against the Fascists. Alexander Dubcek joins the partisan brigade of 'Jan Zizka'.
	20 Nov.	Dubcek is twice wounded in the thigh.
1945	May	Slovakia and the Czech lands liberated; the Czechoslovak Republic reformed. Dubcek goes to work as a labourer in a yeast factory in Trencin, West Slovakia.
1948	February	The Communist Party takes total power in Czechoslovakia; Dubcek later called it 'a great milestone in our history'.
1949		Dubcek enters the Party *apparat*. Works in Trencin.
1951		Dubcek is sent to work in *apparat* in Bratislava.
1950-4		Stalinist trials and purges in Czechoslovakia.

1953		Dubcek appointed Regional Secretary of the Banska Bystrica region of Central Slovakia.
1955-8		Dubcek attends the Higher Party School in Moscow. Graduates with a First.
1958		On return from Moscow promoted to Leading Secretary of the Bratislava Party.
1960		Becomes an Industrial Secretary on the Secretariat of the Czechoslovak Communist Party in Prague.
1962		Elected to the Presidium of the Czechoslovak Communist Party.
1963		Replaces Karol Bacilek as First Secretary of the Slovak Communist Party.
1963-7		Works in Bratislava; most important, but still obscure official in Slovak Party.
1968	5 Jan.	Alexander Dubcek replaces Antonin Novotny as First Secretary of the Czechoslovak Communist Party.
	20 Aug.	Troops of five of her Warsaw Pact allies invade Czechoslovakia.
	21 Aug.	Dubcek abducted from Prague to an unknown destination.
	27 Aug.	Dubcek returns to Prague.
1969	16 Jan.	Jan Palach sets himself on fire.
	19 Jan.	Jan Palach dies.
	17 April	Dubcek resigns as First Secretary of the Czechoslovak Communist Party.
	18-22 Aug.	Violent rioting in Prague, Brno and other Czechoslovak towns.
	26 Sept.	Dubcek is dismissed as Chairman of the Federal Assembly and from the Presidium.
1970	26 Jan.	Dubcek arrives in Ankara to assume the duties of Ambassador of the Czechoslovak Socialist Republic to Turkey. Resigns from the Central Committee of the Czechoslovak Communist Party.

(A more detailed Chronology appears in Appendix Two).

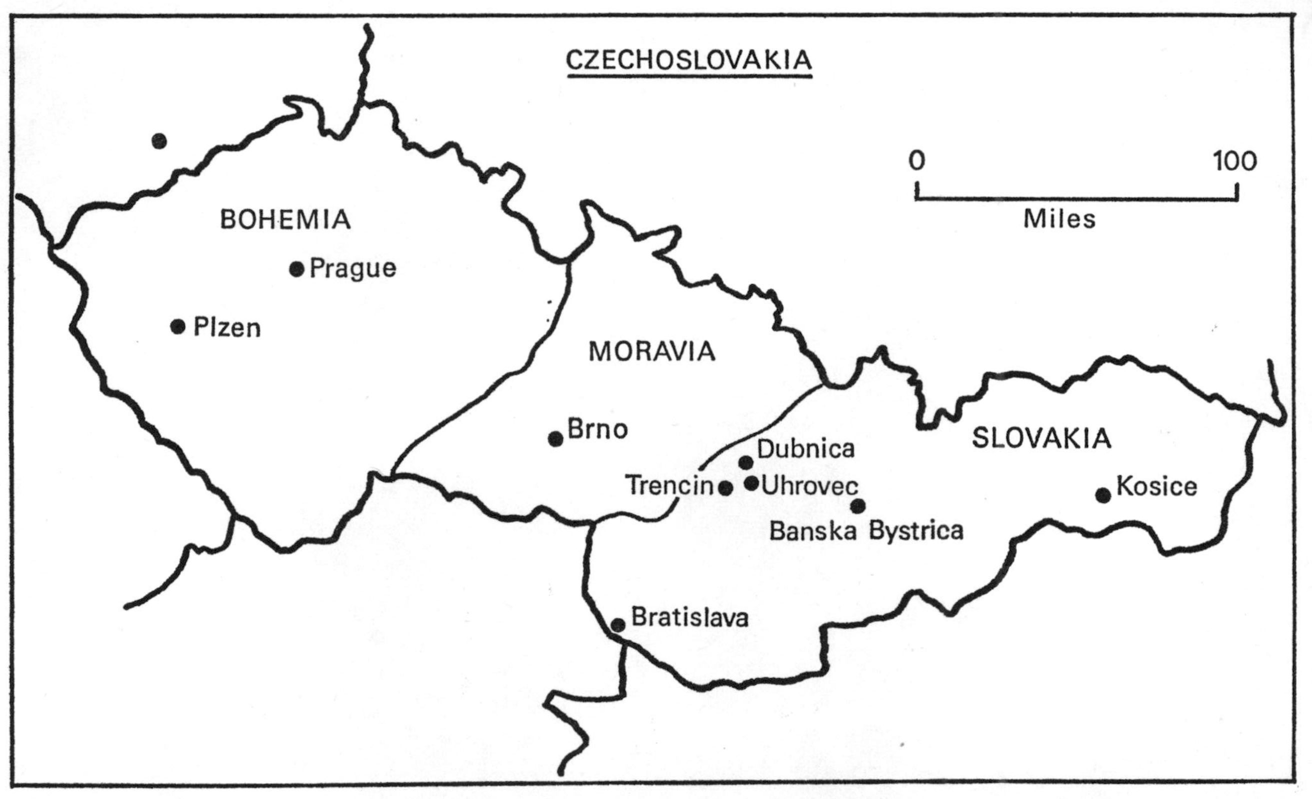
CZECHOSLOVAKIA
0
100
Miles
BOHEMIA
Prague
Plzen
MORAVIA
Brno
SLOVAKIA
Dubnica
Trencin
Uhrovec
Banska Bystrica
Kosice
Bratislava

PROLOGUE

AT ZIJE DUBCEK!

'I ask you not to put me where I do not belong. Do not ascribe to my personality and character motives which, as you very well know, are alien to me.'

Alexander Dubcek to the Central Committee, 26 September 1969

At midday on Thursday 21 August 1969 some eighty thousand Czechs and Slovaks of all ages and professions filled Wenceslas Square in Prague. One year after the Warsaw Pact invasion of their country they demonstrated their utter rejection of the Russians and of the government that the Kremlin had imposed upon them. Weeping and singing, they paraded their devoted loyalty to the personality and policies of Alexander Dubcek. 'AT ZIJE DUBCEK! DUBCEK!'* was the cry. There was no policemen in sight but 'AT ZIJE DUBCEK' called back a few of the young and unhappy soldiers whose lorries had been stationed in the square.

The crowd stood to attention, sang the Czechoslovak National Anthem and lugubriously intoned the name of Husak. They moved up the square towards the museum at its head. Two boys leapt on to the huge statue of St Wenceslas and one of them flung his arms into a crucifix of despair. The people cried its approval at this symbolic gesture of defiance and the police moved in. They ran down from the museum and the streets above the statue, driving the panicked crowd before them by baton blows and tear gas rockets. The demonstrators rallied, the police called in massive reinforcements and within half an hour had emptied the square with violence and water cannon. All roads leading into it were at once sealed off by army trucks and nervous troops.

The non-violent demonstration for Dubcek lasted only thirty minutes, but a bloody, perhaps misguided, fight for

* 'Long live Dubcek!'

what he had represented continued in the side streets all day and well into the night. The people's dilemma was well expressed by a young student who, blood streaming down his face from a baton blow, said to me:

> We came here because we had to. We did not want to. We had to show the world that the people of Czechoslovakia are not beaten. We wanted to show them that we still resist the Russians. Of course we understand that we will probably make the situation worse, but *Jesus-Maria*, what can we do? If we stayed at home the Kremlin would say that we were happy and the world would believe either that or that we had given up. We have not; we still regard Dubcek as our true leader. Despite his mistakes he is the only man we have ever trusted and the only one we want . . . No one who is here today is here by arrangement. Nothing has been planned. There are no student demonstrations as such. We are each here because we chose to be.

At six o'clock that evening seventy-five tanks rumbled out of the quiet suburbs, where they had been waiting all day, over the bridges and for the next three hours clumsily prowled the centre of Prague. But they did not frighten the people off the streets and it was one o'clock before the fighting in the city was finally won. For an hour the bridges of Prague shook to the weight of long columns of tanks and trucks, and into the city moved another army – of street cleaners and roadworkers. They replaced torn up paving stones, collected cobblestones, swept away broken glass, destroyed nearly all the evidence of the battle.

The next morning the town was very calm. There was little to remind anyone of the violence of the previous day. The post-office was working as normal – there was nothing to suggest that only twelve hours ago it had been occupied by the police and militia and used as a temporary prison for the most brutal beating of the demonstrators they had arrested. Only the tankprints in the city tarmac served as a reminder that the nightmare was real. But by ten o'clock that evening it was clear how deep was the damage done and how high would be the price of the repairs. The Government News Agency, Ceteka, published a Proclamation of the Presidium by which the power of the police was substituted for the rule of law. These 'Emergency Measures', which were allegedly necessary in face of the widespread disturbances of the week and which eliminated all traces of his reform movement, were signed by Alexander Dubcek. The Russians had gained their greatest success since January 1968: the Socialist With the Human Face had endorsed the imposition of Stalinism on his country.

This is not a book about the Czechoslovak crisis of 1968–70; nor is it a study of the seductive ideology of 'Prague Spring'*; it is the story of an East European politician. Much of the material for it was collected in Prague and Slovakia in the late summer of 1969. Conditions were not ideal. Even in July many people were frightened to admit any association with the 'discredited' Dubcek and after the imposition of the Emergency Laws, when it was widely feared that he might be brought to trial, very few who had worked with him were willing to talk about their experience.

I needed to be careful in my choice of people to approach. Obviously the most interesting were Party officials in the towns where Dubcek had worked. But had I told one anti-Dubcek *apparatchik* – and there were many in the Party – of what I was trying to do, I might have had my work confiscated and been thrown out of the country at once. This meant that I was not able to speak with as many people as I should have liked.

I have drawn extensively upon Dubcek's speeches. They form a fascinating theological study. So much of the Party's work in any East European country is *in camera* that a politician's public discourses are usually the only hints which the people is given of his attitudes. Audiences become very skilled at reading between Marxist platitudes and clichés in order to see if the speaker has anything new to say. I have quoted his speeches at some length because to extract only the in-

* Probably the best account of the 1968-70 crisis is Pavel Tigrid's *La Chute Irrésistible d'Alexandré Dubcek*, Calmann-Lévy, 1969. For the ideology of Prague Spring, see Roger Garaudy, *La Liberté en Sursis*, Fayard, 1968.

teresting and unfamiliar phrases would have offered a totally distorted picture of the man and his ideas.

There are footnotes elaborating many of the points I consider most important. As it is impossible for any study of Dubcek written today to be completely authoritative I have often merely suggested what his motives in any given situation might have been. Where I have asserted what, in my judgment, were his feelings and intentions I have usually indicated my reasons in the notes; unfortunately, it is obviously impossible to reveal the identity of any Czech or Slovak sources.

I want to thank Bruce Page, Neal Ascherson, Pavel Tigrid and Deryck Viney for their very patient reading of scruffy manuscripts and for giving me invaluable advice and criticism. Also Hugh Lunghi and the entire BBC Czechoslovak Section, Radio Vienna and Radio Free Europe for unlimited use of their files. For encouragement and consolation throughout that terrible Czechoslovak summer of 1969 Mauro and Wanya Santayana, the East European Correspondent of the *Jornal do Brasil*, and Sonia Winter reading the final manuscript; above all Caroline Ritchie for essential research and criticism in Prague, Bratislava, Munich and London.

Without the devotion to Dubcek that inspired so many Czechs and Slovaks – sometimes at considerable personal risk – to help me, this book could never have been written. I cannot thank them personally but I can dedicate my work to them, in the hope that it goes some way towards explaining the complex character of the man whom *Zycie Warsawy* (a Polish Government paper) on 4 September 1968 – only one week after it denounced him as a revisionist – described as:

> . . . an emotional leader, easily influenced by moods, not a strong, cool politician. He trusted people too much, to the point of naivety, and that is why many events took him by surprise. He was devoted to the cause of socialism, and for too long he thought that everyone around him thought the same. One should recognize his moral calibre, but must make reservations about his political acumen and his ability to act decisively when this is essential.

1
UP THE RAINBOW

If a goose flies across the sea, there comes back a quack-quack.

German Proverb.

Alexander Dubcek was conceived in Chicago, at the beginning of the year 1921. In the spring his father brought the family home and Alexander was born, on 27 November, in Slovakia.

Stefan Dubcek, international idealist and Slovak carpenter, had been wandering the world for eleven years. He had left home because, uneducated and only semi-skilled, he was unable to find work in a Slovakia dominated and depressed by its Magyar rulers.* Perhaps more important still, he longed to break out from under the harsh cords of feudalism by which the ramshackle Austro-Hungarian Empire was held together. He was certain that somewhere was a life in which he would not have to work as a peasant for ever subject to alien exploitation, and he was determined to find it.†

And so, in 1910 he left his native village of Uhrovec, which lies hidden in the Strazovska mountains of West Slovakia, and walked down the bank of the Danube into Budapest. He found a place in a furniture factory and organized a socialist cell to conspire against a monarchy which, for political and for national reasons, he found so repellent. This activity cost him his job – after six months he found himself on the streets

* In 1910 'Slovakia' did not exist as such. The territory was an integral part of Hungary, exploited by the Magyars. During the eighteenth and nineteenth centuries the Magyars had successfully sought to establish themselves as the superior, governing race in the Hungarian Empire. All other ethnic groups – Slovaks included – were forced to remain subject communities with no rights at all. Magyar oppression was violent and total.

† Information on Stefan's early life and beliefs is mostly derived from talks with those of his relatives still living in Slovakia and from an examination of some of his letters home.

again, with little chance of finding further work and every chance of being arrested. Disgusted by the political restrictions of Hungary, he decided to go to America, a land in which, so he had heard, egalitarianism and democracy were taken for granted and to which imperialist exploitation was utterly alien.

He was nineteen when he landed in the United States. He made his way to Chicago and rented a room in the Slovak community. But, finding that life there was too introspective and that he was learning no English, he moved to the Irish quarter, took a carpentry job and earned $25 a week.[1]

To his dismay, Stefan discovered that the American way of life was less egalitarian than he had been led to expect. Nevertheless, it afforded him considerably more liberty than did that of Slovakia or of Budapest: at least he could expound his political beliefs – those of an unconvinced social democrat – without fear of arrest. Moreover he did not risk having to fight for Hungarian landlords in a monarcho-imperialist war. In 1916 he saw little reason for returning home and decided to take out US citizenship; the following year he joined the American Socialist Party of Eugene V. Debs.* But almost immediately after that America entered the war and Stefan received his call-up papers. To evade the draft he tried to flee across the border into Mexico. He was caught and, unable to pay the $1,000 fine, was imprisoned for eighteen months.

When he was released, he found lodgings in Madison Street, which cuts through the 'Loop' District of Chicago, took a job in a piano factory at $40 a week and married. His bride, Pavlina, was a young Slovak who had run away from home 'so that I could see the world'. All that she had seen was Chicago from the scullery of a Jewish merchant and the experience had made of her a dedicated Communist. Stefan was by now disgusted with what he saw as the American fraud and needed little to persuade him that his scant remaining hopes for social democracy were entirely misplaced.

* Debs. President of American Railway Union, jailed in 1894 for leading strike against Pullman Car Co. Founded Socialist Party in 1898; its programme was based on that of the American Populist Party, demanding social democracy without capitalism. Debs stood for the Presidency as Socialist candidate five times.

Under his wife's influence he began to study Marx. He was delighted by what he read and believed that at last he had found the Utopia for which he had so long been searching; within twelve months he was a committed Marxist.

It was now that he began to realize the immense promise of Lenin's seizure of power in Russia, and in 1919 he wrote home: 'In America you can have most things but you certainly can't have freedom. The only free country in the world is the Soviet Union.' The following year his younger sister wrote to him from Slovakia that she wanted to get married. Concerned lest her fiancé should be petty-bourgeois, Stefan sent him a long questionnaire on his political beliefs. He was satisfied with the answers and, with her brother's blessing, she embarked on a long and happy marriage.

By the end of 1920 Stefan was feeling very restless in Chicago and Pavlina was homesick. They decided that it was time they went back to Slovakia. His boss offered Stefan a pay-rise, but he turned it down saying that he was off to build socialism and, in the spring of 1921, sailed for home with his baby Julius and a pregnant Pavlina. He took them to his village of Uhrovec and there, in a whitewashed cottage below the *château,* Alexander Dubcek was born.

Alexander had just missed the opportunity of being an American citizen – an option which his brother possessed but never considered – but he was born into a nation no less hybrid and extraordinary. Since Versailles, Slovakia was no longer a down-trodden province of Hungary. For the first time in a thousand years the Slovaks had been recognized as a people almost in their own right. They were joined with the Bohemians and Moravians in an exciting, independent and incredible nation – Czechoslovakia – the figment of the imagination of Tomas Carrigue Masaryk, the evangelist professor from Prague.

Masaryk can fairly be described as both the architect and the builder of the Czechoslovak State; but for his almost single-handed and tireless crusade throughout the world the idea of conjuring up this new nation would never have been realized. However, he must take blame as well as credit for its construction, and one of his greatest mistakes lay in his treatment of Slovakia. He was a man of principle and of conviction verging on rigidity; on the Slovaks he held very pronounced opinions: 'They had long been oppressed by the Magyars, deprived of education and deliberately kept in a backward, nay, a primitive condition.' This was, in 1917, an understandable and sadly accurate assessment. But Masaryk went on to say, and here his prejudices appear to have overcome his discretion: 'In general culture and political maturity they were decades, perhaps generations behind the Czechs and, despite the presence of a Protestant leaven among them, they were apt to be fanatically Catholic and priest-ridden.'[2]

However arrogant Masaryk's judgment, it does point up a vital difference between the Czech lands and Slovakia. During the nineteenth century Bohemia and Moravia were rapidly industrialized and this encouraged the growth of a Czech national consciousness. There was no such 'secular regeneration', as the Czech transformation has rightly been called, in Slovakia. Whether the Magyars intended it or not, the post-1880 industrial development in Hungary gave scant benefit to the Slovak people. By 1919 35% of Czechs worked on the land, 40% in industry. In Slovakia only 19% were employed in industry and 60% in agriculture. The Czech working class had a reasonable standard of living whilst in Slovakia peasant poverty was so acute that most Slovaks had much more in common with the Slavs and Rumanians to the east and south than with the Czechs to the west. Bohemia and Moravia had produced a strong middle class which was quite capable of taking over the civil service and running the state after her independence. In Slovakia there was no such group. In 1919 perhaps the main thing that the two nations shared was half the vocabulary of their separate languages.

This in no way deterred Masaryk; he was convinced that the two people should be one. But perhaps he betrayed in his writings a precognition that Slovakia was, although necessary, bound to remain an unequal partner of the Czech lands. It was Bohemian and Moravian independence that he was fighting for; Slovakia was included in order to strengthen the other two nations, not to share fully in their freedom. 'My programme as early as 1914 was a synthesis of Czech aspirations in the light of our constitutional, historical and natural rights,' he wrote, adding for good measure, 'and I had kept the inclusion of Slovakia constantly in view for I am by descent a Slovak, born in Moravia.'[3] It is true that Masaryk's father was a Slovak, but his wife was American and he had spent little time in Slovakia; his academic work had been mostly in Vienna, Prague and Hampstead.

During the war Masaryk travelled all of Europe and much of Asia trying to convince the governments and peoples of the world of the validity of his visionary 'Czechoslovakia'. In 1918 he was in America, still pursuing with extraordinary single-mindedness his fantastic dream. He spent some time making himself known in official government circles and communicated his ideas 'through mutual friends' to President Wilson. From him Masaryk gained his greatest success; on 3 September 1918 Wilson agreed in principle to the concept of a unitary Czecho-Slovak state.* Although Masaryk claimed the credit for this coup, the American government had accepted the idea even before he began to apply his formidable powers of logic and persuasion. On 29 May, Lansing, the Secretary of State, had announced that 'the nationalistic aspirations of the Czech-Slovaks and Jugo-Slavs for freedom have the earnest sympathy of this Government.'[4] Nevertheless, this commitment from Wilson was the turning point in Masaryk's campaign; from then on his cause was almost assured.†

* This was the spelling favoured by Slovaks before and, indeed, long after the creation of the state.

† Despite Masaryk's energetic gospelling, Czechoslovakia could never have been established but for the enthusiasm of the Western Allies. Until the end of 1916 both Britain and France hoped to be able to arrange a separate peace with the Austro-Hungarian empire and refused to lend any support to Czech or Czecho-Slovak demands for independence, for fear of complicating such negotiations. Only after the death of Francis Joseph in December 1916 did the Allies begin to mention amongst their conditions for peace the political freedom of the Czechs.

The Czech cause was much helped by the activities of men such as Seton-Watson and Wickham Steed in Britain and the historian Denis in France. Their publications—such as *The New Europe*, *La Nation Tchèque* and *Le Monde Slave*—helped to create a consciousness of Czechoslovak rights and prospects. But most important of all was the desire of the American, British and especially the French governments to create a *cordon sanitaire* around the eastern flank of Germany which would also act as a bulwark against the new and looming threat of Soviet Russia. It was not out of respect for Masaryk or in recognition of Czech rights that the Allies came to support the independence of Poland, Yugoslavia and Czechoslovakia, but out of blatant fear and self-interest.

Czechoslovak independence was confirmed and its frontiers established by

Whilst in America he did not concentrate only on the Government. He also spent considerable time and energy in eliciting the approval and support of the large Slovak colony in the States. The emigrant community was very clearly divided in both its political and its territorial aspirations for its homeland. Some – by no means the majority – agreed with his idea of a unitary state with the Czechs, others wanted a federal union of the two nations within a dual state, some demanded full autonomy for Slovakia, others, union with Poland and a few, perhaps Stefan among them, thought that union or federation with Russia might be the best solution for their country.

Masaryk did his best to convince these varied Slovak factions that in reality their best interest lay in a close alliance with Prague and that the idea of a separate Slovakia was 'absurd even preposterous'. He was not altogether successful, despite his claim that 'I was able to show the Slovaks how little they were known in the political world' by contrast with himself, the globe-trotting Moravian philosopher

> . . . and how serious a failure we should have courted had they acted independently. The idea of an independent Slovakia could not be taken seriously, though there might be a theoretical possibility of Slovak autonomy under Hungary. But since this possibility was not practical in the circumstances, there remained nothing save union.[5]

Unable to convince them all, Masaryk decided to try and extract some sort of agreement from those Slovaks least hostile to his cause. Accordingly he met with Czech and certain Slovak *émigré* leaders at Pittsburgh in the June of 1918. The Slovaks demanded an assurance that, if a Czecho-Slovak State (*sic*) were to be formed, they would not be completely submerged by the Czech majority. They also wanted guarantees of a measure of autonomy, and a promise that the Czechs would never try to assimilate them. Masaryk agreed and 'there on 30 June 1918, I signed the Convention between the Czechs and Slovaks of America'.[6] By this Convention the Slovak

three of the Peace Treaties drawn up at the Versailles Conference: that of Versailles, June 1919, of St Germain-en-Laye, November 1919, and that of Trianon in June 1920.

émigrés approved the founding of a single Czecho-Slovak State (*sic*) but Masaryk conceded that Slovakia should have its own administration, judiciary and parliament, and that Slovak should be the official language in both schools and government of Slovakia.

Unfortunately Masaryk did not see in this document the commitment that the Slovaks thought he had made. The Convention, he said 'was concluded in order to appease a small Slovak faction which was dreaming of God knows what sort of independence for Slovakia'.[7] It is perhaps not surprising that Masaryk should have been so intransigent, but what is curious is that he did not appreciate that the 'small faction' constituted the great majority of politically conscious Slovaks, both at home and in America. To these people the Convention appeared a guarantee that in the future state Slovaks would be free from Czech domination and would practise at least a measure of self-government. Masaryk, however, regarded the agreement as merely a basis for future discussion between Czech and Slovak Deputies in the new Republic.

> I signed the Convention unhesitatingly as a *local* understanding between American Czechs and Slovaks upon the policy they were prepared to advocate . . . It was laid down that the details of the Slovak political problems would be settled by the legal representatives of the Slovak people themselves . . . And so it was . . . the legal representatives of Slovakia [later] expressed themselves in favour of complete union, and the oath sworn upon the Constitution binds the Slovaks, the Czechs, and me too.[8]

It was a pity he did not say this earlier; as it was, most Slovaks assumed that the Convention was binding and were accordingly disillusioned when Masaryk declared it to be of only temporary and parochial importance. Their grievance was not alleviated by the fact that Masaryk was at least technically correct: no émigrés have the authority to deliver their home country into any form of government or unto any manner of people. Slovaks could with some justice later complain that

> . . . the Czechs discovered the document to be non-binding

only after they had extracted full value from it as evidence, at home of their intentions towards the Slovaks, and abroad of the Slovaks' sentiments towards them, and that its existence was at least partly responsible for their securing international approval for the creation of a Czechoslovak State.[9]

Perhaps Masaryk's greatest mistake was to imagine that the Slovaks had little or no national pride. It is true that before the First World War they appeared a totally subservient peasant people meekly tilling the ground for their Magyar landlords, but their nationalism was only dormant. Its greatest outburst had been in 1848. On the 10 May that year a group of Slovak patriots had assembled in Liptovsky Svaty Mikulas and adopted a resolution entitled 'Demands of the Slovak Nation'. This was a revolutionary document claiming full constitutional rights and liberties for all Slovaks. It demanded seats for Slovak representatives in the Hungarian Diet and for Slovakia a legislative assembly. It claimed the recognition of the Slovak language and the right to a free press. It asserted that all citizens should have the vote and that the peasants should be entitled to own the land they occupied.

This programme remained the basis of all Slovak national demands for the next eighty years and its author, a brilliant journalist and politician named Ludovit Stur, became Slovakia's greatest national hero. By a haunting coincidence he had been born in 1815 in the very same cottage in which Pavlina gave birth, 106 years later, to Alexander Dubcek.

Stefan had returned from the United States in order to experience the new Czechoslovakia and to visit Lenin's Russia. He was soon disappointed by the first because although Slovakia was finally free from Hungarian domination he found it subject to a new tyranny: the feudalism of Budapest had simply been exchanged for the capitalism of Prague. In Marxist terms this was a move in the right direction, but for Stefan it was not fast enough: under neither system did he consider that the aspirations of the Slovak people could be met. He was a Communist before he was a nationalist but he found (as have many genuine Slovak Communists since) that in his country the two ideologies were inseparable.

There was no piano industry in Uhrovec and so he went back to straight carpentry. He also founded a branch of the new and legal Czechoslovak Communist Party in the village and spent most of his free time recruiting. But it was not enough; he wanted a bigger part in the building of socialism and began to consider how he might go to Russia. When, in 1923, the 4th Comintern published an appeal to the international working class for help in the building of socialism in the Soviet Union, Stefan realized that this was his chance.

Throughout Slovakia hundreds of workers, skilled, unskilled, Communist, Social-Democrat, Nationalist and Catholic, were thinking the same. To some of them it offered the best opportunity of escaping unemployment in Slovakia, to a few like Stefan it was a chance of serving the cause. Dozens of small groups formed to discuss the idea all over the country.[10] The largest of them had the somewhat extraordinary but perhaps appropriate origin in the Ido Club of Turcansky Svaty Martin.* Ido was an artifical international language, rather less successful than Esperanto. In the widespread desire to build a better world which accompanied the founding of the League of Nations and later the United Nations, many esoteric international clubs and associations were born. In most cases the intensity of their commitment was matched only by the shortness of their lives, and Ido was no exception. But in 1923 it was still extant, and to the Club in Martin came a magazine from Moscow. It contained a description of that offshoot of the Comintern, the International Workers' Aid Movement, and suggested how groups of foreign workers might organize themselves into self-contained agricultural or industrial co-operatives and come to the Soviet Union. On 1 May 1923 the Ido speakers of Martin, and others who spoke only Slovak but had come along to the Club to hear about the movement, resolved that they would answer Lenin's call, form a co-operative and call it Interhelpo.

The organizers wrote to Moscow, asked for permission to come and work in the Soviet Union and, in due time, received

* This town is the cultural hub of Slovakia. It contains the Matica Slovenska, the Slovak National Museum.

the reply that they were very welcome. They were sent photographs of the site that had been assigned to them. It was in Kirghizia, near the border of Sinkiang; the area at the moment so fiercely disputed with the Chinese.

A sub-group of Interhelpo was set up in the West Slovakian market-town of Trencin, and it was here that Stefan Dubcek came and registered as a member of the scheme. He and Pavlina had decided that this was the moment to go to the Soviet Union; according to a letter of farewell he wrote to a friend, they hoped that by the time they returned to Czechoslovakia the Communist Party would have taken power and that all economic and national problems would have been miraculously but automatically solved.

In March 1925 the Dubceks set out, with 105 other families, on the thirty-day train journey across the Soviet Union to Kirghizia and to the little village of Pishpek, where Alexander was to spend the next eight years.

Kirghizia was at that time one of the most primitive and backward areas in a primitive and backward Soviet Union: illiteracy was almost total, for the Kirghiz language had never been committed to paper; the peasants were totally unskilled – metal plowshares were non-existent and they did not even have any idea of how to make hay.

Donat Lanicek was a Slovak workman who was with the Dubceks that cold morning when they first came to Pishpek:

> It was terrible, [he wrote home in 1928.] We did not have anything at all. We had to build ourselves houses, and we had no tools. We tried to borrow some from the villagers, but they did not trust us at first and, in any case, they had hardly anything of any use. The Soviet Government gave us very little help. I think their attitude was that they had enough problems of their own. They thought we had come to help them, and that there was no reason why they should help us. It was very cold and the children were most of them ill. The peasants from Pishpek and thereabouts had no idea how to cultivate the land and so we had little food. Nor could we look after the children properly. Our first problem was to build huts and to feed ourselves. We were

Julius (far left) and Alexander Dubcek (far right), photographed while on holiday with their aunts and uncles in Trencin, Slovakia, 1935.

Julius Dubcek (left) and three comrades in arms in the Slovak Revolt against the Nazis, September 1944.

Stefan Dubcek: On release from Mauthausen Concentration Camp in April 1945 he weighed seven stone (left). Right: His normal appearance.

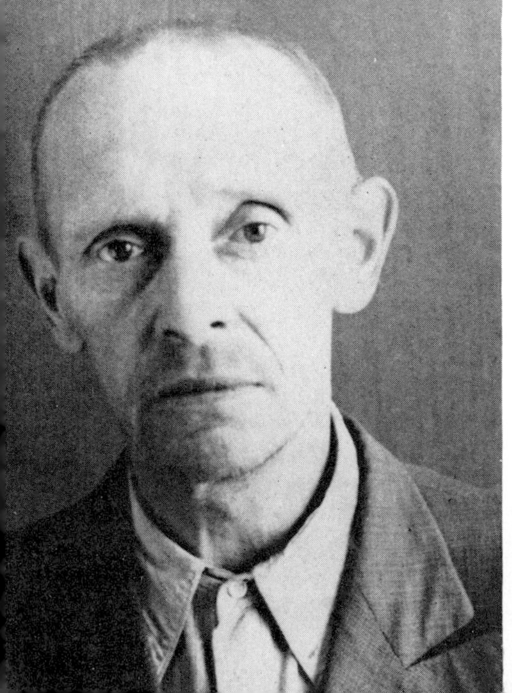

terrified of malaria. But we went ahead, trying to build Interhelpo as we had planned.

They were to be disappointed. The Articles of Interhelpo, published in the Slovak paper *Pravda Chudoby* on 9 April 1924, had stressed that every member must be a Communist; this was logical enough as the group was pledged to live and work as a commune and: 'In the commune everyone works and is expected to contribute according to his capacities and everyone receives according to his needs and requirements, that is, equally, since all are equal and in equal conditions of life and labour.'[11] Such was the idealistic theory by which the members of Interhelpo were supposed to live. They failed.

Until 1926 they worked without payment. They were clothed and fed by the commune and given pocket money for tobacco. Few, however, were devoted enough to the ideals of Communism to find this satisfactory and by the end of 1926 many of those who had come to Interhelpo merely to escape the unemployment of Slovakia had left in disgust. They found working in the commune, without pay and in very primitive conditions, less attractive than the high wages they could command in Soviet towns, where the shortage of even semi-skilled labour was often acute.

Reluctantly, those members of Interhelpo who persevered decided that their experiment in communization had been premature. It was a bitter disappointment to some, for it was above all in the communes that the ideas of the Revolution took a constructive form; in the perfect commune the joy of sharing was paramount; the members slept, ate and worked together.

This much Interhelpo did achieve. Whether joyfully or not, families lived together in open-plan communal houses. They were grouped according to trade, and so Alexander Dubcek grew up in a house full of carpenters and woodworkers – in this one long, draughty clapboard building he lived as a child the practical problem of idealism.

The commune movement was essentially utopian in the same way as the Revolution, originally, was utopian. But as the Revolution ceased to be revolutionary, as the Bolshevik leadership was able to impose more and more of its selected pattern upon the disorder that was Russian society, so the communes became increasingly unacceptable. There was simply no room for their naive impracticality in a society fast becoming defined, rigid and bureaucratic. The Bolshevik leaders were wary of the chaos which, they felt, might result from any attempt at full-scale communization. It is true that Lenin was willing, at first, to allow the communes to succeed, and in 1919 he said: 'If the communes show in practice that they really improve the peasants' life then, no doubt, the authority of the Communists and the Communist Party will increase.'[12] But he was unprepared to do anything to encourage or precipitate this success – if they were to flourish it must be because of their innate worth and not because of government help.

By the beginning of 1930 Interhelpo had long abandoned the attempt at communism, and the members had tried to reconcile their ideals to the harsh practicalities of Kirghiz life by rationalizing their failure and arguing that they must pass through a socialist stage of development before they could even begin to attempt communism. It was at this time that Stalin, who had previously rejected the idea, seemed to have second thoughts about the system and considered whether communes could in fact be imposed upon the reluctant peasantry. But he decided that both the economic and the political risks of such a truly revolutionary step were too great and later the Party Congress resolved that forcible communization would have 'threatened a breakdown of the collectivization of agriculture, undermining the very basis of the Soviet Government, the union of the working class and the peasantry.'[13] In other words, the peasants would not stand for it.

Stalin's decision was the correct one, for enforced communization is really a contradiction in terms: it is difficult to compel people to participate in the 'joy of sharing'. Lenin saw that communization must be a spontaneous grass-roots movement if it was to be successful, and it failed because of the understandable, conservative reluctance of the peasants to sacrifice their tiny properties.

But the failure of communal methods in such voluntary organizations as Interhelpo was of a different nature, for here it was largely a reflection of the convictions, ingrained habits and stamina of the members. For in many voluntary Soviet communal experiments, when and if material failings were overcome, then human failings became all too apparent and the temptations of the surrounding market economy all too great.

The parents of Interhelpo were anxious that their children should profit fully from their Soviet experience and fraternization with local children was not only encouraged – it was virtually compulsory. During his eight years at the camp Alexander attended a school for both Slovak and Soviet children. At first there were no proper teachers, and, with fifty children of varied ages to a class, not very much was learnt. But in August 1926 Petr Jilemnicky and Frantisek Svozil, both Slovak writers, came with a second batch of families from Slovakia to the settlement. Jilemnicky had been sent out by the Party in Zilina which had suddenly realized that no one amongst the first flock of families was either qualified or indeed even capable of instructing the children. Until his arrival teaching had been in Czech and in Slovak. This meant that the Kirghiz children found it rather more difficult to benefit from their instruction than did the others. Jilemnicky decided that this was very wrong and that in future all teaching should be in Russian.

The application of his plan aggravated the confusion and difficulties in the already chaotic atmosphere of the school, but the parents, still enthusiastic for all things Soviet, agreed 'in a democratic fashion' that Russian should be the official and only language taught to their children. The subsequent arrival of twenty-five Soviet teachers did something to restore order and to improve the efficiency of the school which from then on was run 'in the Soviet fashion'. According to Pavel Pollak, authoritative and eulogizing chronicler of Interhelpo, 'The life of the children there was very gay . . . everywhere one could see the smiles and hear the songs of young children.'[14] Apart from those who were suffering from malaria.

For in the first year of Interhelpo's existence over half of the children under three years old died of the disease.* Alexander and Julius were lucky: they both avoided it. But in

* Jilemnicky had caught malaria soon after his arrival. He left Interhelpo at

1933 each of them caught some fairly serious form of influenza and Stefan, who had by now become a little disappointed by life at Interhelpo, decided that this was the time to leave. He took them away from the village school at Pishpek – which they had attended for twelve months – and the whole family entrained to a healthier climate.

They went to Gorkiy, an industrial town 250 miles east of Moscow, where conditions were much less rigorous. This was a town in which Lenin had spent all the last months of his life and that gave it an added attraction for Stefan. He found work at the Likhaevsky car factory where his English came in useful as they were apparently producing cars in collaboration with the American firm of Adams and Co.[15]

The move from school in Pishpek to school in Gorkiy was very important for Alexander. In Pishpek the classrooms had, as at Interhelpo, been overcrowded and ill equipped, textbooks almost unobtainable, teaching methods obscure to say the least, the atmosphere anarchic, and the incentive to learn non-existent. When he arrived at Gorkiy he found a much better appointed school and, more importantly, an attempt to re-establish many of the practices that had been accepted in pre-revolutionary Russian schools.

The problems of education in Pishpek had been shared throughout the Soviet Union. For the first ten years after the Revolution all Soviet children had suffered not only from an understandable lack of facilities and books, but also from the pedagogic methods of the hastily trained revolutionary teachers. By 1931 it was evident even to the leadership that the system was not working as it should, and on 5 September of that year the Central Committee of the Soviet Communist Party passed a resolution 'On the Primary and Secondary Schools' charging them with having failed to prepare students adequately for entry into technical college and university'. In August 1932 the Central Committee went further criticized the way in which subjects were taught and called for a rapid revision of the school curricula. This had the effect of restoring to the teacher the role of leader of the class and of stressing the importance of school discipline. So at the Gorkiy

once and hastened to the more temperate climate of Anapa on the Black Sea, where he established a Slovak village.

school Dubcek found the atmosphere much stricter than at Pishpek where the children had largely been able to behave as they wished. Whereas during the first twelve years of his life he had learnt almost nothing but Russian, he was now able for the first time to work quite seriously and to take advantage, if he wished, of the reasonable facilities that his new school had to offer.

He did wish, and it appears that he worked extremely hard at Gorkiy. Whereas his brother Julius had always been extrovert, amusing and rather lazy, and was becoming more so, Alexander developed through these years into something of a subdued and serious-minded student though, according to Stefan, he enjoyed ice-hockey, and swam with the rest of the school in the Volga every day of the year until it froze over.

According to a friend who was with him at school in Gorkiy*, Alexander Dubcek marvelled at what he saw of Russia in 1937. He had been taught to do so, and he had little reason and still less opportunity to question his instruction. He had been told that before the Revolution the peasant died of starvation on his tiny and unproductive acreage, cruelly exploited by absentee and callous landlords. He had learnt of the evils of the Tsar and his loathsome Tsarina; he had been regaled with the iniquities perpetrated in their divine names. He had been shown that since 1917 the industrial working class no longer had to toil under the oppression of capital and that for the first time in history the Russian was free of his chains.

He also understood that Stalin had forced Russia through the most ambitious and intensive programme of industrialization to which any nation had ever been subjected. So successful had it been that by the end of the thirties the Soviet Union, which only twenty years before had seen the most backward feudalism in Europe, had outstripped even Germany in industrial production. It was by any reckoning a fantastic achievement and it was there for all to see.

What fewer people saw, and what some refused to recognize, was the cost at which all this had been achieved. Dubcek

* This source is used for description of many of Alexander's attitudes for the rest of this Chapter.

must have known something of it. In Kirghizia he had seen a little of this misery of the peasants; he had witnessed the bitterness with which they had resisted collectivization, and he probably knew that for their resistance millions had died and millions more had been imprisoned. But of this treatment he seems to have been largely uncritical. The khulaks were, after all, trying to thwart the revolution and the wishes of the proletariat – they deserved to be punished. Those who impeded the instructions of the Party leadership were petty-bourgeois allies of the Capitalists.

It was also while he was living in Gorkiy that he began to realize the extent of the Terror*, and the degree to which it affected ordinary men's lives. For by 1937 the Terror was not something that touched only the members of the Party: the entire population was threatened. For every Party man who suffered arrest, imprisonment or death, eight or ten citizens endured the same. As Conquest has explained:

> What is hard to convey about the feeling of Soviet citizens through 1936–38 is the long drawn-out sweat of fear, night after night, that arrest might arrive before the next dawn. . . . While under dictatorships arrest had been selective, falling on genuinely suspected enemies of the regime, in the Yezhov† era . . . anyone at all could feel that he might be the next victim. Fear by night and a feverish effort by day to pretend enthusiasm for a system of lies was the permanent condition of the Soviet citizen.[16]

As an alien in Gorkiy, Alexander Dubcek must have understood the situation as well as any Soviet citizen. For he lived in the same fear as everyone else – foreigners were not exempted from arrest. Indeed he found that many friends he had made in school now refused to have anything to do with him, because contact with a foreigner often meant death for a Soviet citizen.

It must have been a horrible experience for him, but there is no evidence that he blamed it on Stalin. Indeed he did not hold the Great Leader responsible for the Terror at all. With his usual skill, Stalin had managed to keep himself largely in

* The years 1936-8 in the Soviet Union.

† Stalin's Chief of Police.

the background. In the public mind the man responsible for the informing, the police, the arrests and the deaths was Yezhov rather than Stalin. And if Boris Pasternak could not realize at the time the extent of Stalin's guilt, there is little reason to suppose that the sixteen-year-old Alexander Dubcek would have been any more successful. He, like most Russians of his age, was convinced that Stalin was the saviour of mankind, that if there were abuses committed by the Soviet authorities then these must be despite, not because of Stalin. Indeed, Stalin must be unaware of them. This belief was strengthened by the fall of Yezhov, just after the Dubceks had gone home to Slovakia, on 8 December, 1938. Beria took over the NKVD and a number of prisoners were at once released. Haphazard and totally arbitrary arrests began to occur less frequently, and the Terror became institutionalized. It was a brilliant exercise in public relations, for it convinced millions at home and, perhaps more important, liberal sympathizers abroad, of Stalin's own blamelessness. To Dubcek himself this must have been a great relief, for it vindicated his trust in Stalin; it was now quite clear that the Terror had been a temporary maladjustment which the Great Dictator had corrected.

It is hardly surprising, considering his education and his entire upbringing, that Dubcek did not question more closely the nature and the cost of Stalin's achievements. Indeed, it would have been quite unnatural for him to have done so.

Perhaps one further point should be made about his schooling, for his childhood was so completely different from that of all his future colleagues in the Czechoslovak Communist Party. This aspect is best described by Wolfgang Leonhard, the son of a German Communist, and also in a Soviet school (in Moscow) during the Terror.

> We learned to form radically divergent judgments on developments and phenomena and situations which at first sight appeared familiar. All depended on whether the context was capitalist or Soviet society . . . A rise in the price of food in capitalist countries was assessed as 'fresh evidence of the intensified exploitation of the workers' but a rise in the price of food in the Soviet Union was 'an im-

portant economic contribution to the construction of Socialism' . . . We learned to condemn or approve every event without hesitation by observing where it had taken place. This habit of thought so deeply impressed itself upon us all, including myself, that for many years I at least was incapable of imagining any other way of thinking.[17]

It impressed itself upon Alexander Dubcek also. Perhaps less intelligent than Leonhard, he too found himself 'incapable of imagining any other way of thinking', and probably for rather longer. In fact, until about 1962.

2
PARTISAN

'The Sudetenland is the last territorial claim I have to make in Europe.'

Adolf Hitler, speech 26 September 1938.

'War is much too serious a thing to be left to military men.'

Attributed to Talleyrand.

In 1938 Stalin decreed that all foreign residents in the Soviet Union must either take out Soviet citizenship or leave at once. Stefan, who is believed to have been by now somewhat disillusioned by his Soviet experience, saw little point in staying, and in spring 1938 he and Alexander travelled back to Czechoslovakia, a country disunited, unhappy, about to be betrayed and on the verge of destruction. They went to join Pavlina and Julius* in Trencin and a few months later Chamberlain met Hitler at Munich.

Chamberlain must be given much of the credit for the subsequent growth of the Communist Party in Czechoslovakia; his activities in 1938 did a lot to produce the conditions that made the Party's take-over of power ten years later so bloodless and so painless an operation.† Few Slovaks and far fewer Czechs had imagined that a betrayal as grand as England's was conceivable; when the inconceivable occurred they were horrified and disillusioned. But to Dubcek, weaned on hatred of the class-enemy, Munich did not come as such a surprise: it was behaviour typical of the bourgeois-imperialists. At that

* Pavlina had brought Julius home in 1936 as he was still ill.

† At Munich in 1938 Chamberlain handed over to Hitler all the German-inhabited territories of Czechoslovakia. Two months later in Vienna Hungary was given all the Magyar-populated regions of Slovakia. Benes, who succeeded Masaryk in December 1935, abdicated the Presidency and left for the West. In March 1939 Hitler's army occupied the Czech lands of Bohemia and Moravia and made of them a Protectorate of the Reich. But he did not occupy Slovakia, which was turned into an 'independent' but puppet republic, governed for the next five years by the clerico-fascist Catholic People's Party, under Monsignor Josef Tiso.

time Stalin was promising to help Czechoslovakia should it require assistance against the German menace, and should France also be willing to march. This would have dispelled any doubts that Dubcek might have had as to the Great Leader's integrity. As a result of Stalin's attitude the Communists were the only political party in Czechoslovakia wholeheartedly to condemn the treachery of Munich and for this gained, at least in Bohemia and Moravia, a respect and a following it had hitherto been denied.

In Slovakia, Hitler's partition of the country was greeted with less dismay than in the Czech lands, for

> . . . the [Czechoslovak] Government has been obliged more often than not to rule Slovakia against the wishes of most of its inhabitants, maintaining itself only by the expedient of restricting the powers of the self-governing bodies to within the narrowest possible limits . . . and utilizing freely the weapons of censorship and police supervision.[1]

If this judgment was a little too harsh, Slovaks were quite convinced in 1938 that they had been discriminated against by Prague in a shameless way; the treatment they had received since 1919 seemed to bear out the thesis that Masaryk had deliberately deceived them with the Pittsburgh Convention. In 1938 only 7% of the entire civil service was Slovak – even in Bratislava the best jobs in the administration were reserved for Czechs. In the army there were few high-ranking Slovak officers, and worst of all, Slovak children were usually taught by Czech teachers.*

Slovak discontent was something that the Communist Party might well have exploited. In 1926, on Stalin's orders the Party did issue a proclamation 'Against the Kramar-Hlinka Fraud with Autonomy – For Full Independence of Slovakia'† and in June of that year a national Communist Party Conference issued a manifesto entitled 'Clear Out of Slovakia'.

* Inevitable, given the disparity between Czech and Slovak standards of education and levels of culture.

† Dr Karel Kramar was a prominent right-wing Czech nationalist. Andrej Hlinka was a Slovak Catholic Priest who led the Slovak People's (Catholic) Party. An ardent Slovak nationalist, Hlinka had a habit of recalling the terms of the Pittsburgh Convention to demonstrate how far Masaryk had betrayed his promises to the Slovaks. This so infuriated the old President that he once wrote to Hlinka and denounced the Convention as a forgery.

If the Party did not have as much success in Slovakia as such a programme warranted, it was because these sentiments were not sincere. Stalin had forced them on the Party largely in order to weaken its first chairman Bohumir Smeral who was not suitably obeisant and who was convinced that Czechoslovakia should remain one nation.

The Party's insincerity meant that it made the same arrogant mistakes as the government in Prague. Instead of allowing the Slovak section to be controlled by Slovaks, Czechs were sent in to the country. For example, Klement Gottwald ran the Slovak Party paper *Pravda* until 1925, and after that remained very influential within the Slovak branch. There were even German Communists who were given authoritative positions in Bratislava. It was an absurd miscalculation not to have given most of the best jobs to Slovaks. Had this been done then the growing nationalist feeling within the country would undoubtedly have hitched itself to the Communist wagon. But a party staffed by Czechs did not encourage confidence when it demanded Slovak independence and the nationalist vote was scooped up by the clerico-fascist Catholic People's Party. In October 1923 the local Communist Party group in Bratislava had asked that the Central Secretariat of the Czechoslovak Party consider setting up a branch in Bratislava to serve as the focus of political activity in Slovakia. 'Of course,' the request rather servilely continued, 'the office should be headed, if possible, by a Czech comrade.'[2] Even on such terms the suggestion was turned down by the Czechoslovak Party Conference in Kladno; only in 1930 was a Slovak Regional Leadership set up, and it was not until the proclamation of the independent Slovak State on 14 March 1939 that, thanks to the efforts of Adolf Hitler, the Slovak Communists really became independent of Prague.

From its inception the new Slovak Party was illegal. This did not prevent it from recruiting hundreds of Slovaks anxious to struggle for the liberation of their country from a regime which enjoyed considerable support amongst the Catholic peasantry and bourgeoisie; amongst the first of those who enrolled were Stefan, Julius and Alexander Dubcek.

The Party which they joined was unique. It was the last

major European Communist Party to be formed before the beginning of the war, it was led by men of considerable calibre and it owed no allegiance to Stalin. Not all Slovak left-wing politicians had willingly accepted the pre-war system under which almost all parties treated Bratislava as a provincial town in Moravia rather than as the capital of Slovakia. During the last ten years there had grown up in Slovakia a group of left-wing intellectuals, most of them Communists, who combined with their socialism an ardent nationalism. The group was centred on *DAV*, a Slovak political, cultural and literary review, which had been founded in 1924 by students then studying at Charles University in Prague. The paper took its name from the initials of its three founder members: Daniel Okali, Andrej Siracky and Vlado Clementis. (‘*Dav*’ also means ‘crowd’ in Slovak.) The group was soon joined by others who were to be prominent politicians: the writer Laco Novomesky, the teacher Petr Jilemnicky (after his return from the Black Sea) and the young lawyer Gustav Husak.

These young men were of great importance for they were perhaps the most talented ‘intellectual socialists’ within the Czechoslovak Communist movement. Stalin had done his best to see that the Party was fully bolshevized* by the mid-1930s and that any members with the slightest pretension to bourgeois ideology were weeded out, but he had been able to do nothing about the members of *DAV*. This was because the group was only loosely affiliated to the Czechoslovak Communist Party before the war; though the Party leaders frowned upon its activities, they were unable to stop them. When the Slovak Communists declared themselves an independent party in 1939 it was these young men who stepped into the leadership, for most of the previous leaders of the Czechoslovak Party were either in prison or in exile.

The most important aspect of the ‘bolshevization’ of the Communist Parties was that they should accept without question the strictures of Stalin. After the resolution of the ‘Great Debate’ over ‘Socialism in One Country’ this meant that

* The term ‘bolshevization’ was coined at the Fifth Comintern Congress in 1924. It was aptly defined as ‘bringing into all sections that which is international and generally valid in Russian Bolshevism’.[3]

national leaders understood quite clearly that – in Trotsky's words – they were to be the mere 'frontier guards' of Soviet Russia. Gottwald and Novotny, Siroky and Bacilek all appreciated that their purpose in life was not so much the serving of their own working class as the abetting of the international proletariat – and by 'international' was meant the various nations of the Soviet Union. According to Trotsky, Stalin held the foreign Communist Parties in ineffable contempt, but this was a prejudice which the leaders of the Czechoslovak Party were quite prepared to indulge.

It is easy to be over-critical of this total dependence on the Soviet Union and of this apparently unquestioning toadying to Stalin, not only by Czech Communists but by Party members throughout the world. But one should remember the importance of internationalism in Marxist ideology and that until the end of the war the Soviet Union was the only ruling Communist Party in the world, and that for much of the time it was struggling against very great odds for survival. It was vital for every Marxist throughout the world that this first experiment with Communism should succeed. He might consider it a historical tragedy that it had to be Russia rather than an industrialized country of Western Europe that was the guinea-pig of the new system; undoubtedly this made the growing pains infinitely harder and harsher than might otherwise have been necessary; but such was the situation and the best must be made of it.

But Husak, Clementis and their friends were less eager than most to accept this orthodoxy. They were independent, impetuous and flexible. Whereas other Party leaders were Stalin's handmaidens, the Slovaks were above all patriots leading a national crusade against the clerico-fascist* government of Tiso and Hitler. They did not consider that the experience of other Parties bore any relevance to their own situation and they refused to accept advice from such quarters.

Between August 1939 and June 1941 the Czechoslovak Party leaders accepted the logic of the Hitler-Stalin Pact. Although Vlado Clementis was the only prominent Slovak Communist to condemn the Pact in public, the Slovak Party as a whole pursued its own independent policy of doing all it

* The clerico-fascists were still nationalists – but only by courtesy of Hitler.

could to build up an underground of resistance against Hitler and his allies. This was reassuring for all those Slovak Communists who had been disturbed at the cynicism of Stalin's alliance with the Nazis. Whether or not Dubcek was one of those who doubted its morality is not quite clear. What seems very likely is that with Communists all over the world he contrived to shift the blame for it on to the Western bourgeoisie. Nevertheless, he joined with the rest of the Slovak Party in making his own contribution towards the overthrow of the Nazis. In 1940 he managed, despite his political convictions, to get a job as a locksmith in the Skoda armaments factory at Dubnica-nad-Vahom, about fifteen miles from Trencin. There, in conditions of considerable danger, he helped to build up a communist cell which organized minor acts of sabotage. He also contrived to steal small supplies of arms which he hid in caches in the hills round the town in preparation for the 'inevitable' armed struggle against the fascists.

In August 1943 Gottwald sent Karol Smidke from Moscow to help re-establish the Slovak Party leadership as the previous leaders (the fourth group in succession) had been arrested by the secret police. His task was to see that the new leaders appreciated the policy of the exiled Czechoslovak Party and 'to organize the national liberation struggle according to the directives of the Comintern Executive Committee of January 23, 1943'. In other words he was to convince the Slovak Communists that their duty, as well as their best interests, lay in following the directions of Moscow. With him as radio operator went Karol Bacilek.

Bacilek appears to have had trouble with his transmitter and Smidke had trouble with his new colleagues. For although he was duly elected to serve on the 5th illegal Central Committee of the Slovak Party he found that already very powerful on that body were Dr Gustav Husak and the poet Laco Novomesky. They soon made Smidke realize that they had no intention of carrying out the instructions of a bureaucratic and isolated leadership in Moscow and that they intended to act according to their own interpretations of the situation around them. Gottwald had chosen badly in Smidke for he was an extremely intelligent man who quickly realized that Husak was correct, abandoned his instructions from Moscow and enthusiastically adopted the Slovak cause of independence.*

The Slovaks took their most important and self-assertive step in December 1943: Husak and Novomesky ratified the 'Christmas Agreement' with the social-democratic forces of the Slovak underground. By this treaty the two most important resistance groups in Czechoslovakia pledged themselves to restore the pre-war republic, 'a common state of Czechs and Slovaks based on the principle of equality'. It was a significant doctrine which enormously increased the authority of the Slovak Communists. Before the war they had been inconsequential creatures of the Czechoslovak Party; now, thanks to Husak's skill, they entered the resistance movement in full and equal partnership with the democratic forces. They thus laid claim to a share in the spoils of victory and were assured a place at an eventual peace conference in their own right and irrespective of the wishes of the exiled Czechoslovak leadership in Moscow. It was a brilliant tactical move by Husak which was seen by Gottwald and Stalin as a serious deviation from the sacred doctrine of democratic centralism. It was a deviation which was to be brutally punished.

Moscow did not appreciate as well as did Husak that by 1944 Slovakia was ripe for revolt. To the Czechoslovak Communist leaders in Russia it appeared that the Slovak Party was still a hopelessly small, insecure group with no popular base and in constant danger of destruction by the Slovak authorities. They did not realize that by the end of 1943 the right to print their own banknotes and stamps and to maintain ambassadors in other German puppet states no longer held much attraction for many Slovaks who had initially greeted their 'independence' with some enthusiasm.

The greatest mistake that Hitler had made with regard to Slovakia was to compel its army to fight his war. It was first deployed against Poland and although the Slovak army had never before been staffed by Slovak officers (and their German 'advisers'), it was not a popular fight in Slovakia. But worse was the fact that at the end of the year 1942 the Tiso

* It should be said that General Ferjencik (now in Chicago) who flew out with Smidke and Bacilek surmised that Smidke worked for the NKVD.

Government agreed to send two Slovak divisions to the Eastern Front to fight alongside the Germans against the Russians. This was ill-judged, for Slovaks had never had any tradition of anti-Sovietism – indeed there had been a long-standing affection between the two countries. The Slovak soldiers reacted to this order by deserting *en masse* to the Red Army they were supposed to defeat; at the battle of Melitopol alone some three thousand fled across the lines and joined up with the Czechoslovak Brigade which was fighting in Russia under the Czech Colonel Ludvik Svoboda. Husak understood this disaffection in the army and knew that, if he called a revolt, large sections of the Slovak troops would rise up against the Government and its German allies.

He was also confident that many Slovaks in the civil service and in the police force now realized that Germany might not win the war and were beginning to think of their futures. They would have slight prospects in a Slovakia relieved of Nazi protection unless they had played some part in that liberation and thus compensated for their previous collaboration.

The Christmas Agreement was the first step towards coordinating the plans of revolt. At that time it appeared that one of two things might happen in the war as it affected Slovakia:

1. The Red Army struggling towards the Carpathians might reach the passes leading into Slovakia and then thrust down to the Danube Basin before the Germans were able to occupy the country, or

2. The German Army, distrusting the Slovak forces, might decide on a full scale military occupation of Slovakia in order to defend its vital lines of communication and the Carpathian Passes.

The Slovak National Council decided, under Husak's guidance, that the army and the entire Slovak people should begin an armed insurrection in order to drive the Germans out of their country and back into Czech lands. It was also agreed that when the Red Army reached the Dukla Pass in northeast Slovakia the resistance in Slovakia should concentrate on clearing its path through the country so that it could drive straight down to Bratislava and Vienna. The Partisans in the west of the country were to try, with the help of the army units stationed there, to forestall a German invasion from Moravia. In case the Germans were to enter Slovakia before the Red Army had reached the Carpathians, all resistance was to be concentrated in the mountainous Banska Bystrica region of Central Slovakia.

In fact the German Army did invade Slovakia before the Red Army had arrived at Dukla. This appears to have been the fault of an over-enthusiastic group of resistance fighters who attacked the small German garrison in the village of Vrutki near to Martin on 24 August 1944. The Germans realized that this was only the first incident in a long-planned assault upon their position in Slovakia and at once sent in reinforcements from the Czech lands. So when the Uprising really began on 29 August only two Slovak garrisons from Western Slovakia were able to join in – the rest had already been immoblized by German troops. Most serious was the fact that the Germans surrounded and contained the two crack Slovak divisions at Presov in eastern Slovakia. This meant that Husak had to abandon the plan by which these two divisions were to have cleared the Dukla Pass to enable a swift occupation of Slovakia by the Red Army. The Revolt thus immediately became much more of a guerrilla affair than had been hoped. Nevertheless, the Partisans held out in Banska Bystrica for sixty days before the Germans were able to take it. Surrounded on all sides by mountains the town is perfect for defence and seven German divisions were needed before it was won.

Even its final fall did not mean the end of the Revolt, for groups of Partisans and soldiers fled to the hills and continued their guerrilla activity into the winter. During the worst months of January and February 1945 they spent their time holed up in mountain camps and villages, but with the spring approach of the Red Army they again started to harass the Germans, if only to impress the Russians that their stamina and fighting qualities had well survived the winter.

There were nine main groups of Partisans fighting in Slovakia from September to December 1944. The Jan Zizka*

* Jan Zizka: near-legendary, one-eyed Hussite military leader who co-

Brigade, in which Alexander and Julius Dubcek served, was five hundred strong and led by Commander Teodor Pola. This group had been organizing itself for the past two years. Its nucleus had been in the Bata Shoe Factory at Banovce where there was a very strong Communist group.

Alexander Dubcek had tried to co-ordinate the work of the Party members in his factory at Dubnica with that of the Bata group. But conditions at Skoda were extremely difficult. As it was an armaments factory, the secret police kept a very careful, though clearly not always successful watch for subversive movements and organizations. The Party cell was therefore very small and it was able to act only in conditions of secrecy greater even than those imposed on the Party in the rest of the country.* An official account states that:

> The outbreak of the Revolt found the whole Dubcek family well-prepared. On the night before its outbreak Julius swam the river Vah near Dubronice together with four comrades. Only Dubcek was armed. They spent the night at the house of Dubcek's grandmother, and on the morning of 29th August joined the ranks of Jan Simek. In the meantime Alexander Dubcek came stealthily over the hills from Dubnica together with Misa Adamek and a sizeable group of French Partisans who had worked in Dubnica as prisoners of war.[3]

On the night of 27–28 August a Douglas DC3 flew over Vrutki. From it dropped nineteen parachutists. As they landed, seven of them either broke or sprained their ankles so badly that their comrades had to carry them away. Such was the arrival of the Slovak and Russian guerrillas who had been specially trained at Kiev and were supposed to lead the Jan Zizka brigade. The following night they began to limp through the Tatra mountains to Fackov where they met their men, amongst them the brothers Dubcek. The next day this

ordinated the resistance of Tabor against the anti-Hussites; until his death in 1424 most successful opponent to Sigismund's claim to the Bohemian crown.

* The following, sometimes contradictory accounts of Dubcek's war are derived from two sources: the official records in various Slovak libraries, and conversations with men involved in the Slovak Revolt and especially in the Jan Zizka Brigade.

new band marched to Cicmany, where they informed the villagers that the glorious revolt had broken out. The villagers appear to have been unimpressed; there is no record that any of them left his plough to join the Partisans.

For the next three months Alexander Dubcek roved around the hills of his birthplace, Uhrovec, where the thickly wooded terrain is ideal for partisan fighting. His war was not particularly glorious. There have been attempts to make it appear so, not least by Dubcek himself, but more revealing than the official Party histories published later and than the continual eulogies of Slovak politicians, are the diaries kept by the men at the time.*

Dubcek was in a unit led by a Captain Zalman. In the account of Zizka's commander, Pola, the activities of Zalman's unit do not figure very large, and in Zalman's own notes on fighting there is not one reference to Alexander Dubcek. It is safe to assume that neither he nor Julius distinguished himself in any way.

The group followed the tactics of all partisans, hiding up in villages where most of them were known but few were welcome. On the appearance of German search parties they left for the hills, in order to escape or to ambush the enemy. Their aim was to harass the Germans as much as possible whilst avoiding a pitched battle. This is of course a well practised and often successful guerrilla tactic the efficiency of which has most recently been demonstrated by the Vietcong. But the result of such fighting – in South Vietnam as well as in Slovakia – is that the civilians suffer most. It is the villagers, who want nothing better than to be left alone, who are used and abused by both sides. In 1944, food was scarce in Slovakia and the uninvited Partisans consumed most of any village's scant supplies; as soon as they moved on, the villagers' beds were taken by hungry German soldiers hunting for the newly departed guests. Any villagers who refused to co-operate with the Partisans were shot. So were any who would not co-operate with the Germans; and most of those who co-operated with both. As many villages were occupied first by Partisans, then by Germans and then very often once more by Partisans, the villagers had a hard time

* I have been able to study some of these journals.

deciding where their best interests lay. In the village of Sliac eleven villagers were liquidated by Partisans because they refused to leave their families and fields to join the guerrillas in the hills. Their reluctance to fight was explained by one Partisan leader as an object lesson in the thoroughly undesirable effects of the ownership of property upon revolutionary ardour. Had they been working in a collective, he suggested, they would not have hesitated to join the freedom fighters. Given the hatred with which most peasants later came to regard the collectives, he was probably right – they would have left them for anything.

Until the fall of Banska Bystrica, Zizka concentrated on harassing the rear of the Germans engaged in attacking the town. But for these activities it is probable that the town would have fallen earlier. But once it had been taken, the Nazis could give more attention to destroying the Partisans; on 20 November they managed to force a battle in which Zizka suffered such heavy losses that the group was finished as a plausible military unit. This attack also meant the end of Dubcek's war: he was twice wounded. 'His life was saved by the devoted Partisan Bilka, who carried him on a stretcher to Selec near Trencin. Here he lingered between life and death, and his mother made a trek through the hills to report on the situation in Trencin and Nemcova and to visit her Partisan sons.' So reads the official account; in fact Dubcek received two wounds in the thigh – they were not as serious as this source suggests. Nevertheless, his comrades in arms were no doubt sorry to see him go for, if he had played no very distinguished part in the fighting, they 'found him during the worst trials a man of courage and honesty, a fighter for the new Czechoslovak Republic and for the interests of its working people. He was an exemplary, modest and self-sacrificing Communist.'[4]

Alexander was lucky to escape with mere thigh wounds, for Julius was killed. Julius was an attractive, boisterous young man, very different from his studious younger brother, for whom he had an amused and indulgent affection. Julius's communism and partisanship were a lark; Alexander's were very serious.

Once again there appears to be a certain discrepancy between the official account of Julius's death and what actually happened. According to a tract glorifying the Dubcek family published in 1968:

> On 28 January 1945 Julius Dubcek heard how the Fascists had attacked Michal Zajac the miller of Zitna, how they chased the gipsies of Zitna through the woods and then entered Kasian where they continued their plunder of homes and abducted a number of Partisans; he immediately left with his troop for Vestenice, near Jankovy Hill, where he overtook the band. His platoon of brave partisans dispersed the Fascists and freed their comrades. Unfortunately Julius Dubcek was killed in this battle near Vestenice.

According to a good friend of Julius only the time and place of his death in the account are true. Julius was in fact the camp cook, and on that day he had left the camp to spend the evening drinking with his uncle. He was shot by a German patrol as he tried to find his way back to his tent at midnight.

The Slovak Revolt has passed into legend without suffering the purge of history. The Slovak Communists have, since 1963, transformed it into the most glorious moment of their past and have used it as an excellent method of taunting the Czechs, whose own fight against the Nazis was much less spectacular.

It is difficult, therefore, to gauge the precise significance of the Revolt. It failed in its aim to allow the Red Army to thrust through the Dukla Pass and down to Vienna. But it did immobilize for at least two months of 1944 seven divisions of the German Army. And even after the fall of Banska Bystrica the Germans had to maintain large garrisons and thousands of patrols in what was now a largely hostile nation.

Another important result of the Revolt was that it enabled Benes – in exile in London – more easily to persuade the Allies that Slovakia should not be treated after the war as an enemy state but as an integral part of Czechoslovakia which had been struggling for its freedom and for the reconstitution of the State destroyed by Hitler in 1939.

Even more significant was the Revolt's political effect on Slovakia. The successful militancy of the Slovak Communist Party convinced the Czechoslovak Communist leaders in Moscow that Slovak nationalism was a force to be exploited rather than denied. Accordingly they adopted the demands of the Slovak autonomists and these were formally accepted as part of the postwar Coalition's policy and published in 'The Kosice Programme' of April 1945.[5]

This promised the Slovaks greater freedoms than most of them had ever dreamed possible. Chapter Three assured Slovakia the creation of 'Slovak military units', Chapter Six explicitly stated that 'Slovaks should be masters within their own country', and Chapter Fifteen guaranteed that 'education in Slovakia will be, within the framework of an overall state policy, entirely independent in both its system and its spirit – in accord with the Slovak national ideology'.

The Communists were vital partners in the Coalition Goverment which ruled Czechoslovakia after the liberation of the Czech lands and Slovakia in 1945. For three years they paid lip-service to the spirit of the Kosice provisions. But in the February of 1948 they disrupted the Coalition and assumed total power in the country. They then decided that the Kosice formula had served its purpose and began systematically and ruthlessly to destroy every vestige of independence they had either promised or granted Slovakia. They murdered Vlado Clementis, imprisoned Husak and Novomesky and outlawed Karol Smidke. To thousands of Slovaks, Stefan Dubcek amongst them, it was a disillusioning shock to learn that a Communist government could discriminate against them just as blatantly and a good deal more savagely than either a feudal or a democratic-capitalist regime.

3
APPARATCHIK

> 'The Party can never be mistaken,' said Rubashov. 'You and I can make a mistake. Not the Party. The Party, comrade, is more than you and I and a thousand others like you and I. The Party is the embodiment of the revolutionary idea in history. History knows no scruples and no hesitation. Inert and unerring, she flows towards her goal. At every bend in her course she leaves the mud which she carries and the corpses of the drowned. History knows her way. She makes no mistakes. He who has not absolute faith in history does not belong in the Party's ranks.'
>
> Arthur Koestler, *Darkness at Noon*, 1940

Alexander Dubcek celebrated the liberation of the Czech lands and Slovakia and the reconstruction of the Czechoslovak Republic by marriage. He had known his bride, Anna Ondrisova, as a child, for her family was also at Interhelpo. He had not seen her after 1932 because her father had taken her and her brother and sister back to Slovakia just before the Dubceks moved to Gorkiy. They met again in 1944: it was to her house that Dubcek was carried when wounded in the Revolt. She hid and nursed him through the winter of 1944–5, and they were married in the middle of November 1945 – in church.

Dubcek is apparently the only East European Communist leader to have the Pope's blessing upon his marriage; it says something about him. Of course it was not abnormal that even Communists should have church weddings in what Masaryk had described as 'priestridden' Slovakia. Moreover, despite her background, Anna was not as dedicated a Communist as her bridegroom – it was perhaps her idea that they should have a white wedding. Probably as important was the fact that the priest who married them was a good friend of them both. He had fought alongside Dubcek in the Jan Zizka Brigade and it was he who had carried his wounded comrade to Anna's house: he was undoubtedly anxious that his two young friends should be extended at least this one chance of saving their souls.

But more important was Dubcek's own attitude to the affair. As an orthodox member of the Party, he might well have refused to be married in church, despite his bride's entreaties and despite his friendship with the priest. But he was not the rigid theorist who could deny either his bride or his companion the pleasure of a religious marriage if that was what they wanted. He was not, and still is not a man who allows dogma to interfere in his private life. His loyalty to the Party later became more complete than it was in 1945 but he has nevertheless always managed to prevent ideology from interfering with his personal commitments and beliefs.

He and Anna were married in Trencin and there they stayed. It is not an immediately attractive town; the official tourist guidebook describes it as a good stopping-off place for expeditions to more beautiful parts of Slovakia. It has a castle and a few trees, but otherwise it is a seedy, light-industrial slum in what is still a predominantly agricultural area. It has not changed much since the days when Dubcek worked there, and today its run-down and drab appearance illustrates well the failure of Prague-directed socialist investment to transform the peasant economy of Slovakia into one in which industry plays a major role.

Dubcek had been in Trencin before the war. After his return from the Soviet Union he had come to the town in search of work. In 1939 in Slovakia this was difficult to find, unskilled labour was cheap and Dubcek had to take what jobs he was offered; he worked successively, and without particular distinction, as a pageboy at the Tatra Hotel, as a petrol pump attendant and as a chauffeur.

When he came back in 1945 work was more easily available but he was still largely unskilled. His four years as a locksmith at Dubnica do not seem to have qualified him for similar work in Trencin. He took instead a job at the local yeast factory.

Since 1948 every factory and office has automatically had its own Communist Party organization. Before 1948 the existence and activities of such groups depended on the energy and enthusiasm of local workers. In the yeast factory Dubcek gave much of his time to Party work, and in 1946 he was appointed secretary of the group. This was an unpaid job which consisted of collecting dues, arranging meetings, recruiting new members, organizing demonstrations and, when ordered, provoking strikes against the management. Strikes were never wildcat for the Party maintained very strict control over its lower organizations. Dubcek's job was to convey to his members the instructions of the town committee of the Party, received in turn from the district committee which was acting under the orders of the regional section, which was being advised by Bratislava.

Most of his remaining spare time he spent in studying the problems of land reform. After his childhood in Interhelpo he considered, not without reason, that he had experience which could be useful to the Party in solving this difficult question.

In 1945 what had been expected to be a fairly revolutionary Land Reform Act had been passed by the Government. The Slovak National Council decreed that the agricultural property of 'Germans and Hungarians, as well as traitors and enemies of the Slovak people' was to be confiscated and redistributed among the landless peasants and smallholders. This order did not have much effect. Very few Germans lived in Slovakia, and most of the Hungarians and 'other traitors' were able somehow to evade the rigours of the law. The Land Transfer Scheme had been conceived as a nationalist, if not a racialist, act directed against enemies of the country and not of the class. Eighty per cent of the land that was in fact confiscated lay in the Sudetenland – Slovakia, whose agricultural problems were far more severe, benefited least from the redistribution. This had an effect on peasant attitudes towards the Party. In the Czech countryside according to a Party history, 'a considerable number of new medium peasants emerged, aware of the fact that they had received their land from the people's democratic regime with the aid of the working class and of the Communist Party. This is why these medium farmers became a political force supporting the Czechoslovak Communist Party as the May '46 elections clearly showed'.[1] The Slovak peasantry felt proportionately less grateful towards the Slovak Communist Party and this also was reflected in the election returns.

But if many Czech peasants supported the Communists in 1946, their enthusiasm was short-lived. For it was based on a total misunderstanding of the Party's intentions. Policy before 1948 was to profess the highest regard for individual private enterprise; both Czechoslovak and Slovak Parties constantly reassured small shopkeepers that their businesses would not be nationalized and promised peasants that there would be no collectivization. Undoubtedly this encouraged many people to believe that there was nothing to lose in voting Communist – it was merely a more efficient form of social-democracy. In February 1948 the Prague Congress of Peasant Commissions enthusiastically endorsed the Party's takeover of power. Dubcek later said of their activities:

> . . . the confidence which the working farmer demonstrated in the Communist Party at that time can without hesitation be described as one of the most positive factors in constructing socialism not only in the villages but throughout the country. Without this confidence, without a firm union between small and medium farmers and the working class it would not have been possible to carry out the revolutionary changes in our agriculture.[2]

What he should have said was that without the peasants' aid it might have been impossible for the Party to gain power in February 1948; after that the Peasant Commissions found that the Party considered they had outlived their usefulness and, despite repeated promises to the contrary, the government went ahead in 1949 with a large-scale programme of collectivization. It is an important moment in the life of every young and idealistic politician when he first realizes that his loyalty to the Party and to his own career is coming into conflict with his duty to his conscience and to the people. He must decide to abandon either his politics or his moral qualms and, if he decides upon the latter, must feverishly seek to rationalize his choice in terms of unimportant present means to vastly significant hypothetical ends. The betrayal of all that he had promised the peasants apparently did not shake Dubcek's confidence in the Party. For in 1949 he decided to enter the *apparat* full-time.

It was neither a surprising nor a difficult decision. He had been active within the Party ever since his return from the USSR, and the last four years had seen enormous Communist successes, culminating in February 1948 with their taking over complete control of the nation, and ousting the bourgeois-democrats from the Government Coalition.* Dubcek was overjoyed at this victory, which he later described as 'a great milestone in our development'. Now, he thought, a brave new socialist Czechoslovakia would be built, the cause of the international working class would flourish. Perhaps he even believed that Czechs and Slovaks could now be great partners and good friends. He wanted a part in the building of the new society, and when the chance came to enter the Party machine, he jumped at it. Possibly he was not influenced by the thought striking so many people at that time – that the future of those outside the Party was less assured than that of those within. But it would be unjust to ascribe to him the same opportunistic motives as prompted thousands of people to seek to enter the *apparat* – he had, after all, long

* The Communist assumption of power in February 1948 is still very controversial. At the time it aroused rather more horror in the West than had Hitler's destruction of the state ten years before. The absence of any physical violence in 1948 (February) has always enabled the Communists to claim that it was a legal transfer of power. The West, on the other hand, asserts that it was a blatant *coup d'état*. The truth lies somewhere between the two. The Communist Party gained power as much as a result of the irresolution and blunderings of the bourgeois-democratic parties and the weakness of President Benes, as of its own extra-legal strong-arm methods.

On 20 February 1948 all the bourgeois-democratic ministers in the National Front Coalition resigned, ostensibly in protest against Communist manipulation of the police force. In fact they were trying to force a show-down with their Marxist partners over the increasing powers which the Communists had been arrogating to themselves. The democrats believed that President Benes would refuse to accept their resignations and would call for a General Election in which, they were confident, the Communists would suffer heavy losses. There is considerable evidence to suggest that an election would indeed have been disastrous for the Communists. But the success of the democrats' plan depended on two factors: Communist readiness to abide by the rules of parliamentary democracy and to forswear extra-parliamentary methods, and their own ability to bolster Benes in his resistance to Communist pressure. After their resignation the democrats behaved remarkably foolishly – they did nothing to help Benes and made no attempt to inform the public of their intentions. The Communists were left the field and they very skilfully manipulated public opinion and Benes until they induced him to accept the formation of a new government controlled by themselves.

Of course the democratic parties suffered from the built-in disadvantage of all such groups: they were by definition unable to resort to the same effective methods as their opponents. Nevertheless, had they acted with a little more circumspection and political skill, they might have been able to carry out their original intentions and thwart the Communist victory.

been a Communist and had already proved his allegiance through the very difficult years of the war.

During the war membership of the illegal Slovak Communist Party had been rather an adventure. It also had something élitist about it; it was at that time almost a genuine bolshevik movement. But in 1948 when the Party became the government a complete rethink of its whole organization and *raison d'être* was needed. It had to expand at once both its membership and its *apparat*. The first problem was not difficult. There was a recruitment drive, and by May 1948 the Party membership had risen from 1½ million to over 2 million in a population of only 13½ million. The bolshevik notion was forsaken in an attempt to create a genuine popular movement.

Expansion of the *apparat* had to be more selective to keep out enemies of the people. There was, understandably enough, a distinct bias towards working-class entrants and Dubcek had everything in his favour; he had lived most of his life in Russia, he had experienced at first hand, albeit very young, the problems of a co-operative, he had shown himself a militant Communist in the fight against the Fascists, and since the war he had worked long, loyally and without pay for the good of the Party. Participation in the Slovak Revolt was not yet regarded as a symptom of bourgeois-nationalism, and there was only one slight question-mark against his name. This was placed there by the Slovak Party Chairman Viliam Siroky and was occasioned by his dislike of Dubcek's father Stefan. Stefan and Siroky had both been arrested in 1943 for their illegal activities within the Slovak Communist Party. They were imprisoned together in Bratislava. Stefan, whose wanderlust had not diminished, arranged an escape and offered to take Siroky with him. Siroky not only rejected the idea but also betrayed Stefan's plans to the head warder. Stefan was put under closer scrutiny than ever.

In February 1945 the Germans, overruling the Slovak authorities, insisted that at least two hundred of the Communists be transferred to Mauthausen Concentration Camp. Stefan and Siroky were both in this group, but the night before they were to be moved Siroky escaped with his friend the warder. Although Stefan had previously tried to help him, he made no attempt to aid Stefan, who was herded with the other 198 into cattle trucks. Stefan was furious at this betrayal and later told Siroky in no uncertain terms how much he despised him.

On its way up the Danube Valley the train was attacked by American fighter-planes and in the ensuing chaos Stefan managed, with two friends, to make his way to the border.* But just before they crossed into Austria they were informed against, recaptured and taken to Mauthausen after all.

Then Stefan found to his disgust that Antonin Novotny, a leading Czech Communist, had contrived to insinuate himself into the position of *kapo*, a sort of trusty who, in return for certain privileges and comforts denied the others, helped the camp authorities to control the prisoners. Conditions in the camp were terrible: when Stefan came out he weighed only seven stone – Novotny had enough to eat. This did not endear the future President of Czechoslovakia either to Stefan or to his son Alexander.

After May 1945, and when he had recovered from the Mauthausen ordeal, Stefan could reasonably have expected a good job in the Party hierarchy, given his exemplary record of service to the movement. He never got it and many people, not least Alexander, attributed this to the malign influence of Siroky. Some reports have it that Siroky was also against Alexander being given a job in the *apparat*, but at that time Husak was Premier of Slovakia and his influence was still substantial: he was prepared to extend what help he could to any Communist who had fought for him in the Revolt.

Appointments to the *apparat* are made in Prague, via Bratislava. Alexander Dubcek was told to stay in Trencin and his first job – as one of the fifteen junior Party secretaries in the town – involved work in the nationalization of both land and the retail trade.

He should have found the agricultural side of it fairly straightforward because even before 1948 Slovakia had had a well organized system of rural co-operatives; indeed, amongst a large proportion of the peasantry the co-operative idea had been accepted. Dubcek and his colleagues now set out to

* A peasant woman who lived near the Slovak-Austrian border hid them for three days. After the war Stefan left his first wife Pavlina and married this protectress.

persuade the farmers that the proposed collectives were different only in degree and not in kind from the traditional co-operative movement. They even went so far as to drop the hated name 'collective' – in future it was to be called a 'Unified Agricultural Co-operative'. Nevertheless peasant resistance was widespread.

Apart from collectivization there was plenty of work for Dubcek to do within Trencin itself. In 1945 all enterprises employing over 150 persons had been nationalized; in 1948 began the task of taking over the rest. To begin with those concerns with less than fifty employees were left outside the state sector, but within the next two years the denial of raw materials and the inducement, by threats and by bribes, of workers into public concerns, forced all small-time capitalists to liquidate their family businesses or at least to join the socialized sector and relinquish the ownership of their plant. This progress towards complete socialization in industry was duplicated in the retail trade. In 1946 about 88% of it was in private hands, by 1949 only 46%, and by 1952 virtually none at all.

The takeover by the state of small enterprises and shops was carried out entirely by the local *apparats*. It was at this level, in dealing with minor capitalists, that the greatest hardships were felt, the worst persecutions and injustices occurred. Dubcek, though humane, was quite uncompromising in forcing through the programme of nationalization. He considered it essential, he regarded private property as iniquitous, and he was not inclined to allow any wretched petty-bourgeois to resist the aspirations of the proletariat.

The Central Committee of both Czechoslovak and Slovak Parties normally met once every three months; they need large bureaucracies to carry out whatever resolutions they pass and whatever recommendations they make. It was to the *apparat* of the Slovak Central Committee in Bratislava that Dubcek was summoned in 1951.

He left his job in Trencin with reluctance. There he had been a figure of some importance; if his orders came from Bratislava and Prague, at least he had a certain discretion in their execution. During the first two years after the Party took power many problems arose which, despite the help of Soviet advisers, had not been foreseen; many were settled at local level, and it is probably true to say that a small-town Party Secretary had, during these very early years, more freedom in his work and less interference from Prague than he has ever since been allowed. By the end of 1951 the rules had been drawn up to cover almost every possible contingency; rather like the district manager of an international oil company, to any conceivable question Dubcek could find an answer in the book. This left no room at all for individual initiative.

His new job in the Central Committee was much more the work of an anonymous civil servant. Whereas in Trencin his work had taken him all over the town and into the surrounding countryside, he now spent nearly all his time in the Central Committee building on the hill behind the castle of Bratislava. In Trencin he was in constant contact with ordinary people – both Communist and non-Communist – and was continually called upon to solve, even in a dogmatic way, the thousands of human problems that accompany the advent of socialism into a social-democratic society; his only contact now was with other Party clerks doing the same work as himself.

It was work similar to that of bureaucrats the world over – quite humourless, often boring and very often frustrating. It was especially so for Dubcek: having spent three years at the grass roots of the Party and having lived all his life as an ordinary working-class Communist, he found it a curious and not altogether pleasant sensation to be dealing with problems at second-hand and to have to give text-book answers rather than his own.

The new Communist Constitution of 1948 retained a surprising number of the articles of that of 1920. The system remained basically one of parliamentary democracy and only minor adaptations were made to enable it to work as a Stalinist dictatorship. It retained amongst other things a Legislative Assembly, or Parliament, and to this Dubcek was elected in 1951.

In theory his election should have been by 'universal, equal, direct and secret suffrage'. In Czechoslovakia everyone over the age of eighteen had the right to vote and an astonishingly high proportion of the electorate exercised its right – far higher than in most European countries. Moreover the background of the deputies reflected to a much greater extent than in England the structure of the population. The deputy is compelled to make periodic reports to his constituents who are supposed to be able to recall him from office if they are dissatisfied with his conduct of their affairs. In fact, however, this representational system is sadly less perfect than it might appear, for the voter has no real choice.

This is of course true in England; the candidate is chosen by an unrepresentative local party organization from a list more or less approved by Central Office or Transport House. In this sense the voter in Czechoslovakia is no worse off than the English elector. The difference is that in Czechoslovakia the Communist Party has a pre-ordained and irremovable majority. Everyone votes, but his vote is an endorsement of the Party's candidate rather than a choice between two competing interests. His only freedom in the voting booth is to spoil his ballot paper, and in the early 'fifties even this elementary but satisfying right was often denied him. For in many towns and villages the Communists insisted upon open-balloting. Anyone could demand to be allowed to vote in secret, but he was both courageous and unwise if he did so.

The Communists were not the only political party in Czechoslovakia: there were six, all of them incorporated within the National Front which represents 'the union of toilers, peasants and working intelligentsia, the fighting bloc of the Communist Party of Czechoslovakia, the Revolutionary Trade Union Movement, the Czechoslovak Youth League, the Czechoslovak Socialist Party, the Czechoslovak People's Party, the Party of the Slovak Rebirth, the Freedom Party, and other organizations of the working people'. But these are all dominated by the Communists and have no political significance. Their independence was removed in 1948 by the use of a single ticket in elections and by the fact that candidates could be nominated only by the National Front itself.

Dubcek's election to the Assembly was quite typical; it is

In November 1945 Alexander Dubcek married Anna Ondrisova, in Trencin and in church.

Two young Slovaks in search of Communism. In 1945 Alexander Dubcek (below) was 24, Gustav Husak was already 32. Dubcek was an unknown rank and file party member, just married and working in a gin factory in Trencin. Gustav Husak was a national hero, had defied Stalin, led the Slovak revolt and was about to become Prime Minister of Slovakia.

almost a required part of the training of any *apparatchik.* But when he arrived there he found it impotent. According to the Constitution 'the supreme organ of the legislative power', in fact the Assembly, is merely the Party's rubber stamp. The body of deputies is completely controlled by its officers – the Chairman, the Presidium and the Committee Chairman. It meets very seldom, and then for only very short sessions – perhaps for three days ten times a year. Debates were, until 1967, quite predictable and often pointless.

At the beginning of 1953 Dubcek was promoted. He was ordered by the Central Committee to take up the post of Regional Secretary of the Banska Bystrica area in Central Slovakia. He was delighted. For one thing Banska Bystrica is an exceptionally beautiful town at the foot of the Lower Tatra Mountains. For another, the Regional Secretary was at least on paper, a very powerful man, controlling not only the Party apparatus but also the machinery of government in his region. The Regional Secretary might well be described as the nabob of the area. But his powers were closely supervised by the secret police who could, if inclined, completely circumscribe and indeed ruin him. If they felt that the Secretary was interpreting his duties in a manner not in the best interests of the Party, then it was quite within their scope to suggest to Bratislavia that he be removed. In the early 'fifties it was difficult to survive in the Party machine. Only the most loyal, disciplined and unremarkable succeeded in doing so.

Dubcek's move to Banska Bystrica coincided with the death of Stalin and, a week later from a cold caught at the master's funeral in Moscow, that of President Gottwald. Gottwald was succeeded by Antonin Zapotocky in September 1953 and Antonin Novotny was appointed First Secretary of the Czechoslovak Communist Party. Novotny was forty-nine at the time and had been in the Party since the age of seventeen. With his accession a new generation of Czechoslovak Communists came to power – and almost without exception they were men of lesser calibre than those they succeeded.

Dubcek's new job involved directing the work of the other Secretaries in, among other occupations, forestry, transport and town planning. Banska Bystrica is predominantly an agricultural area, but it is so mountainous that the yields of potato and grain crops are low by the national standards. It was Dubcek's task to try and increase agricultural output by the extension and improvement of socialist methods of farming. 'Agricultural policy,' he said in 1953,

> must show how we are to fulfil the plan in this sphere of the economy, how we are to help the political and economic establishment of co-operative farms, to broaden the exchange of goods between town and village ... We must make greater demands on the people today. We do not want a single backward co-op farm, and we shall fight the theory that there exist idle or bad people as such; our task is not only to lay the foundations of a co-op farm – we must see to its development as well.[3]

Despite the Party's efforts, the indoctrination of the peasants and the collectivization of the farms remained difficult, but Dubcek tried to gloss this over:

> The 9th Congress in May 1950 formed the general plan for the building of socialism ... The slogan that 'there will be no socialism without transforming the village into a co-operative' became the leading principle of the Party's work ... In the years of the first Five Year Plan the socialist building of our villages continued. In 1948 only 3% of them belonged to the socialist sector, in 1953 it was 44%.[4]

In other words 56% still resisted.

Dubcek was also concerned with carrying out the industrialization of Slovakia's agricultural economy. His years of Secretaryship saw the building of a large number of factories in the area, the most important of which were the Biotika drug centre, the Slovenska textile factory, the Smrcina woodmill and the Cimentarum cement works. There is an interesting story connected with the construction of this last enterprise.

It was due to be built in 1954 and all the plans, including the choice of site, had, according to the rules of democratic centralism, been drawn up by officials in Bratislava with little regard to the conditions obtaining in Banska Bystrica. The site selected had ludicrously small limestone deposits and, worse still, the planners had not taken into account the prevailing winds of Banska Bystrica: in its proposed position the new factory would continually shower the lovely town with a fine and unpleasant dust.

28 August, 1954 was the tenth anniversary of the Slovak Revolt and there was a celebration in Banska Bystrica. The occasion was remarkable for the absence of most of the men who had played a prominent role in the revolt; they were in prison. The guest of honour was Karol Bacilek, First Secretary of the Slovak Party and a man not noted for his patronage of anything Slovak or for playing any useful part in the Revolt.

After he had made his uninspiring speech, Bacilek was approached by Dubcek and other officials of the town. They wondered, respectfully, if it might be possible to change the siting of the cement plant. Perhaps it could be built to the lee of the town, where the dust would not affect Banska Bystrica itself and where, furthermore, the limestone deposit was much larger than in the proposed site. They had drawn up a detailed plan of how this change might be effected and sought to assure Bacilek that the new scheme would involve the government in no increase in costs; any additional expense that might be incurred would be met by the town itself.

Bacilek would have none of it. 'I won't have my industrialization programme ruined by any narrow-minded bourgeois in Bystrica,' he shouted, and stalked off. The cement plant was built on the original site, the town was continually showered with dust and the limestone deposits very soon ran out. To obtain supplies an overhead cable railway had to be built around the edge of the town to the quarry in which Dubcek had suggested the factory be constructed.[5]

The story illustrates the appallingly inefficient methods of planning at the beginning of the Second Republic, the way in which money, materials and labour were squandered and also the limits upon the powers of the Regional Secretary. He could suggest to Bratislava that a plan might be changed but it was by Bratislava or even by Prague that the decision was made – even on an issue of such obvious local and much less national importance. Dubcek was allowed occasionally to question, but his real job was simply to implement the decisions of Prague and Bratislava.

His period in Banska Bystrica coincided with the first great economic crisis since 1948. In spite of all the political and economic propaganda campaigns of the last four years, the goverment had been unable to curb inflation in the economy. As one commentator put it:

> Unrealistic targets of Communist planning, forced collectivization of agriculture, growing dependence of the country's economy on the Soviet Union . . . orientation towards heavy industry expressed in such megalomaniacal industrial projects as the Huko steel combine in Slovakia (which was never completed) – all resulted in an economic crisis of unprecendented gravity.[6]

In June 1953 a remedy was sought in a reform of the currency. The announcement of this move brought 'bread riots' amongst the workers of Pilzen, Ostrava and other industrial towns. Dubcek was naturally concerned to play down the importance of these incidents. He tried to ascribe their outbreak to 'anti-socialist' forces, and blamed the Party for not exercising strict enough control over the workers:

> In pressing for the quick and successful reform of the currency, our organization has passed through a great test of maturity . . . . It was a manifestation of the power of the Party and of the confidence our people has in it. [This is difficult to credit.] Though there were no serious difficulties, we were able to locate the weak spots. Some Party members agreed with the reform in principle but were not strong enough to fight for it. The reform showed us what changes we need to make in the field of commerce. We must get rid of the capitalist forces in this area which are acting as a brake on the continued development of the socialist economy. The reform showed us, moreover, that some of the local Party organs are weak and do not exercise enough influence on the masses. The reason for this is that there are not enough Party organizations in schools, factories and workshops.[7]

Dubcek was at this time too good a Party-worker to allow

his immense dislike of Siroky to interfere with his duty towards the Slovak Party Chairman. Siroky unquestioningly accepted the orders of Prague and was one of the men most responsible for the Stalinist excesses of these years. Nevertheless, Dubcek's speeches are full of quotations from and praise for this man whom he later helped to have removed from power.

At the beginning of his term of office he spoke to the Banska Bystrica Communist Party about the recent 10th Congress of the Slovak Communist Party. This speech, a long string of Marxist catchwords and Party clichés which could have been made by any other *apparatchik* in the country, illustrates well how colourless a bureaucrat he appeared to be:

> Comrade Siroky showed in his report to the Congress the speed at which we have been building socialism in our country. In spite of the great harm inflicted by traitors* the development of our economy has not been hindered. In the past three years the building of new factories in Slovakia has enabled our industrial production to leap ahead. In 1952 our output was 4½ times greater than in 1937. This is indisputable proof of the value of Lenin's and Stalin's national policy . . . Comrade Gottwald has taught us that the quicker we accept that the experiences of Russia are our own experiences, the quicker we will approach the Soviet model, and the faster will be our progress on the road to socialism. The proof that we have well understood this thought of Klement Gottwald is shown in the development of socialist competition and in the use of new methods of production . . . industrial production this year is up 14½% on 1952.

'But,' he admitted, 'we must not rest on our laurels, we must see the defects in our system,' and went on to describe not the flaws in Party ideology but the deplorable fact that the plans in various industries had not been fulfilled. This failure he ascribed to the incomplete way in which the resolutions of the Party Congress had been realized: 'At the Congress Comrade Siroky said: "We must follow the spirit of the Party and its articles – we must truly unite all like-

* A reference to Slansky and other revisionists and 'Titoists'. See below.

minded people, we Communists, in the Party organizations. Every Party organization must be filled with the strength of ideological unity." ' This, says Dubcek, is most important. He was sorry to have to confess that in some of the organizations in his region, ideological unity had not been absolute. By this he meant that there had been some areas in which the adoption of the orders from Prague had been less than a hundred per cent enthusiastic.

> In some of our district organizations members of the Party did not understand the meaning and importance of ideological work of Communists and of non-Party members also. They did not understand that ideological work is the most important part of the Party's work and the first duty of every Party member. They did not realize that every time the study of Marxism-Leninism is even slightly neglected the influence of bourgeois ideology is strengthened. Many of our functionaries assert that of course ideological work is of the greatest importance, but I am afraid that they do not always carry their assertions into effect.

Much more propaganda work was needed, he thought and added, in an interesting contrast to his later views on the subject:

> The best way in which our Party can re-educate the people is by the Press. With its help our workers can be kept in touch with the resolutions of the Party and Government. We must encourage our working people to use the Press to help them in their work.[8]

Even on the question of Slovakia Dubcek appears to have accepted almost completely the prevailing doctrine of Prague centralism which had been so eagerly accepted and endorsed by Siroky and the Slovak Party's First Secretary, Karol Bacilek, and which often amounted to rank exploitation of the country for the benefit of the Czechs. In 1954 he said:

> Five years ago Slovakia was a backward country. The characteristic feature of its economic and social structure was its agrarian base. Following the policy of the 9th Congress, Slovakia has over the past five years been built and

> rebuilt. Now the Slovakia with undeveloped industry and backward agriculture belongs to the past. Industrial production is five times higher than in 1937 and our industrialization continues, thanks to the help of Bohemia and Moravia . . . When socialist industrialization began Slovakia had no technical intelligentsia. This shortcoming was also made good by the Czechs. The facts show for themselves that Slovakia could have reached its present position only in close unity with the Czechs and with the help of Czech workers and intelligentsia . . . The present epoch in our nation is characterized by huge national development and the organizing element in this development is the Czechoslovak Communist Party and its loyal section, the Slovak Communist Party.[9]

To make any fair assessment of Dubcek's work in Trencin, Bratislava and Banska Bystrica it is essential to examine his attitude to and his part – if any – in the trials of the early 'fifties. For from 1949 to 1954 the Communist Party of Czechoslovakia indulged in whole-scale terror as brutal and as masochistic as any which a 'Marxist' government had imposed since 1937. Every Czech and every Slovak had some role to play in the tragedy of the trials: as suspect, as victim, as juryman whose verdict was always 'Guilty!' or as the one who kept silence in the court.

Dubcek was not a victim of the trials. He cannot fairly be accused of being an executioner. He did not, as far as can be ascertained, at any time come under suspicion – except in so far as every Party member was potentially revisionist and every Slovak Partisan a possible bourgeois-nationalist. The problem is to decide whether he was a member of the careless and obedient jury or whether, caring but impotent, he kept his peace.

The 'Terror' of the 'fifties assumed two main forms in Czechoslovakia: the purging of Party members and indiscriminate harassing of non-Communists. The Party purges were stage-managed from the very top of the hierarchy under the orders of Beria, Mikoyan and Stalin; it is the trial of Rudolf Slansky that is the most notorious. It is in this indictment that the Party is usually thought to have most degraded itself, and it is his death that is traditionally supposed to represent all that was most cruel and absurd in the cancer of those years. Perhaps this is because Slansky was the most senior Party official to be brought to judgment and executed on trumped-up charges. Even Loebl has explained how the evidence against Slansky was invented and how the defendant, after making his 'confession', was forced to write the script for his own trial, supplying the questions for the prosecutor and endlessly rehearsing his answers.[10]

One must admit the horror and the mockery of Slansky's fate but it is difficult to have much sympathy for the man himself. It is only in a strictly legal sense that his punishment can be considered the greatest perversion of justice of those years: in human terms that palm probably goes to the execution of Vlado Clementis. Slansky was quite innocent of the espionage, high treason, sabotage and military treachery of which he was accused and for which he was killed. He was guilty of far worse crimes.

Until his arrest in November 1951 Slansky, one of the Czechs closest to Stalin, had led the 'Terror.' It was he who had instituted the arrests of non-Communists in 1948. At a meeting of the Politburo in September 1948 he had proposed that the government build forced labour camps ... 'they will have a good influence upon the workers. Educating and convincing people is not enough.' Nor was his attention confined to non-Communists. By 1949 he was, at Beria's request, insisting that the Party be thoroughly purged: 'The enemy is penetrating our ranks ... It is necessary to examine every Party member. Our Party must pass through a purification process.'[11]

It is certainly true that many petty-bourgeois opportunists had jumped on the Communist bandwagon in 1948 and that the Party needed to disembarrass itself of such men (very often extreme right-wing Catholics). But in fact it was not the time-servers who were arrested – it was the true Communists, men like Loebl, Goldstuecker, London and Smrkovsky who suffered. For the arrest of all these men Slansky, in charge of the State Security apparatus, was responsible. It is ironic that the monstrous machine which he created and which, he had said, needed to find a 'Czechoslovak Rajk'*[12] should be used to destroy himself. It provided a horrible but perhaps not altogether inapposite end to his career.

Dubcek said nothing at the time of the trial, but two years later he attacked Slansky in terms which showed a complete disregard for historical truth:

> 'The 9th Congress [of the Slovak Party in May 1950] foresaw that the imperialists would try to corrupt the minds and hearts of our people, would try to infiltrate the Party and attempt to influence its policy. When these words were spoken at the Congress, Slansky and his companions did not know that this was the beginning of the end of their criminal activities. They did not realize how close was the moment when the mask would be removed from their faces and when the great power of the never-dormant Communist watchfulness and patriotic vigilance [*sic*] would wipe away their group of emissaries of imperialism.'[13]

This was ridiculous. At the 9th Congress Siroky had denounced his Slovak rivals – no mention had been made of Czechs like Slansky. It was not until September 1951 that Slansky had the slightest hint of what was to happen to him. Only six weeks before that his birthday had been celebrated by the Party and hailed by the Press as a historic occasion, the anniversary of a loyal son of the people, a guiding light of the Party and a champion of the international workers' movement. Slansky could not have known, over a year before, how close he was to destruction for the simple reason that he had not yet been selected as the principal victim in Stalin's ritual demand for blood.

That Dubcek could not have realized. He might have known that Slansky was an evil man and might have rejoiced at his departure. But that, too, is unlikely. For Dubcek lived in Trencin during those years in which Slansky had been at the peak of his career. Busied with the problems of local

* Rajk: Tried in 1949 along with other 'accomplices', most of them members of the Hungarian Communist Party, on charges of plotting with the Yugoslavs against the Hungarian Government, aided by American and British intelligence agents. His trial produced 'irrefutable proof' that the Yugoslav Communist leaders were American agents and war criminals and that Rajk himself was a police-spy, traitor, deserter and international adventurer. He was hanged.

nationalization this junior and insignificant young Secretary could have had little idea as to what was really happening in Prague. The real truth about Slansky's activities and the extent of his guilt was revealed to the public only in 1968.[14] Like most Party members, Dubcek probably accepted unquestioningly the validity of Slansky's cooked-up trial.

Nevertheless, the timing of his attack was curious. As far as can be ascertained, it was his sole rendering of the chorus of execration of the 'Fascist hyenas', and it has been suggested that he was forced into making this isolated and belated assault by pressure from the extremer Stalinists within the Banska Bystrica Party. For during his time at the town he must have caused no small displeasure by his consistent refusal to have any truck with the slanders of the 'bourgeois-nationalists'.

Stalin and Gottwald had been angered by Husak's refusal to obey their orders and abandon his independent policies during the war. At the 1946 election the Slovak Communists polled only 30.4% of the vote while in the Czech lands the Party won an average of 38.9%. This gave the Czech leadership the excuse it was seeking to clamp down upon Slovak autonomy. On the pretext that the Slovak Party was incapable of running its own country, there followed a complete castration of the Slovak organs set up by the Kosice Agreement in 1945, and Slovak Party officials began to receive warnings never to mention that there was any difference between their country and the Czechs'. The policy of discrimination was made official and complete after 1948: any Slovak who showed the slightest inclination to question the authority of the Czechs was immediately accused by Bacilek, Siroky and the other stooges whom Gottwald had imposed upon the Slovak Party of the dread and un-Leninist crime of 'bourgeois-nationalism'.

This is a Soviet term which means an 'excessive consciousness of belonging to a given ethnic group and an undue emphasis on local government'.[15] Within the Soviet Union such a label has always been attached to Ukrainians, Latvians or Tartars; there is no record of any Russian having been accused of excessive patriotism. Similarly in Czechoslovakia no Czech has been thus indicted, although it is probably true that the average Czech despises the Slovak as much as the Slovak dislikes him.

The witch-hunt against the Slovak bourgeois-nationalists began in 1950. At the 9th Congress, Party Chairman Viliam Siroky charged Vlado Clementis, Gustav Husak, Laco Novomesky, and Karol Smidke with the terrible sin. Clementis, Jan Masaryk's equally attractive successor as Foreign Minister, was dismissed, arrested and executed. Husak and Novomesky were thrown off the Slovak Board of Commissioners, arrested and tried. Husak escaped with life, Novomesky with ten years' imprisonment.

Dubcek was clearly confused by the problem. He did not, apparently, publicly accuse Husak, Novomesky or any other individual Slovak of practising bourgeois-nationalism. But he did admit its existence, and in so doing he was once more paying tribute to the supremacy of the Czechs and consciously denying the Slovak Party any independent rights. Thus:

> The organizing element of this epoch in the life of our nation is the Czechoslovak Communist Party and its faithful collaborator the Slovak Party. In the period between the 9th and 10th Congresses [1950–4] the Party developed considerably and underwent many experiences. By broadening the merciless fight against bourgeois-nationalism and its standard-bearers, who were discovered and condemned as enemies of the Party and people, our Party played its part in strengthening and educating our people. It educated Slovaks in this spirit of Czechoslovak nationalism.[16]

He made much the same assertions in a splendidly unattractive rabble-rousing dissertation to the Conference of District Party Organizations in Banska Bystrica in 1954:

> Comrades! The period since the last conference of our organizations has been characterized by the peaceful policy of the Soviet Union and the whole peace-loving system, and on the other side by the war-mongering, arming and seeking of new fighting places by the capitalists . . .
>
> In our organization we still can find the remnants of bourgeois ideology which weaken the unity of the Party and brake the activity of the working people. In the southern parts of our district we can find bourgeois-

nationalism which is used by the class enemy to brake progress. A serious brake on the political work of the Party is the leftovers of social-democratic opportunism, clearly seen in the undervaluing of ideologic work, in denying the importance of democratic centralism, is disregarding mistakes.[17]

The thoroughness of the purges of the Slovak bourgeois-nationalists and Czech traitors* meant that the leadership of both Parties was quite emptied of genuine Marxists and staffed largely by men whose first duty lay not to the proletariat but to themselves. For them the most important thing was to see that they kept their jobs, their big black Tatra cars, their privileges and their power. They managed very well; until 1963 their authority was unchallenged and it was only in 1968 that they began to be replaced by men who genuinely cared about the aspirations of the people. But now, in 1970, they are back and once more ruling Czechoslovakia in the depressingly careless and autocratic fashion of the 'fifties.

The arrests, trials and sentences of prominent Party members were authorized at the top of the Party; they had nothing to do with Dubcek. But at the same time as these spectacular public relations displays were being mounted, thousands of tiny trials were staged. These never made the headlines. The imprisonment of former members of the bourgeoisie and other 'class-enemies' was administered at a local level, and it is with these humdrum but equally unpleasant persecutions that Dubcek might have been involved.

The members of other parties, the small shopkeepers, the Jewish traders, the peasants anxious to resist collectivization, all these men suffered after February 1948 for their activities before the 'Revolution'. Some of them, perhaps even the majority, had been engaged in anti-Communist activities before February 1948: every victorious revolution assumes the right to liquidate its unsuccessful opponents. But many of those

* Although Czechs could not be accused of 'bourgeois-nationalism', they could be condemned for being capitalist spies in the pay of Konni Zilliacus and other well-known imperialist agents. Many of them had fought with the International Brigade in the Spanish Civil War; others had fought in the West against Hitler. For this they were punished, as anyone not fighting within the ranks of the Red Army was considered to have struggled against it. Those of these 'traitors' who were Jews were almost automatically accused of Zionism.

imprisoned had played no actively anti-Communist role; their offence lay in their mere class. To have a plot of land or bourgeois ancestry was crime enough; the sentence – anything between twelve months and six years – was scaled to fit the offender's confiscated possessions or the status of his father.

None of the records of these small-town trials is available to Western journalists, and it is impossible to say how many people were imprisoned for political offences during Dubcek's sojourns at Trencin and Banska Bystrica. And even were these numbers known it would be difficult to divine how much responsibility he should accept, because in 1954 Banska Bystrica the Chief of Police was a much more powerful man than the Regional Secretary. Stalin had died but his spirit still stalked Bohemia, Moravia and Slovakia.

All that can be said is that after extensive research throughout Slovakia it has been impossible to find one person who is able to say that he suffered at Dubcek's hands during those years. Most of those who remember what he is like – and he did not appear much in public even in Banska Bystrica – recall him as an unexceptionable, quiet, diligent, rather uninspiring but quite attractive, convinced Communist, who was noticeable only for his lack of pomp and authoritarianism. But a few were able to appreciate him a little more.

One of his favourite pastimes has always been hunting: he is a very good shot. On one of his official tours around his region in 1954 he stopped in a tiny village in the Lower Tatra Mountains and was told by one of the peasants of the suffering caused by a rampant bear which had been ravaging their crops and which had attacked one of the children. All the local marksmen had tried and failed to trap the animal. Would Mr Dubcek now like to try his hand? The fact that the villager dared to make such a suggestion to the First Secretary illustrates Dubcek's reputation both for sharpshooting and for approachability. It is inconceivable that anyone would have asked such a favour of Bacilek, Siroky or Novotny. Indeed one of the Party officials brushed the villager aside saying that of course Comrade Dubcek did not have such time to waste. Comrade Dubcek, however, disagreed, promised that he would do all he could to help and returned, with his hunting gear, at the weekend.

For the next seven weeks he devoted all his spare time to stalking the bear. On several occasions he was advised to abandon the attempt – with his usual stubbornness he refused to do. His persistence was finally rewarded, he killed the bear and he now proudly displays the skin in his Bratislava home. Dubcek was not, as were so many of his colleagues, obviously a member of the *nouveau puissant*.

The best testimony to his innocence lies in the fact that he owed his subsequent rise up the Party hierarchy to the fact that he was unsullied by the crimes of the fifties; although he was part of the administration of the Terror he was too young to have had an executive role; his hands were clean. Had they not been, then he would not have been chosen to replace Novotny. And it is certain that any 'crimes' that he had committed in the 'fifties would have been thrown in his 'human face' by his enemies in 1968–9. They did not, because they were unable to find any. But one accepts the dubious doctrine of collective guilt, Dubcek must bear some responsibility for the abuses of that period. The extent of his responsibility then depends upon the extent of his knowledge of the excesses. He has himself insisted that this was far from complete and it is possible to make a case for his ignorance. In Trencin and also, but to a lesser extent, in Banska Bystrica the enormity of the crimes of the STB (Czechoslovakia's KGB) was unknown: the chain of communication in the Party ran downwards, not upwards or horizontally.

But if ignorance was possible in small provincial towns, it was much less so in Bratislava, and that is where Dubcek was at the height of the purges. All around him men were being removed from their posts and either being quietly forgotten or disposed of more certainly. Moreover Dubcek's job in Bratislava was, in part, to instruct regional and district organizations of the resolutions of the Central Committee and to see that these orders were executed. In these circumstances he must have known very well what was going on. But it is very probable that he simply believed the purges to be essential. He had, after all, had considerable experience of such matters – he had lived through the Yezhovschina in Russia and he had been consistently taught that Communism could be built only in the teeth of a class war and that what was necessary for Russia was essential for Czechoslovakia. If even Stalin had had so many enemies that he must resort to so whole-scale a purge, then how many more traitors to the people must there be under Novotny and Gottwald? 'I must stress,' he once said, 'how watchful we must be in accepting new members. In several cases the class enemies were allowed to enter the Party. The basic organizations of the Party must arrange recruitment so that the number of members is in proportion to the amount of work to be done.'[18]

In other words, the candidates must be chosen more carefully; Party organizations should accept only 'the best sons of the working class, farmers and intelligentsia'. This, he believed, had not been done in the past. He was of course quite right. Furthermore, there must have been some reason for the far from complete success of socialism up till now: the economy was not functioning as perfectly as it surely should. Dubcek sometimes even went so far as to express his concern in speeches, if only obliquely and alongside his fulsome and occasionally merited praise for the progress of industrialization. The main report on agricultural policy to the 9th Congress of the Czechoslovak Party in 1949 had been given by Slansky. Before that he had led the Czechoslovak delegation to the first meeting of CMEA. It was easy for a Party Secretary in Banska Bystrica to reason that if the economy had failed to boom as fast as had been hoped, and if the collectives were not so popular as had been planned, and if crops were as scanty as they had proved, the fault was Slansky's. The fact that the crisis was aggravated by the Korean War and by the resulting alterations that Moscow imposed upon Czechoslovakia's original production plans was neither here nor there.

He should be allowed his own explanation of that period: 'I worked in the Party. I was at home in the Party, I had my friends there. But you have to understand me as a Communist. I was very young. It was not easy to resist the pressure of the Party's central leadership. We felt that everything was passing us by. In the 'fifties I believed that culpability of the condemned existed.'*

* In the summer of 1969 Dubcek gave an interview to a Western journalist Danielle Hunebelle which was published in *Look* (29 July 1969). He later

There is one incident during these five years which stands out and gives perhaps the most important clue to Dubcek's loyalties and true beliefs at the time.

In December 1952 Karol Smidke died.* Born in Moravia he had been a devoted Communist all his life. During the war he had liaised between Moscow and the Slovak leadership of Husak and Novomesky. It was he who, with Karol Bacilek, had been sent to Bystrica in 1943 as a representative of the Czechoslovak Communist Party in Moscow to try and make Husak accept orders from the Kremlin. Once in Slovakia, however, he began to feel greater sympathy for Husak's aspirations than for the plans of Gottwald and Stalin. He was in Moscow when the Revolt broke out but at once returned and played an active role in the Slovak National Council which had been convened without the Kremlin's blessing.

At the 9th Congress of the Slovak Party in 1950 Viliam Siroky accused Smidke, along with Husak, of Slovak bourgeois-nationalism. In Smidke's case the charges were even more incongruous than in the others – above all because he was a Czech, but also because he was never out of touch with Moscow. Nevertheless it is true that by the end of the war he had gained for himself a leading role in the Slovak Party, and had acquired a greater respect for Husak than for Gottwald. It was presumably for this that he was accused of bourgeois-nationalism, while his continued contact with the Kremlin earned him a remission – he was totally ostracized rather than imprisoned.

When he died in 1952 he was in even greater official disfavour than when Siroky had initially condemned him. Indeed it is likely that had he lived he would have been sent for trial along with Husak and Novomesky. No one in the Party wanted to have anything to do with him, and no one was willing to speak at his funeral. All the top leaders made some sort of excuse and not one of them was prepared to taint his

---

asserted that she had distorted his answers and quoted him out of context.

Perhaps not too much faith should be placed in the answers he gave, if only for the fact that in one of them he denied that he had ever attacked the victims of the show trials. This was not, as shown above, true.

* According to *Rude Pravo* of bronchitis, but some unofficial sources have suggested that he committed suicide, in despair at his 'excommunication'.

own reputation by association with the name or even with the grave of Smidke. Dubcek was appalled that this great, loyal and well-loved man should be denied any recognition and, when everyone else refused to attend the funeral, he accepted. So it happened that at Smidke's death his life was lauded only by this very junior and insignificant bureaucrat.

There were only about fifty people at the cold and windy burial service; most of them were from Smidke's family and several others were STB men taking photographs and names. Apart from Dubcek there were only three Party officials there.

Dubcek's speech was courageous. He heaped praise upon the outlawed and disgraced leader. 'Smidke,' he said, 'was a great member of the Party, a true revolutionary who gave his whole self and his every effort for the battle which our Party has fought. His whole life was dedicated to the pursuit of victory for the Communist movement.' Dubcek was weeping as he finished his address.

A Communist journalist who was at the funeral, and who was later to become the editor of one of Slovakia's most important politico-cultural journals, as well as a close friend of Dubcek's, noted in his diary that evening: 'This man Dubcek is remarkable for his innocent honesty. He may well reach the top of the Party – but he is much more likely to find himself in prison. His ingenuousness is ridiculous, but astonishing and refreshing.'

Dubcek must have been terrified by the idea that he was defying the Party. Nevertheless this fear did not overcome an allegiance to Smidke which was both national and ideological; he undoubtedly had great sympathy for the work that Smidke had done for Slovakia during the war and also for the sort of Communism that he represented. But nationalism and ideology were perhaps only incidental to Dubcek's decision to stand up at Smidke's funeral. The real reason was much more personal. It was simply that transparent honesty which has always characterized his public career. Dubcek is not a man who finds it easy to lie. He is a very emotional man whose affections and loyalties are deeply felt. In 1944 he had realized Smidke's worth and he simply did not see that anything had occurred since then to alter his war-time assessment. He was not prepared to break whatever personal commitment he had made to Smidke those nine years ago.

Dubcek's concept of the hierarchical structure of the Party and his belief in its leading role – or total monopoly of power – were wholly conventional. His official speeches at the time betray almost no hint that he was in any way different from his peers; his words display an unquestioning acceptance of prevailing dogma and – apart from his slight reticence on the subject of the trials – total obedience to the assumptions of the Party and of Stalin, whom he occasionally quoted.

Nevertheless, as the journalist saw, Dubcek was not a run-of-the-mill Party hack. He spoke in praise of Smidke in a fashion that was quite untypical. He was prompted by a naive sincerity which, usually well concealed by the standard Stalinist clichés and actions, became apparent on those rare occasions when he did or said something outside of his official duties. This ingenuous sympathy and humanity has remained with him, and it is this that distinguishes him from other *apparatchiks.*

4
TORN TEXTBOOKS

> '"Reeling and writhing, of course, to begin with," the Mock Turtle replied; "and then the different branches of Arithmetic—Ambition, Distraction, Uglification and Derision."'
>
> Lewis Carroll, *Alice's Adventures in Wonderland.*

At the beginning of 1955 Dubcek was selected by the Party Secretariat in Bratislava to take one of the Party's customary places at the Higher Party School in Moscow. Later that year he set off by train for the Soviet Union for his three-year course in Communist management, economics and ideology.

The School has two functions. It is primarily the forcing-ground of bright young party workers – the high-fliers in the *apparat*. But at the same time Communist Parties throughout the world have often filled their allotted places with men they wanted to dispose of for a time. Like the Diplomatic Service of socialist countries the School has been employed as a place of painless exile either for ideological misfits or for those whose work has been so bad that there is no suitable job for them at home.

It is not clear whether or not Dubcek was being shunted off in this way. It is possible, for he had only worked for two years in Banska Bystrica, and the appointment of Party Secretary is normally for three years. On the other hand there is little evidence that his work in Banska Bystrica had been unsatisfactory to the Party. It seems more likely that he was sent to Moscow to improve his education and thus to prepare himself for further, more important work in the Party.

Whether he was being exiled or not, he is believed to have been happy to leave the job in Banska Bystrica for he was beginning to long for a respite from the increasingly limited orthodoxy which his work imposed upon him. He considered it a great honour to be able to attend the most important school in the Communist world and was determined to put the course to good use for he felt he was not well-educated. Whilst in Banska Bystrica he had taken an external degree in law from Bratislava's Comenius University. Apart from that he had only his secondary schooling in Gorkiy to fall back upon – he had no ideological training. This was a deficiency of which he was very conscious and he was delighted at the opportunity to put it right. His letters home from school over the next three years are full of praise for Moscow and for the work he was doing.

There is, unfortunately, very little information available on what exactly that work was. The students of the School are enjoined to secrecy and few of them are the type who betray the Party. Basically they are instructed in the prevailing dogma of the Soviet Communist Party. Their standard texts are traditional enough – Marx, Engels, Lenin, and, when Dubcek arrived in 1955, Stalin.

It was this that made Dubcek's three years at the School quite extraordinary. In February 1956 Khrushchev denounced Stalin at a secret session of the 20th Soviet Party Congress in Moscow. The teachers, the entire curricula, and most of the students at the School were thrown into complete confusion. Overnight all their established values had been rejected and they had nothing to substitute for them. As Khrushchev's speech was never published – only read at Party meetings throughout the nation – there was never any clear consensus on what precisely it meant. A way of life had been totally destroyed and nothing put in its place.

After this, many of Dubcek's fellow-pupils gave up the attempt to learn. Teaching continued at the School, but only in a very hesitant fashion; it was difficult to place much faith in the frightened and uncertain qualifications of bankrupt historians and ideologists. Nevertheless Dubcek, conscious of the importance of a good degree to his career in the Party, worked as hard as he could, given the prevailing conditions. He got a first.

Of Dubcek's reactions at the time a relation* of his has said:

* This relation is to my mind a reliable source; I questioned him very closely.

He was, after a bit of thought, delighted at Khrushchev's decision and imagined that it would make life much easier when he returned home, because he had been worried by the distrust which the people had for the Party in Slovakia by 1955.

But he was horrified by the aftermath of the speech. I mean, when Khrushchev sent the tanks into Budapest, Alexander was very upset. He thought it was right but he thought it was terrible that Communism had to be imposed in this way. I think it was that experience – Hungary – rather than Khrushchev's actual speech that moved him most at the time and made him realize that something was wrong. Of course he didn't immediately think 'We must do something about this'. And you must understand that propaganda in Moscow was hardly conducive to sympathy for the Hungarians. It was only much later that he began to see how things might be made better, and how it should be possible to do something with the ideas that Khrushchev had expressed.

In 1958 Dubcek came home to a Slovakia which he found remarkably unaffected by the shocks which had shaken so many countries in Eastern Europe over the past two years. By now Novotny had assumed the mantle of President of the Republic as well as that of First Secretary of the Party – so supreme power over both Party and State was centred more than ever in Prague and for the first time in the hands of one man.

The fact that the Czechoslovak regime reformed itself so little during the years immediately following the 20th Congress of the CPSU can very largely be explained in terms of Novotny's personality and power. He was the product of Gottwald's Party-machine, a 'faceless man' with few redeeming qualities and no individuality. He had none of the independence or strength of character of Tito, none of the determination and pride of Gomulka, none of the 'pragmatic originality' of Kadar; his was an excellent example of the incurious and stagnant mind that the *apparat* so often produces – a mind dedicated to the maintenance of the status quo, and quite uninterested in any idea of change except insofar as it was critical to his own preservation of power. That was scarcely threatened, for the thoroughness of the purges had created a vacuum. There was not one person who might be capable of leading the Party onto the way of de-Stalinization after 1956. Gustav Husak was still in prison, and Vlado Clementis was dead. There was no one else of any calibre who might suddenly emerge from obscurity to lead either reformist or nationalist forces. Every Czech and Slovak leader not in jail or disgrace was too closely tied to the Soviet Union to show any independence, and too concerned about his own position to give any voice to public disaffection.

This disaffection had been first mildly expressed by the Union of Writers at its second Congress in April 1956, only weeks after the real importance of the 20th Soviet Party Congress had begun to be understood, in a garbled form, amongst the intellectuals. Several writers made unprecedented criticisms of the Party's surveillance of cultural life. President Zapotocky, who had written a novel and saw himself as something of a Tolstoy, visited them and persuaded them to continue supporting the Party; they acquiesced.

The protest was taken up by the students who turned their recently restored 'Majales' Spring Festival into political demonstrations. In both Prague and Bratislava student groups demanded more political parties, an end to the jamming of the BBC and Radio Free Europe, and greater access to Western books and journals.

This mood began to affect the rank and file; in answer to it the Presidium decided to call a special conference of the Party at which the leadership indulged in mild and desultory criticism of bureaucratic methods but ended by roundly condemning all wayward writers, students and journalists. Novotny announced that a commission under Rudolf Barak was looking into the whole question of the political trials; the conference resolved that in future citizens should be able to play a greater part in affairs of State and then happily adjourned.

Such was the extent of de-Stalinization in Czechoslovakia in 1956. It is conceivable that more might have been accomplished but for the autumn events in Poland and Hungary which convinced the Czechoslovak leaders of the wisdom of retrenchment and of allowing no criticism of their own system. The very fact that the Czechoslovak Party was able to emerge so unscathed from the shocks of 1956 served to strengthen Novotny's position in the years that followed. His obvious success in controlling the 'counter-revolutionaries' made it much easier for him later to resist the pressure from Moscow to follow in the footsteps of the Kremlin. In fact such pressure was, until 1962, somewhat half-hearted; Khrushchev had no wish to be faced with the same problems in Prague as had confronted him in Warsaw and Budapest – he was content to let Novotny have his way.

On his return, the newly-educated Dubcek was at once made Regional Secretary of Bratislava – the most important 'local government' job that the Slovak Party had to offer. At the 11th Congress of the CCP in 1958 he was elected for the first time to the Central Committee of the Czechoslovak Party, and during that year he was also re-elected to the Slovak Central Committee.

He thus had three important positions. The first, which was full-time, involved much the same work as he had done in Banska Bystrica; the two Central Committee jobs took up much less time – but they provided work of a very different kind. He was now in effect both legislator and administrator. As Secretary for Bratislava he had to put into practice resolutions that he had helped to pass in the two Committees. To the debates in these sessions he was now able to contribute an all-round knowledge of the present problems facing the Party's administration. This overlapping of executive and legislative work (in 1960 he was also re-elected to the National Assembly) provides an overall understanding not easily come by in a Western democracy. A senior civil servant cannot also be on the Executive of the Labour Party and a government minister. In Czechoslovakia this is quite possible; the disadvantage is that there is no restraint upon the administration or government; when legislators, civil servants and politicians are all the same people the question of checks and balances can hardly arise.

Dubcek appears to have been confused by the discovery

that Novotny had so completely disregarded Khrushchev's lead. It is possible that had he never left Slovakia he might have accepted the First Secretary's judgment without too much question. But coming home after three years' instruction in the importance of the Soviet Union's leadership of the world's revolution enabled him to see quite clearly that Novotny's inaction was based rather on personal fears than ideological scruples. He seems to have been quite uncertain as to how he should react. Now that Novotny was so out of line with Khrushchev where did his own duty lie? He felt no personal loyalty towards Novotny, indeed his dislike of the President probably led him instinctively to question any of his decrees. Nevertheless Dubcek was a passionate believer in Party discipline and democratic centralism and this enjoined him to total obedience to the First Secretary. At the same time, however, his loyalty to the Soviet Union was quite unqualified and he happened to believe that Khrushchev was correct.

It appears that this ideological dilemma led him into something of an emotional or doctrinal crisis in 1959; his conduct during that year was quite untypical of him. He became suddenly and temporarily very much more aggressive in his speeches than he had ever been before or has ever been since. Not only did he attack the Catholic Church in an abusive manner which, perhaps because of his wedding, he has never otherwise employed – he also made what was for him an unprecedented assault upon Gustav Husak.

In 1953 and 1954 when the Czech-inspired campaign against the Slovak bourgeois-nationalists was at its most frenzied, Dubcek had apparently refused to attack Husak or the others by name. But now, five years later, at a time when that campaign was beginning to be discredited and only a few months before Husak was to be released from prison, Dubcek wrote in an article on the Slovak Revolt:

> The Slovak Communist Party's work united the nation and the fight against Fascism became stronger. Communists led the struggle in the army rebellions at Zilina and Roznava, in the strikes of 1941, and in the formation of the first Partisan groups. They were arrested and killed. These

> arrests moved people, and also allowed nationalistically minded people like Husak and Novomesky to take over the leadership of the Slovak Communist Party. These men were concerned, in 1943, to retain their links with the bourgeoisie and even to ask the help of the bourgeoisie. This hindered the development of the Partisan movement.[1]

This attack on Husak is no less inexplicable than it is unjustified. Dubcek knew quite well that Husak's alliance with the bourgeoisie immensely strengthened the Slovak Communist Party, and in other speeches he has often said as much. This one article represents a curious aberration in an otherwise consistent record of support for the leadership of the Revolt.

In November 1959 Novotny announced plans for a complete reorganization of local government throughout the two nations. The old administrative districts were to disappear completely and though 'the principle of democratic centralism remains the basis of the new system', the establishment of 'productive regions' was the aim. The 19 administrative regions and 306 districts were reduced to 11 regions and 118 districts. Although more power was given to the Regional Party Secretaries of these enlarged districts, the influence of the lowest-level Party branches was further reduced. As far as the individual citizen or even Party member was concerned, control became even more impersonal and distant. In fact the territorial reorganization was really designed to prepare the way for a plan of much greater political and ideological significance: the adoption of a new Constitution. In 1960 the world was informed that after twelve short, admittedly harsh, years, Czechoslovakia had completed the building of socialism, second only to the Soviet Union. The country was declared the Czechoslovak Socialist Republic. To many Communists this came as something of a surprise, and it was a mockery of all that the genuine Marxists believed in to pretend that Novotny's bureaucratic dictatorship was really socialist. But there were few such men at the top of the Party machine in 1960, and to the rest the problem of the country's new status was more mundane; what did it mean? Dubcek tried, not very succinctly, to give an answer:

> We have completed the building of socialism in our country and we are now preparing the progress from socialism to Communism ... [the achievement of this aim] depends on our winning people over to solve the problems involved in raising the level of production: we must explain to them that their needs can only be met by following the Party's instructions. Furthermore, in our propaganda we must explain the relation between the past and the future. We are not dreamers – we have revolutionary inspiration, without which it is impossible to make revolutionary changes. The revolutionary aims of society can only be realized when the mass of the people support them. But this support and its resulting impetus cannot be restrained. It must be organized and led by the Communist Party.[2]

Even more important was the effect of the new Constitution upon Slovakia. Speaking on 5 July 1959 at the national conference of the Party which introduced the new arrangements, Novotny announced with, one suspects, not a little pleasure: 'Changes in Slovak national organs will be based on the fact that central direction of the whole life of our society according to a single all-state [nation-wide] plan is progressively deepening [*sic*].' Basically this meant that Slovakia was to be denied even the pretence of self-government that she had maintained since the promise of full autonomy in the Kosice Programme in 1945. The Board of Commissioners, which had played the part of a sort of Slovak National Cabinet, was abolished completely; so were the Slovak branches of many central authorities, such as the Slovak Statistical Office and the Social Security Office. Only the Slovak National Council, created by Husak in 1943, was spared, but its authority was seriously limited. Till 1959 it had served as a regional parliament for Slovakia: the new Constitution down-graded it to the status of 'an organ of the state authority and administration in Slovakia'.

This new Constitution infuriated the Slovak people, as it might have been expected to do. But no one could prevent its enforcement. The leaders of the Slovak Party, Karol Bacilek and Viliam Siroky had little Slovak blood in them, and even that was donated irrevocably to Prague centralism and working for Novotny. The only real Slovak anywhere near the top of the SCP was Pavol David and he, in Ladislav Mnacko's words, was a 'monster'.

Dubcek's reaction showed no more independence than that of anyone else in the Party. His first statement on the proposed Constitution was remarkable for its refusal even to admit that any changes in Slovakia were contemplated – he did not mention his country at all. In a January 1960 issue of *Hlas Ludu,* a Slovak Party daily, he wrote:

> We are trying to work out the resolutions of the 11th Congress. Comrade Novotny has proposed a new State Constitution. This will give more power to the local authorities and will enable us to find new methods of solving the problems of the economy. All this is being done to complete the building of socialism and to broaden our socialist democracy.[3]

Five months later he was hardly more communicative on the problems facing Slovakia:

> We are engaged at the moment in a discussion over the new Constitution. This Constitution represents the fact that we have worked diligently for fifteen years to build socialism. We shall never forget that the first condition for building a happy, socialist Czechoslovakia and the creation of a high standard of living was the victory of the Soviet army in World War II. We are indebted to the Soviet Union for its disinterested help during these fifteen years.

He went on to stress the importance of unity and, although he referred specifically to the unity of the whole socialist camp, it is probable that he was more concerned with the disunity between Czechs and Slovaks which present Slovak anger threatened to make worse than ever:

> The unity of the socialist camp is the guarantee of our progress; faithful to the principles of proletarian internationalism we shall guard this unity as the basic condition of the full and final victory of socialism over defunct capitalism ... We are most indebted to the Czechoslovak Communist Party for the creative way in which it has put the

principles of Marxism-Leninism to work and indeed for all that we have achieved in our socialist development. With the Soviet Union in eternal solidarity for all time![4]

It is quite clear that Dubcek was neither willing nor able to defend the rights of the Slovak people at this stage. Some commentators have suggested that his later championship of the Slovak cause suggests a complete hypocrisy in his inaction in 1959 and 1960. This is too harsh and reflects an exaggerated assessment of the power and independence of junior members of the Party machine. He realized that it was hopeless to challenge Novotny when the First Secretary was at the peak of his power – the new Constitution was supposed to represent Novotny's greatest achievement.

If the leadership of the Slovak Party had been prepared to protest against the cavalier treatment of Slovakia it would have been open for junior members to do the same, and it might have had some effect. But this leadership was servile, and had Dubcek used his *Hlas Ludu* articles as even mild vehicles of dissent his career might well have ended at once and it is certain that he would not have been elected a Secretary of the Central Committee of the Czechoslovak Party. This was an appointment that he had hoped to win and it was confirmed at the Party Conference in June 1960. He replaced Oldrich Cernik as Industrial Secretary of the Committee and went, for the first time in his life, to work full-time in Prague.

Prague has one million inhabitants, and compared with Moscow or with London it is tiny. But set against Trencin, Banska Bystrica or even Bratislava it is huge. For the first time in his life the small-time Party-boss was sent to work in an international centre. In Bratislava he had been involved in all aspects of political and economic life: now he was required to specialize in industrial problems. It took him some months to accustom himself to the new demands made upon him and the new disciplines he had to accept. It took him even longer to begin to feel at home amongst the Czechs.

He devoted the next two years to his industrial work. His

speeches were nearly all concerned with the development of production, the training of scientists, the fulfilment of engineers and the application of Marxist-Leninist work schedules. It was now that he began to realize, probably for the first time, the full extent of the gravity of his country's economic crisis. In 1959 the rate of growth of GNP had been 11%, by 1962 it was 6.2%, and in 1963 it was actually nil. Food was very scarce, always had to be queued for; apartments were unobtainable. There was an increasingly serious balance-of-payments problem and the planners were incapable of equating the total volume of investment outlay with the capacity of the construction sector and machine-building industry. Eventually this knowledge convinced Dubcek of the need for radical economic reform, but in 1960 and 1961 he was persuaded that any defects in the system must be the result of insufficient central control, of a failure to comply with all the instructions of the National Plan. It never occurred to him that any particular plan might be misconceived, and he would not have dreamt of attacking the 'cult of the plan' itself for it never crossed his mind that planning was a cult. If something was wrong then, quite simply, someone, somewhere was being allowed too much independence. Thus: 'We need at the moment greater centralization in administering scientific and technical progress. For the cause of many errors in the development of scientific industries is a lack of co-ordination in this sphere.'[5]

At a Central Committee meeting three months later he was even more explicit in his diagnosis and proffered cure:

> 'The past months show us the need for greater control over the economy. The political bureau has accepted arrangements which are supposed to result in greater scientific and technical progress. They will remove the objective factors which at the moment conceal the laziness and backwardness of economists and scientists . . . For as the number of people working in scientific fields increases, so does the need for effective control over their work.'[6]

The current five-year plan had been adopted in 1960 when the minds of the Party's economists were apparently a little overcome by the exhilaration of the new Constitution. It certainly bore no intelligible relationship with the reality of the Czechoslovak situation. It was designed to increase machine production by 'more than 76%', industrial labour productivity by 43%, agricultural labour productivity 53%, and investment was to go up to 322 billion Korunas (compared to the sum of just over 90 billion over 1948–57).[7]

Dubcek was guilty of exaggeration rather more absurd and unreal:

> 'To implement the 3rd Five-Year Plan [he said in 1960] we have formed special committees at district and local levels of the Party organizations. . . . We have great tasks before us. The production of our chemical industry will increase by 265% and the production of other goods by 334%. In the machine industry, production will rise 90%. . . . We are at the moment discussing this Plan. The principle that we should produce more and produce it more cheaply is becoming universal. It must be put into effect by the use of new technology, reorganization of work-schedules and better running of enterprises. We will succeed only when all working people have their share in running the economy.'[8]

Two years later he agreed to contribute to *Rude Pravo* his views on the problems of housing and the building industry. Such attention was merited because in 1961 only one third of the annual building programme had been completed. During the first quarter of 1962 flats were being constructed at only 75% of the rate that the Plan laid down and the shortage was acute. Dubcek's solution was traditional: 'The Party insists on the authority of the Plan which determines, from the centre, the tasks to be fulfilled and the means of fulfilling them. . . . Working without a plan or with a plan of insufficient detail simply means that projects are not completed on time.'[9]

He was either ignorant or oblivious of the fact that this seemed also to be the result of working with a plan. He was saying simply that if the present Plan were ineffective then make it more detailed and implement it more rigorously.

A month later he took up the same theme: 'The cause of low work productivity is that there is not enough direction and control over projects that are undertaken.' But for the first time a note of self-doubt crept into his words. Almost as an unintended after-thought, and as if he were not certain how to express the heretical notion, he added what was for him a totally original public statement: 'We must consider the important fact that socialism and Communism are built by people. Only their activities, only the results of their work, only their share in the initiation and fulfilment of plans can lead to a rise in the standard of living.'[10]

Dubcek's views on his country's economic problems in the early 1960s were clear and unhelpful enough. His attitude towards the problem of de-Stalinization is less self-evident but just as important, for Novotny's behaviour on this issue played a vital part in the development of Dubcek's career.

Khrushchev's second denunciation of Stalin at the 22nd Congress of the CPSU in October 1961 and the removal of Stalin's body from its Kremlin mausoleum were very embarrassing for Novotny. It was no longer possible for him to prevaricate; he knew that he would have to follow Khrushchev's example with a little more public joy than hitherto.

He was loath to do so. For, despite his plaintive protest that 'I was not in the leadership at the time', a remark which gave rise to obscene and endless jokes in Prague, Novotny knew that any thorough purge of those responsible for the 'errors of the Fifties' must endanger his own position and those of his closest colleagues. At the Czechoslovak Party's national conference in December 1952, Karol Bacilek had stated that the material against Rudolf Slansky was 'acquired from the Party *apparat* and from the Ministries with the great help of Comrades Gottwald, Zapotocky, Dolansky, Kopecky, and most of all Comrade Novotny'.[11] Novotny had never succeeded in getting this statement annulled – it must have been a continual and terrifying reminder to him of his own guilt and of the danger which de-Stalinization represented to his continued rule. He was naturally anxious to try and suppress for as long as possible any real investigation into the crimes of those years. He made his attitude abundantly clear just after the end of the CPSU Congress, in a speech that was remarkable for its defiance of Khrushchev's line:

> 'We shall absolutely refuse to permit anyone to misuse matters which have been solved long ago for demagogical attacks against the Party. The irresponsible demand that those who were found guilty of gross violations of socialist legality during the Slansky era should now be rehabilitated is hereby rejected as totally unfounded.'[12]

This statement was apparently not well received by Khrushchev; he is believed to have suggested to Novotny that he change his mind. So Novotny announced that the decisions of the 22nd Congress of the CPSU were binding also upon the Czechoslovak Communist Party and ordered the huge monument of Stalin on the banks of the Vltava to be pulled down. He also instructed workmen to dismantle the mausoleum on the hill of Zizkov where, embalmed and byzantine, the body of Gottwald had lain, like that of his friend and mentor, Stalin, in a glass case since his death in 1953.

A cynic might have questioned the sincerity behind the symbolic removal of these unattractive corpses, for two days after Gottwald was publicly condemned and his body laid to rest amongst other 'meritorious Party-workers', a new memorial was suddenly erected to him in his 'own' town, the shoe-making centre of Gottwaldov, the former Zlin.

Even Novotny seems to have realized that more was required of him than the abuse of the dead and removal of the petrified. He understood that a living sacrifice was needed if he was to save his own skin, if the gestures towards Khrushchev's attitudes were not to be completely empty. Accordingly he seized on the man who, he thought, constituted the greatest threat to his own position.

Rudolf Barak had been intimately involved in the processes of the 'fifties, but lately he had appeared to take a line that was almost independent of the leadership. It is believed that he had sent a detailed memorandum to Khrushchev listing all the areas in which he considered that the political

Alexander Dubcek and his three sons, Milan, Pavel and Petr, at home in Bratislava, 1957.

Alexander Dubcek with Leonid Brezhnev in Bratislava, Slovakia, 1963 and (below) with Nikita Khrushchev and Antonin Novotny in Banska Bystrica, Slovakia, summer 1964.

and economic structure of the state was in need of drastic change. His report suggested that as Novotny was so obviously reluctant to undertake the burden himself, perhaps he, Barak, might be the man to do it. Whether this story is true or not it is certainly the case that Barak was one of the very few politicians who had at that time even the pretence of a popular following. He had assiduously and successfully cultivated the friendship of local Party officials; their influence on the thoughts and loyalties of members of the basic organizations had helped him to create an image of 'the friend of the people'.

Despite, or rather because of his popularity, Novotny chose Barak as his victim. He was tried, duly found guilty and sentenced to fifteen years imprisonment because he had 'undermined and rendered impossible the proper activity of the Ministry of the Interior in some sectors and seriously impaired the security of our State and of the national economy'.[13] Novotny had had some qualms about impeaching his Minister of the Interior, but he sought the advice of Barak's deputy, Lubomir Strougal. Strougal, whose eye to the main chance has always been remarkably acute, tried to reassure Novotny: 'But Tonda, of course you can imprison Rudolf. You're the President, Tonda!' For his advice and easy loyalty Strougal was rewarded, as he had expected, with Barak's job.

The Barak story* is a vivid illustration of Novotny's real attitude towards Stalinism and towards the attempt to remove from socialism the worst of that dictator's excesses. The charges against Barak were trumped up in exactly the same way as those against Slansky; both men were used as scapegoats for the Party's problems. The trial of Barak represented an undeniable regression to 'the period of the personality cult' at the very moment that the cult was supposed to be finally condemned.

Many of Novotny's associates joined in the condemnation

* Dubcek had Barak released in 1968. In Autumn 1969 Barak is believed to have repeated his previous mistake: he wrote to Brezhnev and suggested that such was the political bankruptcy of the Czech and Slovak Party leaders that he should make a come-back. Brezhnev is said to have forwarded the letter to Husak who gave it to Strougal. This time Barak was not imprisoned but he was told very clearly that any return to work in the Party was unthinkable.

of Barak and none more vociferously than Bacilek, Siroky and others whose parts in the trials of the 'fifties Barak understood only too clearly. Dubcek, however, seems to have learnt something since he yapped around Slansky's scattered ashes. He made no mention of Barak's 'treason'.

5
PINKPRINT

'Anybody can become angry . . . that is easy; but to be angry with the right person, and to the right degree and at the right time, and for the right purpose and in the right way—that is not within everybody's power and is not easy.'

Aristotle, *Nicomachean Ethics,* Bk 11, ch 9.

The year 1963 was vital to the recent history of Czechoslovakia and to the development of Dubcek's career. It was a year in which Novotny found himself threatened by a very serious economic crisis, by the dictates of Moscow, by his own attempts at accommodation, and by the resulting trend to what he saw as anarchy in the Party.

If he had hoped that his half-hearted gestures towards de-Stalinization would satisfy Khrushchev, he was disappointed. Khrushchev was still displeased and in May 1962 he sent Politburo member Leonid Ilyichev to Prague; one of the purposes of his visit seems to have been to convince Novotny that he must pursue much more eagerly the problem of correcting 'the errors of the 'fifties' at the forthcoming 12th Congress of the Czechoslovak Communist Party.

This Congress should have been held in June: Novotny delayed it in order to work out his tactics. By the time it finally met in December 1962 he had realized that he could no longer resist Khrushchev's pressure. During a debate on the political trials he admitted for the first time that the verdicts of most of them had been incorrect, that many of the guilty were in fact innocent. But he tried to absolve himself and to blame Barak who had, he charged, used his position as Chairman of the first Rehabilitation Commission to protect the real culprits and to keep truths further suppressed. Nevertheless he proposed that a new commission be set up under Drahomir Kolder and that it report back to the Central Committee within four months on the justice or injustice of the political processes between 1949 and 1954. Although this proposal gave many senior members of the *apparat* justified cause for concern, it was accepted unanimously. The fact that its terms of reference were to cover also the trials of the bourgeois-nationalists placed Novotny's loyal colleagues Siroky and Bacilek in an unenviable position. If the Commission did its work properly they would hardly escape indictment. Given this, and given Novotny's previous antics it was not unduly cynical to expect the Commission to do a good job of whitewashing. This is probably what Novotny originally hoped of it. But early in the new year Khrushchev sent yet another herald, Anastas Mikoyan,* to warn the unhappy Czech that this time there must be no mistakes; rehabilitation could no longer be delayed.

Dubcek had been elected to the Czechoslovak Party Presidium at the end of 1962. He was a member of the Commission and he is believed to have enjoyed the work greatly. Since 1960 he had been concerned about the validity of the trials and whether or not they constituted a violation of socialist legality. That he had never spoken his mind was a reflection of both his impotence and ambition.

The trials which apparently concerned him most were those of the bourgeois-nationalists. It is possible that he felt some guilt at his 1959 attack on Husak and wanted to see the record set straight. At the same time he must have been delighted at the thought that Husak's rehabilitation would cause at least embarrassment for Viliam Siroky for whom he still felt his father's contempt.

The Commission reported in February 1963 and, partly because of the warnings of Khrushchev, partly because of the convictions of Dubcek and others of its members, its findings, though insufficient, were remarkably fair. The report stated that during the 'cult of personality' gross miscarriages of socialist justice had occurred, that numerous good Communists had been victimized and that the blame lay with the leadership of the time.

* In 1968 it was revealed that Mikoyan had also been used as Stalin's messenger-boy: in 1950 he had come to Prague to encourage Gottwald to hasten the destruction of the 'Titoists, class-enemies, Zionists', etc. Which mission Mikoyan most enjoyed is not recorded.

Novotny knew that after this the only way to protect himself was to abandon some of his friends. The first to go was Josef Urvalek, Slansky's prosecutor; at the beginning of March he was finally removed from the Chair of the Supreme Court 'for reasons of health'[1]. The next casualty was more serious; it was the Slovak First Secretary, Karol Bacilek.

Novotny did all he could to save Bacilek and to disregard the Commission's implicit indictment of his conduct. He attended the crucial meeting of the Slovak Central Committee on 4 April at which the First Secretary's future was debated. It was a stormy session with Novotny alternately shouting and cajoling and succeeding only in alienating more and more of the Slovaks. When he finally appreciated that Bacilek must be dropped he tried to secure his replacement with a Slovak of his own choice – Michal Chudik, a man who had proved himself completely loyal to the idea of Prague centralism. But Chudik, for this very reason, was unpopular within the Slovak Party, and the Central Committee, realizing that Novotny was already on the defensive, disregarded his nomination and elected Dubcek instead. Novotny was furious, stormed out of the meeting and never again attended any session of the Slovak Central Committee or Presidium.[2] It is not clear whether his anger was due simply to being rebuffed over Chudik or whether he already hated Dubcek. Whatever the reason, he had no intention of allowing Dubcek to remain in the job unless he proved himself totally obedient, and he may have comforted himself with the fact that Siroky was still Prime Minister and the belief that Dubcek could soon be removed. He was wrong.

Dubcek was delighted to take up the Slovak First Secretaryship. Quite apart from a predictable pleasure in promotion, he was glad to return to Bratislava – he had not yet grown accustomed to life in Prague.

Bratislava offered then (and still offers today) a parochial existence, a provincial tempo to which Dubcek has always been suited. He is a small town politician rather than an international or even national statesman, a man who feels much more at ease amongst his family in Slovakia than on his own in Bohemia.

For whilst he had been in Prague, his wife and three sons

Milan, Pavel and Peter had remained in Bratislava. Anna had occasionally visited him in Prague and he had often returned home at weekends, but he had been unable to see as much of his teenage sons as he wished. With his assumption of the Slovak First Secretaryship, the family was reunited – he rented a villa for them all, on the hill behind Bratislava's Castle.

The residential suburbs of many East European capitals share a certain drabness. Decaying villas of the bourgeois 1930s, with grandiose porches and heavy steps, suffer sadly side by side with the grey Stalinist creations of the late 'forties and early 'fifties. These houses, joylessly fabricated and perhaps hardly more happily inhabited, covered with thin sheets of peeling plaster, resemble more the disused control towers of minor prewar airports or even glorified coastguard bunkers than the homes of important Party officials. 46 Misikova Ulice is still Dubcek's house and it is as ugly as the rest.

It lies in the most exclusive residential district of Bratislava, on a steep slope below the huge memorial to the Red Army soldiers killed in the liberation of Slovakia. Here, in a radius of perhaps one mile, live all the most important politicians, bureaucrats, journalists and academics of the town. It is a closely woven, even inbred society. There is no one official colony in Prague; as a result there is no necessary neighbourliness between Party officials and their unofficial admirers and critics. Novotny need never have met his opponents socially; Dubcek could not avoid at least passing them in the lane.

A glass and wooden door set in the road wall leads up steep stone steps, through an ill-kept garden, to the house. It is two storey and boxlike; inside it is comfortably and unimaginatively furnished with standard mass produced three-piece suites, ugly wooden cupboards and heavy beds. Low coffee tables in the sitting room, from which to drink slivovica and cups of badly imitated Turkish coffee, on the wall a Breughel print and a photograph of Lenin; tall potted plants all around the room giving a slightly claustrophobic impression. Much the same as thousands of homes throughout Czechoslovakia.

Anna, too, was delighted at Dubcek's 1963 promotion back to Bratislava. It is difficult to say with any certainty how far she has influenced his political career and the development of his ideology. Blonde, plump and charming, she is more a housewife than a politician. Unlike Mrs Novotny or Mrs Bacilek, she has never had a full-time maid in the house. A char came to 46 Micikova Street once a week, but the daily work and cooking was always done by Anna herself. This is not to say that she did any less Party work than her two predecessors – she has always fulfilled her duties as wife of a leading Party official with diligence if not with conviction.

A partisan during the war, after her marriage to Dubcek in 1945 she was quickly converted to his communism. Nevertheless, she never became a militant Party worker and has always been more interested in tending her family than nurturing the Party. She is much more the woman behind, than alongside, a successful politician. She adores Dubcek, but she has never been ambitious for him; on 5 January 1968 she wept, as did Milan and Peter, when she heard that Alexander had succeeded Antonin Novotny as First Secretary of the Czechoslovak Communist Party. They were not tears of joy.

During his first week in office, the new Slovak First Secretary found that he had to deal with a major and unprecedented political crisis, one which required the greatest political delicacy and which was to change the whole tenor of life in Czechoslovakia. It was the revolt of the Slovak intellectuals.

This had begun at the end of March with the publication of provocative articles in *Pravda,* the Slovak Party paper,[3] attacking the slowness of the process of rehabilitation. It had continued through April with the stormy Slovak Writers' Congress* and been brought to a head at the end of May by

* During the Congress Laco Novomesky, the greatest of living Slovak poets, who had been imprisoned along with Husak, was finally readmitted to the Union – the writers approved his re-election by acclamation. Thanking them for their generosity, Novomesky made a long and moving speech in which he spoke of his great affection for his executed friend, Vladimir Clementis, ex-Foreign Minister, seduced back from New York to Prague to be executed. The charges against Vlado, said Novomesky, were totally false; he had been the victim of something 'monstrous and horrible . . . the cult of personality. It wiped out trust, confidence, understanding, yes, even loyalty in the life and consciousness of thousands and thousands of people'.

Kulturnì Zivot's (the weekly periodical of the Slovak Writers' Union)

Miroslav Hysko, a lecturer in journalism and author of the original *Pravda* articles, at the Slovak Journalists' Congress on 27–28 May. There he made a sensational speech. He began by admitting that journalists must accept a share of the collective guilt for the crimes of the 'fifties, and asserted that they must be very self-critical of their inaction during those years. But this apology was really only intended to clear the ground for his attack upon Viliam Siroky, the Prime Minister.

It was Siroky who had first denounced the 'bourgeois-nationalists' in 1950. Hysko now accused him of being a liar and murderer. The Prime Minister, he charged, was guilty of a total distortion of justice and of complicity in mass murder:

> Comrade Siroky's report to the 9th Congress of the Slovak Communist Party as regards the uncovering of bourgeois-nationalists in the Party was not the result of an objective analysis of the facts . . . On the contrary it was based on a prior thesis of the inevitability of the bourgeois-nationalist danger. To this thesis all the facts had to be subordinated. In this atmosphere any disagreement with even one word of the report would have been accepted as an expression of hostility. Reports were at that time automatically accepted as Congress decisions. Only two ways were open to the comrades charged with bourgeois-nationalism. They could either 'agree' with the 'criticism' or accept the charge that they were wilful enemies of the Party. It would, therefore, be an expression of gross cynicism, if not of something much worse, if their 'self-critical' statements at that Congress were to be considered as a confirmation of the correctness of their indictment for bourgeois-nationalism.[4]

The next week the entire speech was reprinted in the Bratislava *Pravda*. Ondrej Klokoc, its editor, was using the official Party organ to insult the Prime Minister – this was an extra-

---

coverage of Novomesky's speech and the echoes it aroused in the Congress was only the first attack in many months that the paper was about to deliver against Novotny and his Slovak counterparts. In April, Ctibor Stitnicky had been replaced as chief-editor by Pavol Stevcek, who was determined to press for justice for Slovaks wronged by Prague. Throughout the summer the articles in *Kulturni Zivot* grew more and more provocative.

ordinary insolence which, even more than the speech itself, constituted an open challenge to Novotny.

In reply the President chose Kosice, 'capital' of eastern Slovakia, as the place to deliver one of his most threatening and abusive denunciations of the Slovak people. In his speech he gave expressive vent to all his hatreds of Slovakia, castigating Hysko, *Pravda* and, by implication, Dubcek himself. 'We will not permit *Pravda,* the organ of the Central Committee of the Slovak Communist Party' – Novotny almost spat out the words – 'to become a platform for the proclamation of incorrect views or for the heaping of hysterical attacks upon the Party. Nor will we permit that with the help of these articles, made public in this organ, not only the Slovak but also the Czech public be influenced falsely.' He warned all Slovak editors and journalists, and Klokoc and Hysko in particular, that they had trespassed along 'a very dangerous path'. They were guilty of the most severe breaches of Party discipline in discussing 'questions which the Central Committee had stated quite clearly must be resolved within the Party'. If there had to be discussion, and Novotny reluctantly admitted that there did have to be, then 'it must take place within the framework of the Party's policy, in the framework of the unity of the people and the country, in the framework of the struggle for the new against the old, for the flourishing of creative constructive effort!'[5]

Novotny would have been wise to leave it at that. He had made his point; everyone realized that he was intent on reasserting his authority. But, not content with lambasting his opponents for their alleged breaches of discipline, a perfectly justifiable – if in fact unjustified – line to take, he had also to indulge his prejudices. His contempt for Slovakia had been thinly masked in his tirade against Hysko, but at least some sort of disguise was there. Now he ripped it away and delivered an entirely unprovoked tirade against those two Slovak heroes whose misfortunes had caused the present crisis – Husak and Novomesky.

Although the Rehabilitation Commission had found them substantially innocent of any offence (not wholly – for Novotny could not tolerate that, Khrushchev or no Khrushchev), the President asserted that they were in fact guilty of serious mistakes. They had, he claimed, committed 'breaches of Party unity' whilst in positions of authority. In effect, he said, charges of bourgeois-nationalism were on the whole correct. The mistake was that they had been insufficiently documented. He even claimed that bourgeois-nationalism was still a very real force in Slovakia and that therefore the Party was amply justified in its efforts to make the economy increasingly centralized; it was important that the country's resources should be directed to the general interests of Czechs as well as Slovaks. There was absolutely no reason for revision of the 1960 Constitution: indeed it was quite clear that the Slovak organs had not properly exercised such powers as they did have.

This last was an obvious criticism of Dubcek, sitting mournfully beside him on the platform. Novotny was in fact demanding to know why Dubcek had permitted these attacks; why had he not forbidden Stevcek and Klokoc to reproduce such slanderous material?[6]

Novotny's speech placed Dubcek in a very difficult position. He knew that the Slovak people was anxious to know what he thought of Hysko – whom it had enthusiastically supported – and his opinion of Novotny's bitterly resented arrogance. Slovaks were curious to find out what sort of man was their new First Secretary, this clumsy emaciated six-foot-three bear with the huge nose, the shy smile and such ill-fitting suits.

Dubcek knew that if he endorsed Novotny's abusive arrogance he would forfeit the support of the vast mass of the Slovak people and of a number of the Party's *apparatchiks*. On the other hand public defiance of the President might at this stage lose him his job and would certainly lose him the support of other Party workers. He knew that on his performance he would be judged for a long time to come. And so Dubcek decided, as Dubcek so often does, to compromise.

On 27 June he spoke to a West Slovakian Party *'aktiv'*. After a long and very boring introduction discussing figures of economic production, he adjusted his spectacles, nervously cleared his throat and began, in his appalling, monotonous, stumbling and unprofessional voice, his ideological statement.

He started by conceding Hysko a point – that the elimination of the personality cult had been only gradual up till now.

But he stressed that all this had changed since the 12th Congress which had firmly resolved to eliminate all vestiges of the 'fifties and promised that demolition work was proceeding fast. He argued that although the Party supported every honest and innocent attempt to clarify the record, the Central Committee could not remain totally indifferent to the views often heard,

> . . . which were at variance with the objective truth – contradictory, muddled, incorrect and ill-considered views, which fail to take into account all historic facts and decisions. Whether the authors of such views realize it or not, the fact is that such views create, and I wish to stress this, a tense atmosphere, and lead to the disorientation of the masses, weaken Party unity, and confidence in the Central Committee which is struggling for consistent recovery and for the liquidation of the personality cult. Such views must not therefore be under-estimated, even if they are isolated, because they jeopardize the Party's ability to act and the unity of its policy.

He then went on to deal with the public interest which he admitted the Slovak Journalists' Congress had aroused:

> Comrade Novotny spoke of some contributions to the discussion at this Congress in his address at Kosice. At the Slovak Journalists' Congress there was, needless to say, much that was positive, but some incorrect views were also aired. We cannot agree with Comrade Hysko's contribution to the discussion, . . . and we must altogether disapprove of the fact that extracts from his address were carried by *Pravda,* the organ of our Party Central Committee.
>
> Against subjectivism Comrade Hysko is fighting subjectively. We have no objections to individual members expressing their views in the right place, but I want to underline that attempts to provoke discussion on grave questions of the Party history and on its decisions call for collective assessment by the Party organs. It is incorrect to conduct such discussion outside the Party. Comrade Hysko, as a Party member, could have submitted his opinion on the 9th Congress and on some matters which he

mentioned in his contribution to the discussion, in connection with Comrade Siroky and other inner-party questions, to his primary organization, which would have notified the Central Committee of the discussion. Alternatively he could have written his views to the Central Committee, and so on. Why, then, did he have to express his opinions before the Slovak Journalists' Congress?[7]

After a glance at this speech most Slovaks were prepared to dismiss Dubcek as another creature of Novotny, a Bacilek, a non-person. It was a pity, they thought, but little else had been expected of him. After all he had never shown the slightest independence before, why should he suddenly start?

This was unfair. Dubcek may have been just a cog in the Party machinery but he was not a tool of Prague as any proper study of his speech should have shown. By a careful reading between the lines it is possible to see that his attack, such as it was, on Hysko, was concerned only with the *manner* of the latter's argument, not with its substance. Nowhere did Dubcek spring to Siroky's defence as both Siroky and Novotny had expected him to do. Not once did he assert that Hysko's allegations had been unfounded. His complaint against Hysko was that he had usurped the Party's role, not that he had slandered the Prime Minister – with that particular slur Dubcek had the greatest sympathy. In order to conciliate Novotny a little he had to pretend that Hysko was an ignorant fool to whose wild statements scant attention should be paid: 'Comrades who pretend to speak authoritatively on matters of Party history after only a very superficial analysis of these matters are guilty of the same mistakes as those made during the personality cult.'

Moreover it is important to compare Dubcek's criticism of Hysko with that made by other politicians. Only then can it be fairly assessed. His attacks on the freedom of the Press must be interpreted in relation to the prevailing conditions, in the perspective of actual sanctions at that time. Against the remarks of Vasil Bilak, a Secretary of the Central Committee of the Slovak Communist Party, Dubcek's appear almost mild. For Bilak asserted:

If there is a lack of discipline on the part of an author, an editor-in-chief, or an editorial board; if they lose their sense of responsibility to the readers; if they persevere in expressing incorrect views in spite of patient explanation of their harmfulness; then administrative intervention is necessary in the interests of the author and the Press itself. The Press does not and cannot replace the Party, nor can it assume the Party's tasks. It is the Party's instrument. Whoever loses sight of this basic principle excludes himself from the family of socialist journalists.[8]

Dubcek, for all his rebuking of Hysko, never threatened him with disinheritance.

In his Kosice speech, Novotny had also attacked Husak and the bourgeois-nationalists. Dubcek's critics complained that his behaviour on this issue was even more devious and compromising than his attitude towards Hysko. In fact it provided him with a rather more delicate dilemma, for Husak and Novomesky were at the time very popular, albeit 'unpublic' figures in Slovakia. Most Slovaks, Communist and non-Communist, were rightly convinced that these two intellectuals had been victimized simply for their Slovak blood, that their imprisonment was totally unjustifiable and that they should be accorded instant, full and public apologies and immediate rehabilitation. Dubcek knew that on this issue, even more than on the freedom of the Press, Slovak public opinion, Slovak nationalism indeed, was a hundred per cent behind the accused and bitterly resentful of Prague and all those Slovaks like Bacilek and Siroky who had truck with the centralist regime. His position was complicated by the fact that he had been a member of the Special Commission investigating the problems of rehabilitation. This Commission, under pressure from Novotny, had agreed to accord only partial rehabilitation to some of the defendants, and Dubcek was bound by collective responsibility to accept its findings: he was forced to ignore both the feelings of the Slovak people and the obvious injustice that Husak and Novomesky continued to suffer. He said: 'As regards Comrades Husak and Novomesky, the confirmation of their expulsion from the Central Committee of the Slovak Communist Party expressed the degree of their political responsibility for the mistakes in the application of the Party programme . . . in the work with which they had been entrusted.'

This bald restatement of the official line without colour and without personal judgment was the least that he could possibly get away with. At the same time it was as far as he was willing to go.

He then hinted that there had been disagreements within the Commission over the action to be taken towards Husak and the other 'bourgeois-nationalists'. He hoped to indicate thereby that he, Dubcek, was not personally in favour of the only limited rehabilitation that was accorded these men but that he remained bound by the decision of the Commission:

> In the discussion on the question of restoring Party membership to Comrade Husak and others who had been accused of bourgeois-nationalism and illegally sentenced as traitors and criminals, problems of an ideological nature arose among us, problems as to what exactly bourgeois-nationalism was. It must be admitted that, despite the Party's ideological efforts in the past, many problems still exist, and many matters are still unclear to people in regard to these questions. This is reflected in our everyday lives; we must remember that momentous matters are involved to which we must react with patience and circumspection.

Dubcek went on to make it clear that on such 'momentous matters' decisions and judgments should be reached only after the most careful, objective reflection based on a proper historical analysis of the situation and must not be the product of 'subjective prejudices or rash conclusions'.[9]

Probably a far more important and accurate statement of Dubcek's true views on this difficult subject was that which appeared on 29 August in *Rocnicke Noviny,* a Slovak farmers' journal:

> A proper analysis of the truth and an examination of the facts shows that the illegal Slovak Communist Party and its leadership successfully developed and led the fight for national freedom in the spirit of the Moscow leadership

> of the Czechoslovak Communist Party ... Over the last few years the work of several comrades in the leadership of the Slovak Communist Party has been incorrectly evaluated – especially that of Comrades Husak and Novomesky. They were accused of betraying the Revolt and, in this connection, of collaborating with the London *émigré* government in its plan for an armed *coup d'état*. They were also accused of expressing the feelings and aspirations of the Slovak bourgeoisie. The 12th Congress of the Czechoslovak Communist Party ... demonstrated the true roles of many important elements in the Revolt and so gave birth to an objective evaluation of the history and meaning of the Revolt ... until now bedevilled by subjectivism and lies in which many events have been shown in the wrong light.[10]

But even this article does not reveal the extent of his support for Hysko and his rejection of Novotny's arrogant thesis. His role in the whole crisis is still more complicated, and also more obscure, than has so far been suggested. It would be quite straightforward only if one could be certain that Hysko's speech and Klokoc's reprinting of it had taken place spontaneously and without Dubcek's prior knowledge. But this is most unlikely. Few people then knew that Dubcek and Klokoc were good friends who often spent a weekend hunting together and staying in a little lodge in the mountains near Banska Bystrica. There is no direct evidence that Dubcek colluded with Klokoc on the publication of the Hysko speech but it is almost certain that he did do so. Even if Klokoc had not been his friend it is most unlikely that he would have reprinted in the Party paper so aggressive an attack upon the Prime Minister without asking the permission of his Party chief. Dubcek read the speech in the week between Hysko's delivery and its publication. He apparently authorized Klokoc to publish because he saw the move as a means of embarrassing Novotny and of increasing the pressure on Siroky. Indeed it has been suggested that his complicity was even deeper than this and that he had read Hysko's speech before the young lecturer delivered it. This appears less likely than that he should have consulted with Klokoc, but it is not impossible.

Whether or not he had consulted with Hysko, Dubcek was certainly playing a very skilful double game that summer. He was trying at one and the same time to consolidate his own position amongst the Party orthodox and to lend all possible unofficial support to those who were trying to bring down the Old Guard. His tactics were almost immediately vindicated, and in the most dramatic way.

Had Hysko made his attack on Siroky twelve months earlier, when Bacilek was still First Secretary in Slovakia, he would almost certainly have lost his job, and might well have been imprisoned. But now it was Siroky who was sacked. On 22 September he was removed from the premiership 'for deficiencies in his work, insufficient application of the Party line in directing the activities of the government and for some faults in his political activity in the past, as well as because of his unsatisfactory state of health'.[11]

This was an extraordinary and unprecedented climb-down for Novotny to have to make. Conversely it was a remarkable victory for Dubcek and all Slovaks. It was only three months since the President had angrily denounced Hysko for his 'incorrect views', and already these views had prevailed.

But for Novotny worse was still to come. By the end of the year Dubcek had managed to extract from him an admission that his Kosice attack had been a gross error, and in December the Czechoslovak Central Committee passed a resolution which admitted that 'the criticism of the Slovak Communist Party has been unjustified, based on an exaggerated inflation and distortion of errors committed by some comrades'.[12] Furthermore Novotny was forced to confess that decisions and actions taken against the Slovak Party had been 'unsubstantiated in toto'.

This retraction illustrates how insecure Novotny's position had become. The last twelve months had seen an unprecedented assault upon his authority. Before the 12th Congress his position had been apparently unchallengeable, the old orthodoxies were unquestioned, at least by anyone of political influence and at least in public, and, most important, all his favourite, best-tried and most mindless supporters were gathered in office below him.

The heretical challenge to his hegemony in 1963 was a blueprint for that of 1967. In both years Novotny found himself threatened by a motley crowd of Slovaks, intellectuals and economists. He survived their first attack, but only by conceding a lot of ground, and in many ways his temporary survival engineered his ultimate defeat.

For in 1963 he was able to maintain his own supremacy only by sacrificing his colleagues; lesser men were offered on the altar of de-Stalinization, and by their political deaths Novotny managed to appease the gods and to continue as High Priest. Although there were no ties of friendship between himself, Bacilek and Siroky, their dismemberment cannot have been a ceremony which he enjoyed. For the dismissal of those most closely involved in 'the cult of personality' contained two very great, though as yet implicit, threats to his own supremacy. First of all he was much more exposed; he was now all alone in the Hradcany. Secondly the men who had replaced his subservient subordinates were all young products of the postwar *apparat,* not men who had grown up in the prewar Party with him. They were not people on whose support he could rely unconditionally. Over the last twelve months the character of the leadership had changed completely – Novotny was the last surviving member of the old regime and below him were bright young partycrats, most of them, he could be sure, coveting his position. The next time the leadership came under attack there was no one with whom he could hope to placate his enemies, for by the end of 1963 he had been forced to destroy all his best defences.

But dropping the 'Stalinists' was not the only factor that had enabled Novotny to survive 1963. Perhaps more important, he had been able to call for and receive support from Khrushchev, who was not willing to see the departure of his most loyal ally, a man with whom he was very friendly. Novotny had asked for urgent support throughout the year and his pleas had been answered. The Soviet ambassador had delivered a long and public eulogy. At a Kremlin reception Khrushchev had embraced him and called him 'our close friend',[13] and Brezhnev, in Prague to celebrate the twentieth anniversary of the Czechoslovak-Soviet Friendship Treaty, had clapped him on the back and hailed him as 'a loyal son of the Czechoslovak people and an indefatigable fighter for Communism'.[14] Four years later Brezhnev was to prove, to Novotny's horror and downfall, less eager to help.

Another important factor was that, although in 1963 the various crises of confidence in Novotny's leadership were acute, they were not yet uncontrollable. The economic situation was certainly catastrophic but there was no genuine discussion of alternatives to the present practice of adopting and subsequently abandoning a series of quite impractical and irrelevant Party plans. By 1967 most serious economists were convinced that political changes, and above all a complete revision of the role of the Party in the economy must precede any meaningful economic reform. In 1963 this was not so.

Intellectual disgust with Novotny's leadership was already immense in 1963, and the writers and journalists made their attitude quite plain, especially in Bratislava. But they were not goaded by any issue quite so provocative as his treatment of them in 1967.

The events of 1963 finally brought into the open the extraordinary Czech-Slovak antipathy but this did not yet become the overriding political issue. Nevertheless Novotny must have known that, now the good Bacilek was no longer in control of Bratislava, he was going to have more trouble there than before. The dismissal of Siroky was not enough to quiet those Slovak voices which inveighed against Prague centralism, and Novotny should have realized the danger of a potential Slovak outburst. But over the next four years he did nothing to improve his relations with the little country; indeed his subsequent treatment of Slovak aspirations betrayed an unprecedented arrogance and contempt.

He was undoubtedly lulled into further false confidence by the fact, that although the opposition to him in 1963 was very real, it was disparate and completely unco-ordinated. There was no one about whom the three groups could coalesce and regard as a common leader. Indeed it was difficult to see anywhere a man who could be considered a serious alternative to Novotny. At the beginning of 1964 the distinguished

Czech observer, Edward Taborsky, concluded, perhaps a little too gloomily: 'Neither Lenart, who has replaced Siroky, nor Dubcek who has stepped into Bacilek's shoes, nor Koucky the leading spokesman on ideology, appears to be anything but a staunch Party *apparatchik* in the fashion of Novotny . . .'[15]

It was only after 1963, in the more relaxed atmosphere that Novotny himself had been forced to allow, that the opposition to him was able to grow and coalesce. That year was the beginning of a revolt which was to take four years to mature around an opposition leader. Novotny, with some justification, did not believe that any such revolt could have a chance of success. For the next four years he played into the hands of his enemies and, until it was too late, was unable to see and thus to prevent the gradual association of hostile forces around a man who was certainly a 'staunch Party *apparatchik*' but not at all 'in the fashion of Novotny, – the insignificant and inarticulate, shambling and hesitant, apologetic Slovak, Alexander Dubcek.

6
AND OTHER SLOVAKS

> 'He who does not make his words rather serve to conceal than discover the sense of his heart, deserves to have it pulled out like a traitor's, and strewn publicly to the rabble.'
>
> Samuel Butler, *Remains*, II, 25. (1759)

Since the Kremlin's destruction of Prague's '1968 Spring' two views on Dubcek's role in that extraordinary movement have become fashionable. The first, which he has himself encouraged, is that he was a surprise and compromise candidate for succession to Novotny, that he only reluctantly accepted a job which he had neither expected nor wanted. This account would have it that he was a rank outsider who got the post at the last minute only because no one else was obscure enough to attract the wide-ranging support from Slovaks, intellectuals and economists necessary to the toppling of Novotny.

The second theory, which he is less eager to propagate but which is even more widespread, is that as well as obscure he was colourless and mindless, that his part in Prague Spring was essentially titular, that he was a mere figure-head of the reform movement. His views, it is often said, were not his own; ineffectual and pliable he could be induced into any shape; it just so happened that the mould selected in January 1968 was that of a human face – it might have been the mask of Stalin and Dubcek's features would have fitted it equally well.

Neither of these theories is accurate; both are based on an ignorance or disregard of Dubcek's work over the years 1964–7.

According to several people who worked closely with him

in Bratislava, Dubcek soon became convinced that much was wrong with the Party's methods. The First Secretary quickly understood and sometimes even admitted what the member of the Presidium and the Secretary of the Central Committee had only vaguely seen and had been quite forbidden to mention, that the administration of the Party was top-heavy and absurdly overloaded by always dogmatic, usually impractical, often anti-socialist and sometimes even inhuman procedures.

Insofar as an East-European politician's speeches are an effective guide to his beliefs and loyalties, Dubcek does appear by mid-1964 to have become a protagonist of mild reform. There is, of course, a danger in reading too much into his public attacks upon 'bureaucratic and administrative methods' and his insistence that the Party approach the people. Many politicians, including Novotny, were making similar noises after 1963. Nevertheless, there is reason to believe that Dubcek was rather more sincere than his superior. His activities in Bratislava were closer to the reforms that he was suggesting than were those of the President.

It is also important to realize that Dubcek worked after 1963 in the context of an ever deeper split with Novotny. He knew that Novotny would not hesitate to take the first opportunity of removing him and – at least until June 1966 – he had to calculate his moves carefully. He had two alternatives. He might have decided that the best way to secure his position was to swallow his dislike for Novotny and to become the same sort of Slovak First Secretary as was Bacilek, for ever eager to do the bidding of Prague. In this case Novotny would probably have abandoned his plan to get him replaced and Dubcek could have rested assured against any attack from within his own Party. On the other hand, Novotny's patronage was no longer all powerful, as the dismissal of Bacilek and Siroky had proven and, in any case, Dubcek had not the slightest wish to become the President's little man in Bratislava. To have done so would have meant the unquestioning acceptance of policies he was beginning to consider misguided, would have completely destroyed his freedom of movement and would have prevented him from building up a separate power base.

The only alternative to working with and for Novotny lay

in working despite and against him. This involved the adoption of a political platform and the assertion of political ideals which could be seen to be different from those of the Presidential First Secretary. It meant, in short, the formation of an unofficial and very tentative opposition in the hope of building up his own grassroots support so that in the event of an attack from the President he could rely for help on his popularity if not on the upper ranks of the *apparat*. 'Humanizing the Party' was a good way of achieving this. It assured him of a popular following that would always be denied Novotny, and it could be used as an offensive weapon against Prague. So it was for political and personal considerations that Dubcek opted early in his tenure of the Slovak Secretaryship to make himself the proponent of reform. This does not mean that his calculations were entirely cynical. Dubcek was simply able to wallow in the rare luxury of having political ideals which were in his own best interests; he could profitably combine principles with expediency.

His decision to make of himself the first independent Secretary that Slovakia had had since 1948 emerged only slowly but it divided the Party very sharply. Against him were, initially, most of those men who had supported Bacilek, who had lived and worked by his grace and who, as a result, both resented and feared the man who, despite the intervention of the President, had succeeded in wresting the Secretaryship from their patron. They had largely transferred their 'loyalty' and affections to Michal Chudik, Novotny's most devoted disciple still near the top of the Slovak Party. Chudik therefore represented a considerable course of opposition of which Dubcek had to beware. He could not always be sure of a majority in the Presidium; the vote on each issue depended too much on the current assessment of the waverers as to how the balance of power lay between himself and Novotny-Chudik. If, at any given moment it appeared that the tussle would finally be resolved in a victory for Dubcek, then he would easily get the vote. If not, not.

This was a highly unsatisfactory situation and one which was not finally resolved until the June 1966 Congress of the Party when Chudik, with Novotny's active assistance, tried and failed to mount a full-scale rebellion and oust Dubcek from the Secretaryship. After that Chudik lost most of his support from amongst the time-servers – an unsuccessful rebel is not someone who attracts much confidence; even those in the *apparat* who were opposed to Dubcek's 'liberalizing' policies and his flirtations with the intellectuals were forced to concede the political reality that he was now too powerful for it to be wise for them to resist him. Furthermore, Dubcek had managed to remove from the *apparat* many of the backwoodsmen; by 1966 there was no one in the Bratislava Secretariat who had held a responsible position in 1948 – all the old school had died, retired or been pensioned off. This must have been a relief for Dubcek who admitted in an oblique and unmistakable attack on Novotny that 'the phase we have just passed through was not simple ... there were certain comrades who wavered and there were sallies from the left as well as the right'.[1] There were few people at the top of the Party more orthodox or more 'left' than Novotny. A supporter of Dubcek wrote later: 'In Slovakia the period between 1963–5 was particularly complicated in the ideological field. There were pressures from right and from left ... Thanks to the leaders ... the atmosphere of dissension with its accompanying passion is behind us.'[2]

But one should realize that he only managed to rebuff Chudik and establish himself with the help of very strange companions. Two of his allies at this time were Vasil Bilak and Viliam Salgovic. Neither of them had any sympathy for the principles of reform which Dubcek occasionally and cautiously enunciated. Their interest in the Slovak leader lay simply in his usefulness in getting rid of Novotny. They regarded his adoption of a slightly different ideological stance from that of the President as a mere tactical move and expected that when it had succeeded he would revert to strict orthodoxy. Bilak and Salgovic were interested in removing Novotny in order to further their own personal ambitions; they had little objection to the rigid and unimaginative way in which he ran the Party. What they do not seem to have realized, at least until it was too late and they had helped him rout Novotny, is that Dubcek was sincere. They did not understand that certain gentleness and humanity which has always been so important a part of his personal and political character. They could not appreciate that he wished to translate these traits into the country's everyday life. It did not concern them – as it did him – that the Party should regain the popularity it had once held; in 1946 it had won 36% of the vote throughout the two countries – in 1964 he knew that it would be lucky to poll 10% in a genuinely free election. To Bilak and Salgovic this would have constituted a problem only if it endangered the Party's leading role; Dubcek considered it a tragedy, and one that could not simply be ascribed to the work of anti-socialist elements. If the Party had lost so much support then it must, to some extent, be the Party's fault; it was not enough to apologize for the abuses of the early 'fifties – something must be done about those abuses that were still tolerated and even encouraged. He wanted the Party once more to be a genuine popular movement; he did not hold either with a tight-knit bolshevik élite directing society or with a vast and sprawling bureaucratic octopus whose clawing tentacles encircled and imprisoned the people's every action.

Later that year there were elections throughout Slovakia to the Slovak National Council. Dubcek endorsed them enthusiastically. They were, he announced, without, apparently, any very good reason:

> a manifestation of the full agreement with our policy of broadening economic, political and cultural co-operation with the Soviet Union, which was and always will be the basis of our foreign policy. . . . The newly elected organs must at once assume full responsibility for their work and fulfil their functions properly.
>
> But, [he continued, with a significant and unexpected qualification] they must keep in continual contact with the electorate, and co-operate with their constituents. *Confidence is not given by the people once and for all . . . it must be continually renewed and reaffirmed** especially when conditions and demands may have changed.[3]

This was a concept that had rarely, since 1948, been so explicitly expressed by a Party leader in Czechoslovakia. It had never been publicly questioned, even by Dubcek,

* Emphasis added.

whether or not the people had confidence in the actions of Party and Government organs. Doubts must have been felt by even the most intellectually dishonest of the leaders, if only because of the frightening anti-Communist feeling revealed in the secret polls that the Party commissioned, but feeling such hesitations and expressing them publicly were two very different matters. The Party had always pretended that it believed it had the confidence of the people and that this had been granted unto eternity in February 1948. It was considered most unwise, quite unnecessary and even wrong to implant in people the suggestion that they might not wish to accord the Party their full and unqualified devotion. Undoubtedly there were anti-socialist elements and there were those who questioned the right and the capacity of the Communists to continue governing the country, but there was no point in encouraging them; above all they should have no possible grounds for believing that such lack of faith was legitimate.

Dubcek tried to counter this attitude. As early as 1964 he was saying to the people he governed that he understood that they could not, had not and indeed should not vote for 'the Party right or wrong'. He continued:

> Lenin said that it is very important to encourage all citizens to take part in the ruling of the State. This, I know, is a very difficult task, but it is not possible for a small minority – the Party – to introduce and maintain socialism. Ideally it should be introduced by tens of millions of people, and it will be when they learn to do so. Therefore Party members must, and most of our members do, pay close and constant attention to these matters – any lack of attention to the electorate weakens socialism. It is no good stressing this only before an election; we must also practise it after the election, so that the newly elected organs will adopt these principles as the basis of their work. Representatives must constantly meet their constituents; they must really understand thoroughly the particular problems of the districts they represent.[4]

Dubcek and the Intelligentsia.

Since about 1961 Marxist philosophers and intellectuals in Eastern Europe have sometimes been allowed to do constructive work and not forced merely to act as the apologists of the Party machine. In part this is the result of a need to readapt fundamental Marxist teaching to the changed economic conditions of the 'sixties, for Socialist economics have not only been overtaken but left far behind by the industrial countries of the West. The more Party machines tend to busy themselves with finding new solutions to economic problems the more tolerant they initially appear to become of ideological questioning.

By 1963 most East European countries had long had their errant philosophers and economists, in the form of a Lukacs, a Kolakowski or even a Liberman. Czechoslovakia was peculiar in producing no philosopher or even economist of any merit between 1948 and 1965. That she did not was a reflection of the degree to which Novotny was both anxious and able to control all spheres of life until then. But with the partial lifting of controls after 1963 – especially in Bratislava – Czech and Slovak philosophers were able to express their ideas and their criticisms more freely. There was, to begin with, a rule that practical affairs should continue to be the domain of the Party's own 'thinkers'; on the organization of industry and the tasks facing the *apparat*, philosophers were expected to exercise a decent reticence. But this did not stop the Czech Karel Kosik from trying to prove, under the influence of Sartre, that Marx and even the bourgeois humanists were agreed in their fight against the inhumanity of bureaucratic society. To prove more important in terms of practical politics was the work of the Slovak legal philosopher Michal Lakatos who tried to devise a system of Marxist political opposition.

The term 'intellectuals' is unfortunately necessary in any discussion of the politics of Czechoslovakia. For such men do form pressure groups within East-European countries in a way that is quite inconceivable in a Western democracy. Intellectuals in, for example, England, have much more freedom to say and do what they wish than in Czechoslovakia but they are, for this very reason, much less important a political force. The persecution and victimization to which the Czech and Slovak intelligentsias have so often been subjected has made of them a fairly tight-knit group commanding respect from the people and attention from the Party on a scale that they could never command in the United Kingdom.

Dubcek's views on the role that intellectuals should play in the government of Czechoslovakia, inside or outside of the Party, have always been far more tolerant than those of most of his colleagues. He has never, since his earliest days in the *apparat,* hesitated to surround himself with the best minds available. He has often found it difficult to convince his colleagues of the wisdom or the 'Marxism' of such an attitude, for the Czechoslovak Communist Party has had a fervent tradition of anti-intellectualism since 1948. Husak and his friends were purged as much for their education as for their patriotism. Nevertheless, even at the moment of their imprisonment in 1954, Dubcek had called on the Party to recruit the 'best sons of the intelligentsia.' It was not in his case an empty phrase – for some of 'the best sons' were already working with him. Indeed, on some occasions while he was in Trencin and Banska Bystrica he is believed to have come into conflict with his colleagues over his tendency to consult academics or experts who were sometimes not even in the Party at all, let alone members of the *apparat.*

After he took over the Slovak Secretaryship he courted the intellectuals not only for their intrinsic value but also for the useful political allies that they made at a time when Novotny was making his disdain for anyone with a university qualification or pretensions to writing so evident. 'Our Party knows that the most important factor in harnessing all the creative forces and enthusiasm in society is a united working class,' said Dubcek.

> Therefore the Party will always defend this unity against intrigues from all sides. Nevertheless, we must not underestimate the role of the intelligentsia in a socialist society. The fact that the working class is the main revolutionary force and initiates all the revolutionary changes in our society cannot be and is not in conflict with the role to be played by the intelligentsia. The harmony of workers and

intellectuals has a moral and political strength which is an important factor in building a developed socialist society. ... We recognize that without the intellectuals it is impossible to build the modern scientific technology necessary to satisfy our needs.

However, he was careful to point out that intellectuals could work only under the direction of the Party and for the good of the working class:

Our socialist intelligentsia must use all its creative ability to overcome all those socially disruptive forces which threaten the speed of industrial advance[5] [and] we have to distinguish between the majority of our intellectuals who are playing a useful part in society and a handful who are intent on confusing the people.[6] [Nevertheless] ... we will never accept the attempt to create artificial divisions between the working class and intelligentsia, between Communists and non-Communists. It is most important that Communists working amongst the intelligentsia should establish and maintain by their example the influence of the Party in such areas.[5]

One of the most important and effective ways in which Dubcek harnessed the support of the writers and intellectuals was by the unprecedented freedom which he extended to journalists.

He had put his friendship with Klokoc, the editor of *Pravda*, to good use in 1963, and this was a relationship that continued to be profitable until the invasion of August 1968. Perhaps even more significant was his friendship with Juraj Spitzer who in 1965 became editor of *Kulturni Zivot*. Under Spitzer's guidance and with Dubcek's approval the paper continued its heretical policy of independence of Prague and the Party which had begun in 1963. Ostensibly *Kulturni Zivot* is the organ of the Slovak Writers' Union but over the next four years few of its readers bought it for its literary merits or for its discussion of fourteenth-century Slav bards. It was the most iconoclastic and exciting political journal in Czechoslovakia, and few issues were without at least one article inveighing against Prague centralism, the management of the economy, the selection of university students on class rather than intellectual merits, or the myopic refusal to recognize the possibility of roads to Communism other than Novotny's.

One of Dubcek's most courageous acts was to allow Spitzer to give space to Gustav Husak, who had not yet been fully rehabilitated and was still officially *persona non grata* with the Party. Husak was allowed to write on his speciality, the Slovak National Revolt which he had done so much to engineer and lead. In one article he argued, in complete contradiction to the official line, that 'the struggle for national liberation was not a struggle of one class or of one party' thus rejecting the Party thesis that only Communists had been active in the resistance movement. It must have infuriated Novotny.

Other articles even dared to question not only the practices but also the basic principles of Party organization, and one rejected the 'dogma of the immaculateness of proletarian origin' and the 'sectarian-dogmatic interpretation of the leading role of the proletariat'. Another condemned the 'scholastic clinging of dogmatists to the letter of classical Marxist-Leninism' and questioned the validity of the concept of collective as against individual happiness. Under Dubcek writers were allowed for the first time to call for 'a humanization of socialism' and 'a return to the ideals of humanist socialism', in hopeful anticipation, perhaps, of 'Socialism with a Human Face'.[6]

Dubcek and the Capitalists

Dubcek's most barren, predictable and uninspiring statements have always been reserved for speeches on international relations. It is probably true to say that he has never had an idea of his own on how Czechoslovakia might better conduct her international affairs. If that is being unduly harsh, then it is certainly true that any original ideas he may have had he has neglected to express in public. It is a pity. But it is perhaps understandable. His whole life, except for the rather exceptional years of 1938–48, has been spent under Communist government. He did not have Novotny's experience of a social-democrat Czechoslovakia before the war. And since 1948 he seems to have visited the West only once: in 1960 he spent two days in Helsinki at the Finnish Communist Party Congress.

Apart from that his only trip outside the Socialist bloc was – also in 1960 – to the Congress of the North Vietnamese Communist Party in Hanoi. Furthermore, he has never been seconded to work in the foreign relations department of the Central Committee in Prague and he has never worked in the Ministry of Foreign Affairs. His interests have been entirely domestic and he has never had the opportunity of reaching his own conclusions on capitalism. There is no reason to suppose that any judgment he might have made for himself would have been more favourable than those he has accepted, but it is important simply to remember that these pronouncements are straight out of the most elementary cold-war textbook.

Until 1968 his attitude towards the West was totally uncompromising and his genuine respect for the Soviet Union almost magnificent in its intensity. He believed that the betrayal of Munich and the events of the war had tied the destiny of Czechoslovakia irrevocably to that of the Soviet Union. He was convinced, furthermore, that this trick of fate or geography was of the greatest good fortune to the Czechoslovak people. For one thing he was sure that the success of the Slovak Revolt, such as it was, was due to the help of the Soviet Union, and particularly to the contribution of the Russian partisans parachuted into Slovakia. He believed that the history of Soviet-Czechoslovak co-operation since the war should be regarded as concrete evidence of and a lasting tribute to the way in which two socialist nations can live together in unity and equality. In none of his enquiries into the economic problems of his country does he seem to have questioned its economic relationship with Russia. He never speculated that Czechoslovakia's low standard of living might be the result of being bled by the Kremlin.

Perhaps because of his happy childhood in Kirghizia and his education in Gorkiy his affection for all things Soviet far surpassed that of a man like Husak. Husak has always maintained a healthy scepticism of Moscow and if, after April 1969, he became the complete collaborator it was probably out of necessity rather than choice. Whereas Husak might well imagine a Czechoslovakia independent of the Kremlin in the same way as Yugoslavia, to Dubcek this was always unthinkable. Nearly all East-European politicians make unceasing protestations of eternal friendship and love for the Soviet Union, but Dubcek's are perhaps more sincere than most. Even in his private letters he has often written of the greatness that is Russia and of its well-deserved premier place in the world Communist movement.

This has led him to take up anti-capitalist positions far more uncompromising than those of Khrushchev, and even on occasion than those of Brezhnev. Whereas both Soviet leaders have often been prepared to pay at least tribute to the idea of peaceful co-existence with the West, Dubcek has been much less so:

> We will stand in all matters at the side of the Soviet Union and will ever back its policies and Comrade Khrushchev in his attempts to prevent nuclear war and to keep the peace and to pursue a policy of peaceful competition between states of different social and economic systems. But that does not mean that we accept the idea of the peaceful co-existence of the two ideologies. Peaceful competition does not provide ideological peace. The class fight continues ... The Soviet Union for ever and nothing else.[7]

This speech was made welcoming Brezhnev to Bratislava on the occasion of the renewal of the Czechoslovak-Russian Friendship Treaty in 1963. It is interesting to contrast it with Brezhnev's apparently less hawkish reply:

> Peace is the ally of socialism ... it is quite a new phenomenon for mankind and in the history of international relations that a group of states should not be concerned only with dominating the world and increasing their own share of the profits, but rather with preserving the peace, independence and equality of all nations. If there are any forces which oppose the policy of peaceful co-existence, they will have to give up sooner or later. The great idea of peaceful co-existence will triumph, and if a third world war is prevented, and if it is possible to protect small nations from imperialism, it is only because the socialist nations have followed a policy of peaceful co-existence ...[8]

That Brezhnev may well have been insincere is not the

point. What is interesting is that he professed himself willing to accept the idea of peaceful co-existence, whereas Dubcek apparently would not. Brezhnev must have gone away from Bratislava thinking that this was a rigid and straightforward *apparatchik* indeed.

Dubcek and his Problems

Dubcek went through something of a watershed in his life in 1966, for it was during that year that he had to make a total commitment either for or against a continued process of reform. It was also that summer that Novotny made his most serious attack upon the Slovak leadership and tried to have him replaced by Michal Chudik. Only after Dubcek had managed to defeat this coup was he, for the first time, unchallenged if not unchallengeable in Bratislava. As a result his personal relations with Novotny, always bad, became execrable.

It was apparently soon after the Chudik affair that Novotny flew to Slovakia to open a factory near Nitra. He brought with him his lunch – sandwiches wrapped up in brown paper. In Bratislava they insist that this was because he was terrified that the Slovaks would try to poison him, but perhaps he simply thought that he might not have time for a proper lunch. In any case, he took the package with him into the factory and placed it on the table beside him while he made his speech. Sharing the platform was Dubcek. He sat next to Novotny listening, his head resting on his hand, and on his features that mournful and rather distant expression that he so often assumes when he is not really concentrating on what is happening around him. Absent-mindedly, he began fiddling with the string that was tied around the sandwich packet. Suddenly a large Czech security man in a dark suit leapt from a front-row seat and snatched the precious parcel from Dubcek's vaguely curious fingers. Dubcek woke up, startled. After nodding to his protector and glancing furiously at Dubcek, Novotny continued with his speech, and Dubcek sank back into even deeper gloom than before.

Even if apocryphal, this story illustrates fairly well the strained relations between Novotny and Slovakia in general,

Alexander Dubcek, First Secretary of the Slovak Communist Party, with Oldrich Cernik, Deputy Prime Minister of Czechoslovakia, and Leonid Brezhnev, First Secretary of the Communist Party of the Soviet Union, at a Czechoslovak Communist Party Conference, Karlovy Vary, April 1967.

Dubcek, Brezhnev and Novotny at Prague airport, 8 December 1967.

The happy human face of socialism, the Mayday Parade 1968.

Novotny and Dubcek in particular. It was a feud that made Dubcek curiously unhappy. After he had finally overcome the Czech's attempts to have him ousted he should have been able to relax. He did feel a little more secure, but he continued to be very upset by the President's increasing truculence. Dubcek is not the sort of man who easily dismisses his enemies with scorn – he sorrows at their hostility.

After the summer of 1966 he and Novotny rarely met except formally and the Czech took to making abusive telephone calls to Bratislava. One of the things that irked him most was Dubcek's receiving any publicity in Press or television; he would often complain both to editors and Dubcek himself that his coverage was disproportionate to his station and smacked of an obsession with his own personality. Late in 1966 he rang Dubcek in the middle of the night and shouted that he had no right to receive ambassadors in Bratislava without permission from Prague. Did he think that Slovakia was a state in its own right? And why had he disregarded the regulations which stated that he should have only still photographs of himself shown on television when welcoming someone at the airport? Dubcek found such sessions extremely depressing and would spend the rest of the day (or night) in blank despair, convinced that Novotny could still find some way of getting rid of him.

Novotny discovered that the most effective way of baiting the Slovak was to accuse him of anti-socialist activities, to charge him with weakening the Party and with playing into the hands of the imperialists. Dubcek's overt flirtation with the journalists was, he would taunt, reminiscent of Slansky's treacherous imitation of bourgeois and anti-Leninist prejudices. Dubcek once answered back in a public attack upon Novotny, asserting that it was necessary 'to stand up against the sectarian-leftist trends whose followers adhered to the bureaucratic administrative methods of Party work and who regarded the method of patient winning-over to the policy of the Central Committee as a manifestation of compromise.'[9]

Despite this bravado, Novotny's insults sank home, for Dubcek was genuinely concerned with the effects of the freedom he had given to the Press and terrified lest anything he did should in fact harm the interests of the Party. During this whole year he fluctuated wildly and anxiously between the belief that what he was doing was for the good of the Party and the conviction that anti-Communist forces were taking advantage of him. On the one hand: 'We must lay more stress on the development of democracy within the Party. We must pay more attention to the thoughts of individual Communists and we must support the development of criticism within the Party.' On the other hand: 'Anti-Communism . . . finds fertile soil in the minds of our people. It flourishes in the most diverse manifestations of negativism, liberalistic trends, social-democratic remnants, religious and national hangovers and so on.'[10]

He hoped that the answer to the problems caused by this ragbag of familiar villains was indoctrination. He thought that the Party, in implementing its new policies, should be meticulous in explaining just how far any new freedoms might extend. There must be no room for doubt in anyone's mind as to what the Party was prepared to allow and what it had no intention of tolerating. The indoctrination must include not only a study of dialectics but also instruction in the Marxist-Leninist use of leisure: 'Within ideological education instruction in scientific atheism holds an important place. It is an inseparable part of our overall efforts to win people over to a materialistic view of the world and for making prevalent the principles of socialist ethics throughout the lives of working people.'[11]

Despite his fears Dubcek was sincere in his assertion that he favoured the development of criticism within the Party and of his own leadership. He saw the broadening of inter-party democracy as the prerequisite of increasing democracy within society as a whole. He never for a moment considered that the Party should abandon its leading role but, to employ a cliché not yet current, he was anxious to increase 'participation'.

Nevertheless, he was very concerned by the use that some journalists had made of the relative liberty of the Slovak press. He could not help worrying whether these anti-socialist aberrations could be justified by his still ill-conceived intention of destroying the conditions in which the 'errors of the 'fifties' could flourish. He wanted to create a Party in which 'violations of Leninist principles' could not again occur, but he knew that this would be taken by some as an admission of weakness which should be fully exploited. Such exploitation he was determined to prevent, for he saw no reason why the Party should allow 'certain individuals . . . to purge themselves at the Party's expense of their own mistakes and errors of the past, to relieve their "consciences" burdened by the dogmatic influences of their own misdeeds'.[12]

His faith in indoctrination he repeated when discussing the problems raised by the partial opening of barriers to the West in 1963 (one result of this had been an obsession with Western pop music which became known in Czechoslovakia as 'Big Beat'). On the phenomenon of Socialist Beatlemania Dubcek had to say:

> The task of the ideological section of the Party must be to counter the uncritical admiration of all that comes from Western countries. We must find ways of educating the young in the spirit of socialism. We must lay more stress on the development of democracy within the Party. We must pay more attention to the thoughts of Communists, to support the development of criticism inside the Party and to correct present and past mistakes. This is the only way in which we can encourage people to have confidence in the Party.[13]

That Dubcek's concern with Party propaganda was not misplaced was demonstrated by a remarkable poll conducted by *Pravda* in 1957. 7,500 Slovak readers gave their opinions on the problems of war, peace and co-existence. Only 51% blamed the imperialists for international tension and 28% said that both sides were responsible. Even more remarkable was that only 41.5% blamed the USA for the Vietnam war; 18% said they had no idea what caused tension in Vietnam. *Pravda* was forced to the sad conclusion that 'in propaganda we are not always able to make successful use of a concrete situation in order to make people take a similar attitude on more general questions'. The poll, must, however, have caused more concern than that. For, apart from reflecting the total failure of propaganda to explain the class interests and proletarian internationalism of socialist foreign policy, it also represented a complete rejection of the Party line. It was perhaps disillusion with their own Party rather than support for the Americans that made so many people refuse to blame the capitalists for the war in Vietnam.[14]

Dubcek and the Economists

By the end of 1964 Dubcek had begun to realize that it was impossible even for a socialist society to ignore the fact that economic advance conditions social expectations. Demands for improvements in the standard of living increase in ratio with economic development and industrialization, and to deny these expectations can endanger the growth rate of the economy. This was not the reason for the disastrous negative growth of the Czechoslovak economy in 1963, but it went some way to explain the dissatisfaction of the vast majority of the people with its economic position; for such expansion as there was simply did nothing to improve the position of the consumer.

The first country to experiment with economic decentralization was Yugoslavia with its workers' councils and decollectivized agriculture. The example of the heretical Tito was followed in the Polish agricultural sector and by the Russians with Liberman's plan for profits and incentives for plant, teams and even for individual workers. During 1964 Novotny, happy to accept Russian guidance, began to listen to the arguments of a Czech reformer, Dr Ota Sik.

If one assumes that there can be two basic forms of economic systems, the one based on administrative control and the other one in which economic levers or 'incentives' are used, then Ota Sik, like Liberman before him, was anxious to break out of the administrative stronghold, simply because he believed the 'lever economy' to be more responsive to the demands and needs of the consumer – both industrial and private.

But Sik, like many Russian economists today, considered that Liberman's economic theories and the reforms he initiated in the Soviet Union had a very limited value. They were useful as a point of departure but they did not go nearly far enough. He argued that to make men work better it is necessary to show them that it is to their advantage to do so; otherwise 'the workers following their own direct interests will act quite unconsciously against their long-term interests'.[15]

One of Czechoslovakia's greatest economic problems was the inefficiency and mismanagement encouraged and perpetuated by the completely centralized and bureaucratic system of planning.

In the early 'fifties Dubcek had believed total and all-embracing central planning to be vital. But after 1963 his attitude towards this 'cult' began to change. On the one hand he saw in planning an effective means of maintaining the leading role and the power of the Party. On the other he was forced to admit that Prague control over industry was not producing the results that it should and that the Czechoslovak economy, directed by the Party *apparat,* was in fact becoming the greatest threat to the Party's success and continued survival. 'We Communists know that the success of our plans depends on how far they are accepted and esteemed by the people. Even the best plans would remain only slogans if we were not able to relate them to ordinary people, so that they could accept them as their own and realize that their own best interests are served thereby.'[16]

By the end of 1964 he had realized that some concessions must be made to market forces, and that perhaps the concepts of supply and demand had some part to play even in a socialist economy. By this time he was prepared to ally himself with the reformers and especially with Dr Sik, who was given official permission in 1965 to draw up a complete New Economic Model. It was to this tentative that Dubcek referred when he said in April 1966:

> The Central Committee is not satisfied with the present state [of the economy] . . . We agree with those people who are seeking more effective solutions to the problems of society . . . . We are prepared to put new plans into effect in order to transform completely the structure of the economy. The new incentive to industry and agriculture will provide a solution to the problems which beset the level of production and the management of industry. The main

aims in the Party's economic policy are based on giving greater emphasis to the basic principle of socialism – reward according to work . . . A great and revolutionary task is in front of the Party, which will need to understand fast the new economic principles – the most important of these is that prices must be linked more closely to costs.

We have two alternatives we can choose: First, we can allow idleness and inefficiency; we can continue to subsidize such failings, and then the standard of living will fall. Or, secondly – and this is the alternative we have chosen – we can decide to end the fallacy of democracy on the shop-floor. We have made a historic change of policy on which we must build a feeling of healthy pride in personal work and achievement.[17]

Sik's New Economic Model, brought into effect in January 1967, was designed to decentralize Prague's control, to allow far greater freedom to individual enterprises and groups of factories. It was in fact intended to permit, for the first time, the actual pattern of demand and the real costs of production to play at least a part in determining the nature and structure of economic output.

It took a long time for Novotny's archaic and stultified leadership to realize the necessity for such reforms. Once appreciated, however, the plans were embraced with considerable enthusiasm by the men at the top of the Party, although to some of the extreme conservatives the emphasis on incentive, on individual achievement, on payment according to results did seem, perhaps justifiably, a betrayal of Marxism. But it was at the bottom of the Party machine that resistance to the proposals was often fanatically intense. To the Party representatives in factories and units, to the small men who owed their livelihood to the Party's centralized economic control, whose work consisted of simply transmitting the Party's orders, the reforms posed an immediate threat. For the first time they were being asked to think; they were being told that from now on they would have to make decisions. For many of them it was an impossible and insupportable change of life. They reacted with despair and took every possible opportunity of inflicting further injury on a plan which was even at birth seriously crippled by the midwife's inexperienced and frightened hands.

The reforms contained a less obvious but no less serious threat to the full-time members of the *apparat*. Insofar as the direction of the economy was to be given to intellectuals and academics from the Academy of Sciences and other extra-Party institutions, then it was clear that there would be fewer jobs for the boys. This was something that should be deplored and resisted.

The conservatives were correct in asserting that Sik's plan represented a betrayal of Marxism insofar as Sik believed that Marx was mistaken in his theory that the market was a purely capitalist phenomenon which would disappear with the system. He contended that Marx could not have foreseen 'in every detail the profound and complex inter-relationships within a socialist economy'. He did not blame Marx for this failure but he did blame those who continued to refuse to admit its existence: 'only a dogmatic concept of Marxist-Leninist theory could lead one to deny the existence of certain new phenomena for the reason that they were not explained and clarified at some time by the founders of Marxism.'[18]

After six months it was already clear that the New Economic Model was not going to be a success. It had been introduced on too limited a scale and resistance to its isolated implementation had been too simple to organize. A Western journalist asked Sik to explain this failure. Sik replied bitterly:

> The government decided that the city fathers had to do something to end the chaotic traffic jams in the streets of Prague. The Town Hall considered the matter for some time; finally someone proposed that we study the English system in order to find a sensible method of regulating traffic. A commission was sent to London. It returned six months later. The first, rather surprising observation of the traffic experts was that in London they drive on the left. 'Ah,' the city fathers said, 'this may be the solution.' So it was decreed that after a certain date everyone in Prague would have to drive on the left. The experts expressed doubt; if a fundamental change of this sort were carried out suddenly in a busy city like Prague, the result could be dis-

astrous. So the city fathers formed a compromise solution. They decreed that the new regulation would apply only to taxi-drivers . . . My plan has met a similar fate. They have strangled it by 'testing' it only in matters that are typical and of small import. Whilst people have recognized the importance of changing the entire system, they do not want to do so everywhere.[19]

One of the problems of this half-hearted reform was that enterprises could not be trusted to set the prices of their own products. It was feared that sudden exposure to the risks of their own decisions might encourage managers to play safe and slap on big price increases, thereby hopefully guarding against any mistakes that they might make and diminishing a demand which they might not otherwise be able to meet. To avoid this prices had to remain controlled, which meant that it was necessary to abandon the New Economic Model's emphasis on market determination.

The problem was not solved and by April 1967 Sik had to admit that wholesale prices had risen by 29% instead of the planned 19%. The Economic Model did not appear to most people to be changing anything for the better – the same shortages and the same poor quality of goods persisted. There appeared to be little difference between Sik's New Model and the ineffectual tinkerings which had periodically been used to upset further an already sick economy in the past. Sik's frustration and impatience grew throughout the year and he began to say more and more openly what he knew all along, that genuine economic reform could succeed only with a reform of the political structure of the country, that economics *was* politics and that, if the necessary incentives were to be introduced into the economic structure, they were bound to affect the work of politicians and political workers. It was a point of view which Dubcek found very convincing.

Dubcek and other Slovaks

Of the three issues – political democratization, economic reform and Slovak nationalism: the last was the cause that came most naturally to Dubcek as leader of the Slovak Communist

Party. It is also here that one finds his most important, original and independent contribution towards precipitating the crisis of 1967.

He became a spokesman for Slovakia only slowly and this has led to the accusation that he adopted the cause out of expediency rather than conviction. It is true that he was never really an ardent nationalist in the way that Husak has always been, and until 1967 he was prepared to give little public encouragement either to the idea of federation or to any of the other nationalist demands being voiced by Slovak patriots. By the end of 1966 these demands had grown into a full-scale movement in Bratislava; the argument over constitutional reform was no longer 'If' but 'How?'. Should Slovakia be autonomous or federated to the Czech lands? Jan Mlynarik, arguing for federation, tried to show the 'Smeral's [founder of the Czechoslovak Communist Party] concept for the building of a state embracing several nationalities was based on a federation system . . . of the Swiss type'. Mlynarik went on to suggest that the reason why so many Slovaks accepted the Fascist government of Tiso during the war lay in the bolshevization and Prague centralism of the Czechoslovak Communist Party after 1929.[20] It was a clear attack on Novotny, and one which Dubcek ignored.

But the fact that Dubcek refused to lend his own name to the nationalist cause should not be taken to mean that he had no sympathy for it. His contribution was in tolerating, even encouraging, the climate of opinion and expression in Bratislava in which such debate was possible. By turning at least a blind eye to nationalist articles in *Kulturni Zivot* and other papers, he was in fact promoting the growth of this all-important political pressure group.

His assumption of the nationalist cause in an active way was, if expedient, also inevitable. Given his evergrowing dislike of Novotny, and the President's attempts to remove him from office and to insult Slovakia, there was really no alternative for Dubcek. Nevertheless he understood that the nationalist issue was a very dangerous as well as a very powerful weapon, and he was initially extremely circumspect in his use of it.

It has been suggested that his reticence on the Slovak

question during his first year as Slovak First Secretary shows that he was bought off by Novotny and that he had been appeased by the apology he had been able to extract in December 1963. It is certainly true that this delighted him, and it is also true that he was more prepared to compromise with Novotny than were many other Slovaks. But Dubcek was all this time playing something of a double game. Januslike, he was trying to prevent the already terrible Prague-Bratislava relations from reaching a real crisis while at the same time surreptitiously building up his support within Slovakia. He knew that he was not strong enough to challenge Novotny in 1964 and, to placate him, he endeavoured to show in public speeches just how much Slovakia benefited from the relationship with Prague. He did not always succeed. Indeed, in at least one set of figures he quoted, he unconsciously proved the converse: 'Since 1938 Slovak industrial production has increased by 12½ times. Since 1948 it has increased 6½ times.'[21] This would seem to be clear evidence of the marked superiority of the Slovak economy during those years when it was independent of the Czech lands and run by the clerico-fascists and the bourgeoisie.

When he referred to the discontent in Slovakia over the country's status within the Republic, it was to dismiss it as either incorrect or unimportant. Thus:

> Some people say that the solution [a united Czechoslovak State] is not good enough. They complain that the Slovak national organs are a mere go-between from Prague to the local organs. But the attitude of both Czechoslovak and Slovak Central Committees is that the Slovak National Council must both in theory and in practice carry out all the functions which have been entrusted to it.[22]

He also argued that the Council's present status provided a perfectly adequate forum for the discussion of Slovak affairs, adding that since the Council had never, even under previous constitutions, played an important or constructive role, there was no reason to expect it to do so in the future. In this he was right; over the years 1950–9 the Council had barely exercised those legislative powers that it possessed. It met only occasionally, and then simply to discuss questions of administration. But this was rather more a function of the attitudes of Bacilek than anything else. He had done nothing to encourage it to act independently of Prague and its refusal to do so reflects only his control over the Party, not the aspirations of the Slovak people for their own government.

Nevertheless, Dubcek went on to try and convince his audience how lucky and how happy they were: 'Only the blind could not see that relations between Czechs and Slovaks are indivisible. The interests of the Slovak workers are the same as those of workers throughout our State – to move as fast as possible towards the faster economic progress of our common country.'[23]

The 150th anniversary of the birth of Ludovit Stur provided, in 1965, an excellent opportunity for Slovak nationalists to assert themselves, for Stur, nineteenth-century journalist, poet and political agitator was the greatest hero the country had. But the celebration of his birth was not only a nationalistic event, it was also a defiance of the Party and perhaps even of Marx. Stur and his colleagues had been condemned by Marx and Engels for their support of the Hapsburg monarchy against the Hungarian revolutionaries of 1848. In that year Stur and a group of nationalistic Slovak writers had organized the Peasants' Revolt, supposedly against Hungarian domination. Stur had tried to strike a bargain with Vienna: if the Slovaks helped the Hapsburgs to crush the Hungarian peasants led by Kossuth, then they should be freed from Hungarian domination. In other words, they agreed to destroy the Hungarian peasantry's bid for freedom in order to gain their own. Clearly Marx's criticism of Stur had some validity – he appears to have acted in the worst tradition of petty-bourgeois nationalism. It would have been much better had he and Kossuth joined forces against their common enemy the Hungarian Hapsburgs. According to many Slovak patriots, this was what Stur wanted, but Kossuth ruined the idea by refusing to admit that Slovakia even existed. In fact Stur did not believe that he was capable of persuading the Slovak peasants to fight alongside their Hungarian brothers whom they disliked so much.

In view of his activities and of Marx's condemnation, Stur had been condemned by the government since 1948. But in 1964 several articles appeared in the Bratislava press attacking Marx's attitude, trying to show that Magyar oppression of the Slovaks was a greater evil than Hapsburg hegemony and endeavouring to prove that Stur really hated the Hungarians for their fanatic chauvinism. This was undoubtedly true, though Stur was hardly less guilty of narrow patriotism. But, said the apologists, he had a right to be.

The attempts at rehabilitation were unconvincing but the xenophobia that the articles encouraged in Slovakia very soon became anti-Czech rather than anti-Hungarian.

Maybe it was because Dubcek had been born in the same house as Stur that he not only sanctioned the publication of these whitewashings but also indulged in them himself. He was asked to make a speech on the anniversary of Stur's birth, 30 October 1965. Somewhat to the surprise of the organizers, he agreed to do so, and their surprise turned to delighted amazement when he, too, asserted that Stur was no petty-bourgeois but, despite Marx, a great national hero. 'We are meeting to pay tribute,' he said, 'to the greatest son of the Slovak people, the founder of the Slovak language, and of the school of poetry, politician and journalist, whose dreams we have been able to realize in our Socialist Republic.' Dubcek might well have been content with this – he might have tried to show that although Stur was no Communist he was at least someone with concern for the proletariat. But he went much further than that and tried to paint a picture of Stur as the first great Slovak revolutionary.

> Stur lived in a period when feudalism was dying, in which the power of the bourgeoisie began to gain ascendancy. It was the period when the revolution began. The ideas and actions of Stur can be understood only in the context of the deep revolutionary movement thrusting through all European countries.
>
> The development of his ideas was very complex. He was inspired by love of his country. His feelings and emotions were in harmony with his reason. With the unity of the people, his personality grew in stature. He worked for his people's language, for their own laws, for education. He showed up the brutality of feudalism which was such a

great barrier to the evolution of society. He demonstrated the great gap between lords and serfs. He understood all the principal social and economic problems and the tendencies of his period, and he understood that everything must change.

Dubcek tried to excuse Stur's attitude in 1848 by explaining that his main concern had been for the welfare of the peasantry and the development of agriculture: 'He understood that the peasants represented not only a productive but also a political force. He realized that the Slovak peasantry was the basis for the evolution of a genuine national movement at that time ...'

Dubcek argued that by his codification of the Slovak language, by blending the various dialects into one tongue, Stur had increased the national unity and consciousness of his people and thus laid the ground for the Independence of 1918, the Revolt of 1944 and, of course, the Glorious Revolution of 1948 ...

Then Dubcek left the problem of Stur himself, and for the first time in a public speech admitted:

> The most important question in our politics at the moment is the question of nationality. As Lenin said, 'Only very careful attention to the problems of all nations can avoid a very dangerous conflict.' The success of socialism has increased and enhanced not only the material but also the spiritual lives of men. For this reason, national pride is not weakened in the heart of a socialist – on the contrary it is strengthened. Therefore, as socialism progresses we encounter a renaissance of national pride. In man is innate a very strong desire for the progress of his party, of his native culture, of his language and, finally, for the development of his united socialist country. This is the opposite of bourgeois-nationalism – we must distinguish between national feelings and pride and that reactionary nationalism that is the core of bourgeois-nationalism.[24]

Dubcek was risking a lot in this attempt to distinguish between bourgeois and proletarian nationalism. If such a distinction can be made, clearly it behoved him to make it.

Although he did not do so very successfully, this is a fascinating and most important speech, for it was the first time on which he could be seen to champion in public the cause of Slovakia and to recognize that the nationality problem was vital.

But it was not until 1967 that he really began to use the Slovak issue as a stick with which to beat Novotny. In March of that year he made a gratuitous speech in praise of one of Stur's band of friends, Josef Hurban. He naturally drew attention to the man's many merits: 'He was a revolutionary agitator and organizer who by his energy and courage is even today a model and example of a man fighting for everything progressive and new . . . He was not a narrow-minded nationalist; he was, as well as a Slovak, a Slav.'

This obviously represented another attack on Marx's assessment of Stur's activities. At the same time it was a direct attack on Novotny's discrimination against Slovakia and Czech domination of the economy: 'Hurban,' Dubcek continued, 'played a great part in improving the relations between Slavonic nations, especially between Czechs and Slovaks . . . *He reminds us today that we need to deepen co-operation between our two races. We must not merely rely on past successes but do all that we can now.*'* This was an extraordinarily blunt assertion that Czech-Slovak relations were not all they could be, and Dubcek went on to accuse Novotny of failing to accord Slovakia her historical rights:

> Stur's ideas on the development of Slovakia were reborn in the Slovak Revolt. During the Revolt the national and international aspirations of Slovakia were clear – soldiers and partisans fought not only for the rights of the Slovak nation, but also for the renewal of Czechoslovakia *as a state of two equal nations,* as a home of Czechs and Slovaks and built on nationally and socially just principles.*

Dubcek was in effect suggesting that Slovaks had been betrayed, that although they had won the socialism for which they had fought, they had been denied their rights as a nation.

* Emphasis added.

But this did not mean that national differences had been forgotten:

> National feeling cannot be thought to be a heritage of the past, even in socialism. . . . There is still a lot to be done to develop to the full the Slovak nation as Stur and his friends had wanted, in the spirit of the Revolt, and *in the spirit of the Kosice Programme,** and to evaluate truly the results of more than twenty years' work by our people in the interest of the progress of our country, the Czechoslovak Socialist Republic.[25]

* Emphasis added.

7
THANK YOU, TONDA

'The fault [of 1968] does not lie in the departure of Novotny —the beginning of the evil lies in the fact that we chose as First Secretary of the Central Committee a person who was unstable ideologically, with marked tendencies towards petty bourgeois ideology in practice.'

Alois Indra, to a Party Conference in Prague, 20 January 1970.

Dubcek's speech in praise of Hurban was an open challenge to the Party line in general and to Novotny in particular; it may have been in response to such provocation that the President embarked upon his most enormous and disastrous insult to Slovakia.

Late in August 1967 he made an official visit to Turciansky Svaty Martin, the cultural centre of Slovakia, to mark the centenary of the Slovak High School. He spoke at the Matica Slovenska. An institute with several functions, this is the museum of Slovak history, culture and folklore; it looks after the interests of Slovaks living abroad, and it disseminates cultural and tourist information. Czechs regard it with suspicion. Novotny's hatred of Slovakia was out of all proportion to the usual dislike-cum-contempt with which many Czechs view 'those primitive peasants', and it may be that he considered the Matica a wholly evil organization, dedicated to the dissemination of Slovak propaganda.

He made a fairly typical Novotny speech – long and quite unsuitable for the occasion – that offended two thirds of his audience and bored the rest. He denied that there was any problem in Czech-Slovak relations; he showed, to his mind conclusively, how Slovakia's interests were best served under a Prague government, and he compared Neville Chamberlain to Harold Wilson – both, he said were supporting Fascist-imperialist aggression, the one against Czechoslovakia, the other against the Arabs. Pro-Israeli sentiment was high in Slovakia that summer. The Israeli victory seemed to vindicate the right and ability of small nations to reject the dictates and domination of larger ones. Applause was brief.

Afterwards Novotny spoke to Juraj Paska, then director of the Matica. Paska asked him for a grant to modernize the inefficient nineteenth-century building. 'Is that really necessary?' asked Novotny. 'Wouldn't it be better to transfer your papers to Prague? And I think it much more sensible that the Foreign Institute in Prague take care of expatriate Slovaks.' A greater snub could hardly be imagined; Novotny was virtually saying that the Slovaks' beloved Matica should shut up shop. Vasil Bilak, standing nearby, was furious and asked Novotny, perhaps a little loudly, how he dared be so offensive. The President summoned his car and his wife and left at once.

The story has a remarkable sequel. The Matica had prepared for Novotny an expensive and reasonably attractive present. It was a souvenir collection, suitably bound in vellum and inscribed to the President, of photographs and reproductions of all the most precious documents in the Matica's archives. As Novotny left in such a hurry, Paska was not able to present it to him as planned. So it was sent by post. Two weeks later it came back. There was no letter from Novotny, not even a covering note; one of the President's secretaries had simply stamped the white wrapping paper with the seal of the Chancellery and written underneath it: 'This gift arrived on 4 September 1967. After inspection it is being returned; it is unacceptable.' The book and the wrapping paper are now jealously guarded at the Matica; perhaps photographs of them will be included in a future documentation of the museum's treasures.

Within a week all of Slovakia knew the story and national feeling ran perhaps higher than at any time since the war. Dubcek took the insult almost personally and he knew that it was a challenge he could not ignore – to have done so would have lost him all support within the country.

At the same time, however, he was beginning to find that there could be a conflict between the demands of the various causes he had adopted. The aspirations of the intellectuals coincided with the political reforms that the economists were demanding, but Slovak nationalism could often be alien to them both. Despite the fact that Sik's NEM had been largely castrated Dubcek had some reason to distrust the possible effects of decentralized economic management on Slovakia's economy. Sik would not allow a separate development plan for Slovakia arguing, surely correctly, that Czechoslovakia's domestic market was already so small that the reforms would have even less chance of success were Slovakia protected from the initial dislocations of redistribution.

Dubcek had to play this very carefully; he needed to guard against giving the economists any reason to believe that he was willing to destroy their plan by demanding preferential treatment for Slovakia, yet at the same time the angry Slovaks must be persuaded that he would never accept any Czech schemes that hurt them.

The Slovak economist H. Koctuch had expressed Slovak fears in the January 1967 issue of *Slovenske Pohlady*. He argued that under the new economic system Slovakia would simply be drawn into the orbit of Prague and that there would be no incentive for re-allocating industry thither; Slovakia would thus remain a supplier of raw materials and unfinished goods to Bohemia and Moravia and the Slovak standard of living would continue to rise less fast than that of the Czechs. He proposed that in order to overcome this anti-Slovak bias an economic council be attached to the Slovak National Council to carry out a separate plan for the Slovak economy.

The first three months of 1967 had convinced Dubcek that some of these fears were justified. After the introduction of NEM the profits of Slovak industry at once fell by 10%. This meant that there were less resources available for reinvestment. NEM also calculated, to the dismay of Slovaks, that the value and efficiency of their country's fixed assets was no higher than those in the Czech lands; this was a shock because Slovak capital equipment was more modern and its industry more recently developed than the Czech. Moreover, it was clear that under the NEM the situation was unlikely to improve very fast because, although Slovakia produced at this stage 20% of the nation's goods (with 30% of the labour force), only 11% of the country's research programme was carried out there.

All of this convinced nationally-minded Slovaks (which meant by now almost the entire nation) that they had once again been sold down the river, this time by Czech economists like Sik. At the plenum of the Slovak Central Committee in June 1967 these fears were openly expressed by at least two members of the Presidium, Michal Sabolcik and Frantisek Barbirek. Chudik predictably sprang to the support of Prague and therefore allied himself, curiously, with the reformers. He attacked all those who sought to show that Slovakia would suffer under the new system of management: 'Unfortunately one cannot say that theoretical discussions, including the discussions in our periodicals and daily press are always marked by the necessary reliability, qualification and circumspection.' Everyone expected Dubcek to speak but he maintained an embarrassed silence, not knowing what best to do. As a result he pleased neither Slovaks within the Committee, nor reformers without.

The Matica Slovenska incident forced him off the fence; he was compelled, for the time being at least, to side with the Slovaks. The Czechoslovak Central Committee met at the end of September and Dubcek decided to use this session to launch his attack on Novotny, and the doctrine of Prague centralism.

It took the form of a denunciation of the way in which NEM had been implemented, especially in regard to Slovakia. In this way Dubcek hoped to keep the support of both reformers and Slovaks. He tried to suggest that Slovakia was suffering now not because of NEM, but because of the plan's emasculation.

> It is no secret that both people and facts testify to the growth of distrust and doubt as to whether or not we shall persist on the course we have undertaken, and whether we shall overcome all obstacles and old habits. These apprehensions are based on the discovery that the economic tools do not always operate in the required direction.

He went on to stress that this did not mean that they should abandon the new system:

> Such loopholes and shortcomings in the economic tools cannot be repaired by a return to the old methods of

> administrative guidance which not only fail to produce the required initiative but . . . damage the unity of the interests of individuals, enterprises and society.

As for Slovakia, he complained at length of the treatment that she had been accorded and alleged: 'The results for the first half of 1967 show that only 21.9% and not the promised 28% of the overall state investment funds came to Slovakia.'

He pointed out that the long-run industrialization of his region came into conflict with some of the short-term objectives of decentralized economic development and he took up Koctuch's proposal for the creation of a central investment reservoir with funds earmarked for regional and underdeveloped (i.e. Slovak) areas.[1]

It was at this plenum that Novotny sought and obtained approval of his treatment of the writers after their unruly and 'anarchic' Congress in June.* Most speakers praised the Party's clamp-down, but some members, amongst them Dubcek, remained silent. This was a disappointment to the would-be political reformers. But Dubcek's tactics seem to have been to force Novotny from one crisis to the next in the hope that he would thus alienate one group after another. Immediately after the debate on the writers Dubcek presented the Slovak demands, and by the end of the session all the Slovak members had appreciated that their First Secretary was now prepared to fight for their rights in the most open way.

But he still had to win the confidence of the 'intellectuals'. His failure to support the writers had alienated many, but others took comfort in the fact that he was the most prominent politician to refuse to uphold Novotny's authoritarian actions. They also realized that since the goverment had banned the Czech Writers' magazine, *Literarni Noviny,* Dubcek had allowed *Kulturni Zivot* to function as the organ of Czech

* Many writers, Ludvik Vaculik, Pavel Kohout and A. J. Liehm amongst others, had denounced in the strongest terms the Party's policy towards the arts and its throttling control of society. As a result Novotny had Vaculik and Liehm expelled from the Party, and the Writers' Union paper *Literarni Noviny* was placed under the control of the Ministry of Culture. By this punishment Novotny managed to alieniate utterly all intellectuals at the same time as he infuriated the Slovaks. It was a powerful combination against him.

as well as Slovak writers and dissidents and that *Kulturni Zivot* was still the country's most provocative broadsheet.

At the next Central Committee session in the last week of October he vastly strengthened his position. It was at this plenum that he first appeared as a vigorous proponent of reform and that many Czech members realized for the first time the potential that this almost unknown Slovak might have. In a debate on 'The Party's role and position at the present stage of Socialist Society' Dubcek demanded a complete change of the Party's structure, in its method of government and relations to both the State and the public. He called for a total separation of Party and State. In effect this was a demand that Novotny should relinquish either the job of First Secretary of the Party or that of President of the Republic. Dubcek's speech was a direct attack on Novotny's monopoly of power and this, taken with his repeated demands for better treatment of Slovakia infuriated the Presidential-First Secretary, who responded by shouting at Dubcek that he was a bourgeois-nationalist. For Dubcek no attack could have been more propitious – it merely confirmed the Slovaks in their support for him.

The debate continued into the next day, and by that afternoon it was clear that a majority of the General Committee was in favour of Novotny losing one of his jobs; indeed a few isolated calls were made to that effect. Novotny understood the danger he was in and managed to get the meeting adjourned on the grounds that he and others had to attend a ceremony to mark the fiftieth anniversary of the Bolshevik Revolution. The members agreed to resume 'this important discussion' in December.

Novotny and Dubcek both spent the intervening month in trying to rally their respective followings. On the whole Dubcek was the more successful. For the first time he came out in public as the unequivocal champion of Slovak nationalism: in a speech published by *Pravda* (Bratislava) he had the audacity to claim that Slovakia deserved the greater credit for the liberation of Czechoslovakia from the Nazis.

We regard [he wrote] the period of the liberation of our

> republic, *which started with the Slovak Revolt,* as the decisive landmark in our recent history ... I recall these generally known facts because without them it is impossible to understand either the course or the result of the political crisis in Slovakia in February 1948 . . . We recall with pride that the progressive forces of the Slovak people fully utilized the historic February circumstances in order to be *the first* to contribute actively to the revival of the Czechoslovak Republic.*[2]

He continued by saying that he favoured greater autonomy for Slovakia, tentatively suggesting that perhaps the adoption of the terms of the Kosice Programme might be as good an arrangement as any. He justified his disgression into history on the grounds that 'it helps to evoke a healthy and constructive dissatisfaction with the present state of affairs ... and a search for new paths to progress'. This was a clear and public statement that he intended to continue his fight against Novotny. To the Slovak population, which knew nothing of what had gone on in the Central Committee, it came as a surprising but welcome attack upon the present structure and methods of government.

Whilst busy drumming up Slovak support in his challenge to Novotny, Dubcek seems to have taken good care not to neglect his external audience. Perhaps in order to convince Moscow of his unwavering loyalty to the Socialist bloc and to the Kremlin he included in this speech one of his very rare attacks upon China. The fact that he so seldom did this suggests that it was a purely tactical move designed to reassure his listeners that, despite his 'reformist' attitudes towards the structure of the Party, he remained steadfast in his belief in Moscow's infallibility and that, whatever changes he might favour in domestic policy, they would be only such as would cause the Kremlin to prosper.

It was a hawkish speech in which he asserted that peaceful co-existence was a necessary evil because the only alternative – thermo-nuclear war – would destroy the world. He abused the Chinese and rejected out of hand 'the adventurous policy' of their leaders. He also gave warning, as a sort of

* Emphasis added.

footnote, of the need for changes within the Party. In order to maintain its leading role it could not live only on past successes but 'it had to win constantly its leading position by the solution of new problems of the revolution, and it must lead the way to the further development of socialist society'.[3]

Whatever the feeling in the Central Committee, the Presidium was at this stage very sharply divided. It met at the beginning of December to decide whether or not the Central Committee should be recommended to separate Party and State. Some reports suggest that the voting was eight to two in favour of Novotny's retaining both his jobs, but it seems more likely that the division was five-five. According to this account, voting with Novotny were Lenart, the Prime Minister; Michal Chudik; Ottakar Simunek, a Vice Premier; and Bohuslav Lastovicka, Chairman of the National Assembly. The rebels, led by Dubcek, were Hendrych, Kolder, an obscure head of the Party's Economic Commission, Jaromir Dolansky, and Oldrich Cernik, best described as a cunning technocrat.[4] Whatever the exact voting figures Novotny appreciated that he was in a dangerous situation. Realizing that he could no longer rely on unconditional support from previously loyal placemen below him in the Party, he fell back on his second and third lines of defence: the Kremlin and the army.

After the meeting he appealed for help through Chervonenko, the Soviet Ambassador in Prague. Chervonenko had been his country's representative in Peking from 1959 to 1962. His activities in the Chinese capital had certainly done nothing to prevent the widening of the Russian-Chinese rift. He had been recalled in disfavour and his appointment to Prague was a demotion. He was undoubtedly anxious that nothing should happen during his stay in Czechoslovakia that might make his own position worse. He was for preserving the status quo at all costs and he at once informed the Kremlin of the need for immediate and active support of Novotny. On 8 December Brezhnev arrived, talked to Novotny, Dubcek and other protagonists, told Novotny, '*Eto vashe delo*',* and left without eating the formal Presidium dinner which Novotny had prepared for him. Some reports suggest that he tried to sway some of the 'undecided' votes in the Presidium

* Russian for 'It's your affair'.

towards Novotny, but there is no evidence that this was so. Novotny is said to have remarked bitterly that he would have been better off without Brezhnev's assistance.

Nevertheless, his chances of survival had not been utterly destroyed; his enemies were still undecided on who should replace him, or indeed whether he should be replaced at all. He tried to buy off the Slovak faction by authorizing State subsidies of up to forty per cent of investment costs in 'certain underdeveloped regions'. That this meant Slovakia was confirmed in January by the announcement of the National Assembly that the 1968 Plan would provide 22 billion korunas for Slovak industrialization. This raised Slovakia's share in the nation's net investment from a quarter to a third. Even more significant politically was the fact that these investment grants were to be at the disposal of the Slovak National Council, as Koctuch and Dubcek had proposed.

This concession was not enough to save Novotny from Slovak anger, and when the Central Committee finally met on 19 December the Presidium, still split, could offer it no programme for debate, no pre-arranged list of speakers. The result was an unprecedented free-for-all in which the most violent emotions and tempers were displayed; everyone used the opportunity to air his pet grievance. The most bitter and impassioned speech came, apparently, from Ota Sik who had watched in hopeless despair the failure of his Economic Model throughout the year. He savagely traduced the government that had emasculated his plan and insisted that only a completely new regime could carry out the programme that was essential to the nation's economic survival. It was a brilliant warning of the disasters attendant upon further inaction, and convinced many of these Central Committee members wavering between Novotny and his enemies that they should support the reformers.

Novotny listened to the violent denunciations hurled at his leadership from all sides and realized that he would be unlikely to survive this crisis if he relied on constitutional means. After three days of debate, with dozens of members still wishing to speak, his supporters managed to get the session adjourned, 'because it's Christmas'. The Committee agreed to reassemble in the first week of January but resolved that a special Commission be appointed to study the separation of Party and State and to recommend any changes in personnel that it considered necessary. The Commission was to consist of the Presidium supplemented by the eleven Regional Party Secretaries; it was to make its report as soon as the Central Committee remet.

Novotny now played his last card – the army. Once again he enlisted the aid of Chervonenko who, apparently acting on his own initiative, began to canvass for the President amongst the generals, especially Lomsky, the Minister of Defence and his deputy General Janko. Novotny's supporters began assiduously to spread the rumour around Prague that the Soviet Union was prepared to intervene to save him; this did not, as they had hoped, frighten waverers to his side but rather served to stiffen the resolve of the nationalists to resist. Major-General Jan Sejna drew up a letter of support for Novotny and had many top-ranking officers sign it. It seems that everything was prepared for the army's intervention 'in defence of socialism' and for the subsequent arrest of Dubcek and his supporters, when General Vaclav Prchlik informed Dubcek of the plot. Dubcek apparently confronted Novotny with evidence of his planned coup; Novotny was compelled to deny any knowledge of it and to give the orders that made any action by the army impossible. He had lost his best hand.

But he did not give up. In his New Year's broadcast to the nation he tried once more to buy off the Slovaks and intellectuals. He promised Slovakia that she should have priority in all economic considerations, he showed himself an ardent reformer, eager to end the worst abuses of the Party, and he lavished praise upon 'progressive art and culture'. In fact he stole most of Dubcek's clothes. It was not an impressive performance. For Novotny was a much smaller man than the ungainly Slovak and these garments hung loosely and awkwardly around his body; he appeared as an ill-dressed scarecrow giving a pathetic last bow and hearing to his dismay no calls for an encore.

When the Commission met on 3 January it decided only that Novotny should lose the First Secretaryship: there was no consensus on his replacement. It appears that Lubomir

Strougal and Deputy Prime Minister Oldrich Cernik were both proposed; both declined. Strougal was Minister of the Interior and Novotny's right-hand man; he must have realized that he had no hope of any support from the reformers, let alone the Slovaks. Cernik stood down because of a previous agreement with Dubcek. They had arranged that, in the event of Dubcek's election, Cernik should be promoted to the Premiership.

It was then that Dubcek was proposed. By Cernik, with Novotny's approval. This was not so extraordinary as it might appear, for Novotny had three reasons: first of all he thought that Dubcek would probably refuse and that everyone would then realize that there was no one prepared to take the Secretaryship. Secondly, if Dubcek did agree, it was quite likely that the Czech majority in the Central Committee would balk at the unprecedented idea of the country's top job going to a Slovak. Thirdly, as well as hating Dubcek, he despised him. He considered him weak and gutless and believed that if he did manage to secure the job he could be easily controlled.

Novotny was three times wrong, Dubcek accepted his nomination, the Central Committee ratified it, and Novotny proved quite unable to restrain him.

After the vote in his favour, Dubcek addressed the Central Committee in a characteristic fashion:

> I shall try to be brief. I should like to say, comrades, what I have said in the Presidium and to the consultative group when I was proposed as a candidate, and I should like to repeat it at least in part to you: anyone who knows me will realize this is one of the hardest decisions I have ever had to make. I do not have to explain this; you will understand it yourselves and in any case I would find it hard to put it before this plenum. This is something that so affects one's state of mind; as I have already said, I do not know how I shall feel after the lapse of time . . .
>
> As for our Czech comrades here and all Czech working men, I should like to say – as it were through the mouth of the Czech man-in-the-street, my brother-in-law Vasek and my uncle in Siany – well, that I shall continue to do everything I can to strengthen our unity, the unity of our

> indivisible Czechoslovak state, and to do everything for what has always been the keynote of our Party's policy – all-round reinforcement of relations with the Soviet Communist Party and the parties of the other countries in the socialist camp; to put it simply, I shall exert every possible effort to work towards the aims which the Central Committee has always had under the leadership of comrade Novotny . . .
>
> I realize, comrades, that everything depends on the collective . . . We talked about this in the Presidium . . . as the most important thing a man can rely on in his work: the collective. And that includes, last but not least, the assistance of comrade Novotny which he has promised me – and that of course is something I value . . .[5]

On 5 January 1968, Radio Prague announced to a surprised Czechoslovakia that A. Novotny had resigned as First Secretary of the Czechoslovak Communist Party and had been replaced by A. Dubcek. The nation was surprised for two reasons. The public had not realized the extent of Novotny's weakness, and few of them had ever heard of his successor. In the Czech lands Dubcek was almost unknown, and even in Slovakia he was hardly a public figure, for most of his manipulations had been behind the scenes.

There is a danger of being wise after the event, but it does appear that Dubcek was the best alternative to Novotny and that, surprised though people were, he was the single man who might be able to topple the President. For Novotny was ousted by a temporary coalition of very disparate forces and no other members of the Presidium could attract such wide support as Dubcek. The Slovaks in the Central Committee, at last seeing power close at hand, would probably not have accepted a Czech and the only other Slovaks in the Presidium were Chudik and Lenart. Chudik was Novotny's man in Bratislava and as such was totally unacceptable to most Slovaks and all reformers. Lenart was a different matter; Prime Minister since 1963 he had come through the same mill as Dubcek – indeed they had been together at the Party College in Moscow. He had gone to Prague in 1963 with something of a reputation as a reformer, but had done little to justify it since. He was a possible successor to Novotny but his credentials were not so good and his hands were not so clean as Dubcek's. He had worked too close to Novotny all the time that Dubcek had been known, at least within the Slovak Party, to oppose him.

It is not possible to accept entirely Dubcek's claim that he was a reluctant leader. It is true that his primary motive in mounting his attack upon Novotny had been to have the First Secretary removed and that promoting himself had been only a secondary consideration. Nevertheless he was a reasonably ambitious and successful politician and there is little reason to suppose that he did not share the conviction common to many politicians – that he would make a great leader. It is true that in the wranglings of November and December he did not play a very prominent part, but this was because he had no need to do so. By the end of October he had already established himself, whether by design or by chance, as Novotny's leading opponent. By his sudden (1967) adoption of Slovak nationalism, by his demands for a separation of Party and State, and by his desire to revitalize and extend NEM, he was already the only man acceptable to all three pressure groups; there was no need to participate actively in the actual killing of the cock.

But if Dubcek's role in the drama was obscure, much more curious was that played by Brezhnev. Novotny was right in complaining that the Russian's visit had done him more harm than good. For it virtually gave Moscow's approval for his removal and it immensely strengthened the will of his opponents.

There are two theories about Brezhnev's behaviour. The first is that he imagined that Novotny could survive without his help and that it was only in late December that Chervonenko managed to convince him that this was not the case. Then, in a panic, the Kremlin ordered Chervonenko to try and organize the military coup which Prchlik and Dubcek so neatly forestalled. According to this dubious account the Kremlin must have been furious when Dubcek took office. But, apart from the fact the *Pravda*'s 6 January coverage of Dubcek's election was minimal and his photograph small and badly reproduced, there is no real evidence to support this argument and it does not give an adequate explanation of Brezhnev's conduct. He must have had a good idea at the beginning of December that Novotny might be ousted and of who might succeed him – for once Chervonenko's information was accurate; it is surely absurd to imagine that the Kremlin preferred to risk having to resort to force rather than to employ discreet diplomatic pressure.

Much more plausible is that when Brezhnev said: '*Eto vashe delo*' he really meant it. If Dubcek was not given a long write-up in *Pravda* it was because Moscow was at that time quite uninterested in Czechoslovakia and its petty political problems; the Russians had far more immediate concerns of their own. Indeed it might not be unduly sensationalist to suggest that at the end of 1967 the Kremlin was punch drunk, its members reeling from the cumulative blows of the disappointments and disasters of the year. The barren failure of Brezhnev's 'collective leadership' had been most dramatically demonstrated abroad by the débâcle of the June Arab-Israeli war and at home, less publicly but perhaps no less importantly, by the collective-farm crisis, by renewed intellectual dissent, by the general failure of Liberman's limited economic reforms, and by the growing problem of nationalist disaffection amongst the various races of the Soviet Union – especially the Tartars and, more decisive still, the Slovaks in the Ukraine.

Given all this, it is hardly surprising that Brezhnev was relucant to involve himself in the internecine squabbles of the Czechoslovak Communist Party Presidium. If he had any views at all, it is probable that he favoured a change of leadership. For he must have recognized the severity of Czechoslovakia's economic crisis and presumably much preferred that the country settle it on her own rather than call upon the Soviet Union for aid. If Novotny would not allow Sik the necessary scope, then perhaps Novotny should go. Secondly, Brezhnev understood very well the threat that a recalcitrant racial group could pose to the fabric of the state. When that minority comprised a third of the nation and when the First Secretary of the Party notoriously loathed that third and they him, perhaps something should be done to meet at least some of their less unreasonable demands.

Brezhnev's third reason for refusing to help Novotny probably lies in his personal relationships with Dubcek and Novotny. Novotny he had never liked, for Novotny had been a very close friend of Khrushchev. When Novotny was in difficulties in 1963 Khrushchev had responded to his call for help by sending Brezhnev to Prague – but it was to Khrushchev that Novotny was grateful. The two men continued to spend holidays together until Brezhnev and Kosygin replaced Khrushchev; indeed the Russian's last trip abroad was to Prague where he busied himself with making unofficial and highly secret overtures to Bonn. Novotny was genuinely upset at Khrushchev's dismissal. This was partly because he considered the new leaders had insulted him – he was not told in advance – but also because he was genuinely fond of the old man. Impulsively he rang the Kremlin to demand an explanation. Apparently he was not satisfied with Brezhnev's hurried answers and slammed down the phone. It was one of the few emotional and human gestures in an otherwise almost faultless political career; it was also a great mistake and one that Brezhnev did not forget. Their relations were never again very good and the next time Novotny asked for help he did not get it.

Nevertheless the conviction that Novotny had outlived his usefulness is not the same as welcoming his replacement by Dubcek, for the Slovak First Secretary had proved himself a man with a certain mind of his own, a man prepared to tolerate journalistic and intellectual excesses which, in the Soviet Union, would result in stiff labour-camp sentences. At the time of the trial of Sinyavsky and Daniel, Dubcek was allowing the publication in Slovakia of views just as heretical as theirs. Worse than that, he was openly expressing cautious agreement with some of those views; he was not only asserting that the intelligentsia had an important role to play in the development of socialist society, but he was actually allowing it to do so, and he was pretending that the Party's leading role should be one of guidance and advice rather than coercion. Perhaps even more sinister, he had shown himself a man not only willing but able to defy the

Party, in the person of its leader. A man who could for five years survive and even flourish despite the hatred of the First Secretary and the President was a man who might possibly be led by previous successes into the fallacious belief that as he had done to Prague from Bratislava so he might do to Moscow from Prague. This was not the type of man the Kremlin liked to have in the First Secretaryship. The Russians must have had reasons for discounting all this seemingly damaging evidence. It appears that these reasons were of the best; one cannot say that the Russians arranged Novotny's downfall, but it seems that Brezhnev at least was party to the plot and that he indeed encouraged Dubcek in his attempt.

There is a story that Dubcek and Brezhnev first met and became friends whilst studying at the Moscow School together. This story is unconfirmed, but Stefan Dubcek, amongst others, swore that it was true. There is no record of Brezhnev having attended the College but the story may be based on the fact that they did meet, outside the School, during those years.

Even if this history is unfounded, Dubcek had, in the Kremlin's eyes, an almost perfect pedigree. Son of working-class parents, brought up and educated in the Soviet Union, loyal *apparatchik*, university in Moscow, a man whose regard for Russia had always been quite unconditional, who seemed, in many ways, more Russian than Czechoslovak – this was someone of whom the Kremlin need have no fear. When Dubcek had been appointed Secretary of the Czechoslovak Central Committee in 1960 his work had brought him into frequent contact with his Soviet counterparts. On his appointment as First Secretary of Slovakia in 1963 these contacts were increased (although Novotny prevented him from travelling very much); when Brezhnev came on his boost-Novotny visit in 1963 he also went to see Dubcek in Bratislava. It was on the twentieth anniversary of the Soviet-Czechoslovak Friendship Treaty, and it provided these two ambitious and successful politicians with an excellent opportunity for slapping each other on the back. Dubcek promised the Russian that 'our people fully realizes the meaning of friendship and co-operation with the Soviet Union', but he did not explain exactly what it did mean. In his reply Brezhnev claimed that 'the pact served us well and became the basis of the real blossoming of friendship between our two nations and encouraged mutual co-operation. It served us well in those years' – he did not clarify whom he meant by 'us.'[6]

But even if it was true that he knew and liked Dubcek of old, this would not have been enough to persuade Brezhnev that this apparently dangerously undogmatic and pragmatic Slovak was a safe choice as First Secretary of the Czechoslovak Party; for him to be convinced of this he must have had more recent and detailed information of Dubcek's intentions. Much would have been provided automatically by the KGB, whose file on Dubcek must have been very thick. What he saw there presumably helped persuade Brezhnev (and the rest of the Politburo) that Dubcek was utterly reliable.

But it also seems likely that the Kremlin had other information on Dubcek; probably the most important came from Janos Kadar. Dubcek was a close friend of the Hungarian leader at that time; their *dachas* (country cottages) were only a few kilometres from each other on either side of the mutual frontier. Insofar as Dubcek was not a reluctant leader he may have taken care to arrange that his friendship with Kadar should pay political dividends and that Kadar should transmit to the Kremlin such accounts of his activities and views that he wished the Russians to receive.

At the same time it appears that he kept in close touch with the Kremlin, and especially with Brezhnev himself.* It is of course unconfirmable, but there is some reason to believe that Brezhnev and Dubcek had at least one secret meeting during November 1967. This took place when Brezhnev flew into Bratislava airport one night to seek and give assurances to Dubcek. These he undoubtedly received, and both men presumably left the rendezvous with the feeling that all was proceeding well.

Had Brezhnev had any anxieties about Dubcek's 'liberal' record in Bratislava, he could reassure himself with the fact that a Slovak First Secretary would find life very restricted

* Brezhnev had come to Slovakia several times since 1963: his last official meeting with Dubcek before December 1967 seems to have been at a Czechoslovak Party Conference in Karlovy Vary (Bohemia) the previous spring.

in the Czech capital; his hands would be firmly tied by a largely hostile *apparat* and he would find it extremely difficult to introduce any changes of which the Novotnyite 'civil service' disapproved. Under any normal circumstances this assessment would have been correct, and indeed until Dubcek showed his hand many Czechs were resentful at this sudden growth of Slovak power. Brezhnev could not be blamed for believing that the Prague *apparat* would control any tendencies to deviate that Dubcek might show.

But the most important thing is that he did not expect Dubcek to deviate. He knew that Dubcek hated Novotny and that he had been working for years to secure Novotny's removal. Any means that he had employed – such as courting the Slovaks and the intellectuals – Brezhnev probably believed to be only to this end. On the whole he was right, but he made the same mistake as had others before and have others since. Dubcek was sincere.

His Slovak policies were largely tactical and expedient, but it was not the case that he championed the issues of extensive economic and political reform simply for his own political advantage. He was in the rare and fortunate political position of believing what he had to say. Certainly he utilized the reform platform in order to build up support against Novotny. At the same time, however, he did believe those policies to be essential for the Party. This Brezhnev did not understand. He expected Dubcek to initiate only that economic reform which was unavoidable for the good of the economy. He probably imagined that Dubcek's devotion to the Soviet Union would prevent him from pursuing any domestic reforms which the Kremlin might consider against its own best interests. What he also did not understand was that Dubcek was an extremely stubborn man, anxious above all to increase the popularity of the Party and thereby, as he saw it, the strength of socialism. Once he became convinced that the reforms he had begun were doing just this, then nothing would persuade him otherwise.

Dubcek ended his short address of 5 January to the Central Committee on a note of gentle irony which was to become so skilful and remarkable a part of his political repertoire:

'I want to thank Comrade Novotny for the work he has done all these years . . . there is no doubt that he tried to do his best, according to his conscience, to help the fulfilment of our Party's policy. I thank you, comrades, for your confidence.'[7]

8
STAND AND STARE

'The Press of the country has decisively influenced the reforms of the last few months and continues to play a leading role in the new development ... This development has been so violent that there are serious fears in Prague of a reaction aiming at the suppression of the freedom of speech. Both the foreign relations of Czechoslovakia and the internal relations between its own politicians are still so tense that all incautious lapses can lead to restrictive counter measures ... It would be very sad if a lack of self-discipline created a new situation bringing about laws restricting the freedom of the Press.'

Helsingen Sanomat, independent liberal magazine, Helsinki, 29 April 1968.

On the night of 20–1 August 1968 some 200,000 troops* of the Soviet Union, Poland, East Germany, Hungary and Bulgaria crossed four frontiers into the territory of their Warsaw Pact ally, the Czechoslovak Socialist Republic.

The Kremlin led this invasion because, by its own account, the future of socialism in Czechoslovakia was in jeopardy, because the Communist Party had lost control of the nation and because Alexander Dubcek had lost control of the Party. Since then, the Russians and their friends within the Czechoslovak Party have tried to portray Dubcek as a weak and mindless man who fell into the clutches of such 'vicious agents of imperialism' as Dr Ota Sik. Dubcek has been accused not so much of leading a counter-revolution as of allowing a counter-revolutionary situation to develop. His vacillation and indecision, it is said, debilitated the Party's leading role; policy was no longer made in the Central Committee Building but in the streets and editorial offices of Prague.

This is not a book about the Czechoslovak crisis of 1968–70 but in order to examine the validity of Moscow's charges against Dubcek it is necessary to recall the main events of

* Estimates vary. There were probably about 500,000 troops in the country by mid-September. See Windsor and Roberts, *Czechoslovakia 1968*, p.107.

that drama. An appendix provides a chronology: here perhaps three points should be made.

The first, and most important, is that Czechoslovakia was the only East-European country to remain virtually unmoved by the 20th Congress of the Soviet Communist Party. Between 1956 and 1963 Novotny successfully resisted all pressure from Khrushchev and, although since 1963 he had relaxed his grip a little, Czechoslovakia had never been de-Stalinized.

The country underwent, in 1968, the emotional breakdown that Hungary and Poland had endured twelve years before. In those twelve years enormous frustration had built up. Whoever had led Czechoslovakia's reform movement would have had difficulty in coping with its release.

The second point is the completely experimental nature of the Prague Spring. What the Czechs and Slovaks tried to effect during those first eight extraordinary months of 1968 was a spontaneous revolution quite without precedent. There were no rules to go by – everything had to be improvized and adapted in response to events.

The third factor is that although he was in office for fifteen-and-a-half months Dubcek was never really in power. This was partly because the experiment which he was trying to conduct involved some of the ideas of 'democracy' as understood in the West. It was an attempt to combine with an orthodox Communist dictatorship a genuine sensitivity to the aspirations of people and pressure groups outside the Party leadership.

But another reason for his lack of power lay in the very limited and unstable nature of his support within the Party. He had defeated Novotny on 5 January with the help of a coalition of very disparate men. He had found even before 1968 that the demands of these various backers were often conflicting – if not mutually exclusive – and when it became clear that he intended to pursue a course of total reform, the grand coalition irrevocably divided. As soon as the Russians began to demonstrate their disapproval those who, like Vasil Bilak and Drahomir Kolder, had supported Dubcek in order to tumble Novotny rather than to reform the system, began to withdraw their help. Dubcek was probably the most popular leader in the world in the summer of 1968, but at no time after mid-February did he enjoy the guaranteed support of a comfortable majority in the Presidium or Central Committee.

It is in this context that the charges that this young, unknown, shy and inexperienced *apparatchik* was also vacillating and mindless must be judged.

The freedom of the Press is a very relative concept but it is probably true to say that for some months in 1968 journalists in Czechoslovakia were subject to fewer external administrative controls than almost anywhere in the world. A study of the Soviet criticism of 'Prague Spring' suggests that this liberty and the use that was made of it was, for the Kremlin, the most disturbing factor in the Czechoslovak experiment.

Dubcek has been accused of gross irresponsibility in suddenly lifting all censorship and in giving journalists, at least until too late, no instructions for self-restraint. In fact, as with so many other events in Czechoslovakia that year, it was despite rather than because of Dubcek that newspapers were liberated from Party control.

Under Novotny each newspaper had its own censor whose job it was to prohibit the publication of anything infringing State or Party secrets.* He could directly embargo any article that was obviously an infringement of the rules. In more doubtful cases he was required merely to draw the editor's *attention* to the questionable material and it was then up to the editor to decide according to his own courage or judgment, whether or not to accept this counsel.†

For this system to work well, the Party leadership needed to convey downwards the slightest change of policy so that

* Censorship of the press had been rigidly enforced, except in Dubcek's Bratislava, since 1948, but it had never had any statutory basis—indeed the 1960 Constitution specifically guaranteed freedom of speech. In 1967 Novotny passed a Press Law which recognized censorship but placed some, inadequate, limits (libel and deliberate falsehood) upon it.

† Censorship had often operated on a more informal basis. Journalists knew the limits of disobedience and exercised self-censorship. Anything they thought might be questionable they submitted to their superiors.

censors should be quite clear as to what, at any given moment, was a 'Party secret' and what was not.

Novotny's replacement by Dubcek naturally raised great speculation in editorial and censorship offices throughout the country and both journalists and censors eagerly awaited their new guide-lines. None was extended. After taking office, Dubcek was for three weeks almost mute. Any censor who cast hopefully around for a clue as to what were the views of the new First Secretary would have found, after a week, only the following comment:

> The period just ended was marked by an appraisal of the values established in the past, and was the test of an ability to support and extend them for the present and the future. What we are now experiencing is a historic turn, a transition to a new quality of socialist society: this has characterized our work and makes enormous claims upon us.[1]

That remark did little to convince anyone that he had a brilliant new leader. Indeed Dubcek's January silence is often cited by his enemies as evidence of his utter lack of original ideas and of his total inability to make decisions and to act upon them.

It is true that he did not have a programme on 6 January. But this was a reflection not so much of his stupidity as of the speed with which the crisis of 1967 had developed. He came into office morally and emotionally committed to right the wrongs done to Slovakia, to increase the efficiency of the economy and to bring the Party back to the people, but intellectually uncertain of how far all this should go and indeed of how it should best be achieved. He later described his problem:

> What happened in January was objectively necessary because serious social problems were coming to the fore. There was an urgent need for a new positive attitude towards not only the principle of democratic centralism in the Party but also towards the relations between the Party and the whole of Society. There was a need for citizens, and especially for the younger generation, to participate more fully. There was an urgent need to solve gradually the interminable problems of economic development, and politically that meant again to increase the participation of

> the people. There was also a more urgent need to settle nationality questions . . . It was necessary to extend socialist democracy to do away with subjectivism and voluntarism and to destroy the political monoply of a small group of Party functionaries.[2]

As he also pointed out, 'we had simply been unable to make preparations' before 6 January because of the autocratic nature of Novotny's rule: nothing could be considered until Novotny had been removed.

And so, on 6 January, Dubcek took a room in the Party Hotel – he did not at once look for a house because he was uncertain how long he would be able to remain in Prague – and began to work. He asked for special reports on every conceivable subject relating to the Party's rule of the country. He worked sixteen hours a day and read everything that was put before him. He tended apparently to be a little too easily impressed by the layout rather than by the content of the reports, but some of the material horrified him. A friend of his has said of those weeks:

> He only then began to realize the appalling things done by the Party in the 'fifties. He saw report after report and heard story after story of the old days. I was with him on several occasions. Dubcek was incredulous . . . he wept when people told him of the cruelties of the past . . . he asked 'How is it possible for Communists to behave like this?' . . . In this way Dubcek became engulfed in the revolution. His basic decency made him respond to his new knowledge and he responded in the typical Dubcek way, which was the tears of pity we all saw and the very tough determination not to let it happen again.[3]

Thus determined, he committed himself utterly to an extensive programme of political reform.* By the end of January he had, after long conferences with such men as Ota Sik, Eduard Goldstuecker, Josef Boruvka, Bohumil Simon, Frantisek Kriegel, Cestmir Cisar and Josef Smrkovsky,

* Designed, according to Eduard Goldstuecker, to extend to Czechs and Slovaks all the liberties enjoyed by citizens of a social democracy except the right to unlimited private property.

enthusiastically adopted the principles of what was to become the Action Programme.

To say, therefore, that the ideas of that Programme were not his own is, in a limited sense, true. However, it is more accurate to assert that the Programme was a compromise. It was not as radical as Dr Sik or Josef Smrkovsky would have liked and Dubcek himself has described it as only 'an outline' on the way to greater reforms. Nonetheless, at that time it probably represented very nearly his own political beliefs and he has never once denied that its principles are close to his heart.

Compromise or not, the Action Programme might, if implemented, have completely changed the face of world Communism. It is perhaps not an exaggeration to describe it as the most significant reinterpretation of Marxist practices by a ruling Communist Party since 1948. If 'to vacillate' is to spend three weeks in pondering such reforms, then Dubcek vacillated in January 1968.

But whether or not such a pejorative description is applicable, Dubcek himself soon appreciated that the consequences of his inaction in January were very serious. On 16 March he admitted to a Party Conference at Brno: 'It would have been much better if we could have come before the Party and the entire public with . . . the Action Programme.' He explained that it had been impossible to rush the programme out any faster than they had done because 'we did not want to place these materials before the Central Committee until they had been thoroughly worked out . . .' But he confessed that: 'The very fact that we do not yet have the contents of a positive programme and a positive plan for action creates a vacuum and difficulty for political work at this moment and is the basis of the problem.'[4]

In this vacuum no directives as to what should or should not now be published were issued to the main censorship office, no new definitions of 'Party interest' were coined, and in the confusion and uncertainty censorship became meaningless, if not non-existent, more by default than by design.*

* One way in which, during this limbo period, censorship was evaded was devised by Josef Smrkovsky, fast emerging as one of the most committed and radical proponents of extensive reform. He and Josef Boruvka are believed to have had at least one meeting at the end of January with a dozen like-minded journalists. They agreed that they should both make outspoken and provocative

By mid-March the censors had decided that their job was quite impossible. They met together on the fifteenth to pass a resolution calling for the complete abolition of censorship. But they still had to stay at their posts.* An editor of *Lidova Demokracie,* conjuring up a delightful image of a tame friendly pet trotting humbly and obediently along, wrote 'our censor comes round just to make the tea and toast', whilst in *Svobodne Slovo,* the paper of the Socialist Party, the censors played cards for an hour or two and at midday wandered down to the nearest *vinarna* (wineshop) for the afternoon.

In an interview on Radio Prague on 6 April Dubcek was asked what view he took on the new freedom of the Press, and his stumbling, confused reply was indicative of his surprise at the licence which journalists were so suddenly enjoying. 'Well, look here,' he said, 'every Press everywhere serves certain aims, a certain policy, this applies in the present period also. That is, the workers of radio, Press and TV have very effectively contributed towards ensuring the public's familiarity with items of information.'[5]

This sudden 'familiarity' was intoxicating both for journalists and for the public. By the middle of March most papers were sold out at 7.30 every morning, despite the fact that they had all increased their print numbers. *Prace* doubled its circulation between January and March to 114,000 in Prague alone, and it was no longer read just for the sports page. Previously indifferent and contemptuous of the political charade and the puppets who performed it, the Czech and Slovak peoples now began to realize that the strings were no

---

speeches in defence of the reform movement. These could then be written up extensively and commented upon in the Press with no fear of censorship—for no one could forbid the publication of the words of two such important members of the new regime. Smrkovsky's own article on 21 January in the Trade Union paper, *Prace*, was indeed the first real statement of intent on Dubcekism and it produced a flurry of replies and response, both favourable and hostile, from all over the Republic.

* Pre-censorship was inoperative from about the middle of February but it was not actually made illegal until a National Assembly resolution on 26 June which was passed by 184 votes to 30 with 17 abstentions. These voting figures give some idea both of the opposition with which Dubcek was still faced and of the freedom which he allowed. Under Novotny there would never have been 30 votes against a Government-introduced motion.

longer being pulled by Moscow and they started to take an intense interest in affairs of Party and State.

The problem that most interested, indeed concerned them was Dubcek's attitude towards Novotny and his associates within the Party. Here lies the core of the Czechoslovak crisis. The synthesis of a free Press and Dubcek's policy towards his enemies was disastrous.

The middle and upper ranks of the *apparat* were terrified as well as surprised by Novotny's dismissal from the First Secretaryship because, with some historical justification, they equated a change in the leadership or its policies with purges of the Party. But no purges were instituted: Dubcek did not attempt to rid himself of the Novotnyites cluttering up the Party apparatus, and made no preparations for convoking an Extraordinary Congress of the Party.

There were at least two reasons for this attitude towards the Novotnyites. The first was advanced by Dubcek's friend Ondrej Klokoc, still editor of the Bratislava *Pravda.* This was true democracy, he argued. The new goverment was not going to tolerate anti-social and anti-socialist programmes of State repression – instead tolerance was to be extended to those who might disagree with some aspects of the Party's programme. What that programme was to be was as yet unclear, but Klokoc's article was an early indication of the way in which the new leaders were thinking.*[6]

Klokoc had summed up the situation well but he did not give enough emphasis to Dubcek's own attitude, typical of that extraordinary streak of unworldliness that has always been so important a part of his political and personal life. He simply hated to sack people and – despite his horror at what

* Another was an article by Gustav Husak in *Kulturni Zivot:* 'The citizen . . . wants guarantees that he can exercise his right of choice, control and responsibility freely. This is the problem of the progressive democratization of the social order and involves the liberation and development of all the people's creative forces, its physical and intellectual potential, and its commitment to act.'

Now that Dubcek was in Prague, Husak was emerging as the most radical reformer in Bratislava; he was the hero of the students of Comenius University, and was brought back into political life by their popular demand.

he had discovered of the Party's past – saw no justification for revenging himself on either Novotny or his acolytes.

As he said, in a typical Dubcek fashion, 'We must treat people humanely, with dignity and in a humanistic manner. Laws must be observed so that we ensure that we do not commit errors which we should have to correct against later.'[7]

He continued to be driven around Prague by Novotny's chauffeur and he dictated his letters to Novotny's assistants. He has little judgment of character and, perhaps because he realizes this, hates to pre-judge anyone: 'Don't worry,' he remarked naively to one Slovak journalist,* 'I'm sure they'll be loyal to the Party and to me.'

It appears that Dubcek's second reason for not pursuing purges lies in a telephone conversation he had with Brezhnev on 6 January. He is thought to have assured the Soviet leader that now Novotny had been removed from the Secretaryship there was no need for further changes in the cadres, and nothing would be done to unsettle the Party workers.

It was also for both personal and political reasons that he insisted that anyone who had helped him in his long fight with Novotny should be suitably rewarded. Thus men whose dislike of the former First Secretary had been either personal or national but certainly not moral or ideological were given jobs in which they were ideally placed to sabotage the whole reform movement. Vasil Bilak was rewarded for his years of support in Bratislava with Dubcek's old job as Slovak First Secretary; in August he was almost certainly one of the leaders of the 'Revolutionary [but puppet] Government of Alois Indra' that the Russians attempted to impose after the abduction of Dubcek.

Oldrich Svestka, editor of *Rude Pravo* for the last ten years, had been a loyal disciple of Novotny. But he had done Dubcek one favour; in 1966 he had published an article of his on the Slovak Revolt, a subject that was anathema to Novotny. This action had probably been motivated by some obscure political jealousy rather than by any regard for Dubcek, but Dubcek took it as a personal favour for which he should be, and unfortunately was, very grateful. In February 1968 he absolutely refused to listen to all those

* I spoke to this journalist.

journalists who swore to him that Svestka was not to be trusted. Dubcek insisted that his was a democratic government and that Svestka could not be dismissed on hearsay. It was a noble but mistaken attitude: Svestka was party to the invasion, tried to prevent publication of the Presidium's Proclamation of 21 August against the invaders, and has never since missed an opportunity of slandering and denying his Slovak protector.

Viliam Salgovic, Chairman of the Slovak Party's Commission of revision and Control, had helped him in his fight against Chudik and so Dubcek, with characteristic lack of insight, gave him the job of Deputy Minister in the most sensitive department of all – the Interior. This afforded Salgovic a unique opportunity to rally the disaffected members of the civil and secret police* throughout the summer. On the afternoon of 20 August he is believed to have given them instructions for helping the KGB that night. It was on Salgovic's orders that Czech secret police arrested Dubcek at dawn on 21 August and abducted him to the airport for deportation to the Soviet Union.

By the middle of February, Smrkovsky, Kriegel and others of his radical supporters were trying to convince Dubcek that he should convoke an Extraordinary Congress of the Party. The Party Congress normally meets every four years. It is composed of delegates from Party organizations all over the country. They are supposed to approve the Party's programme for the next four years and also to elect a new Central Committee. The 13th Congress had met in 1966 and a large part of the Committee then elected was, in 1968, still loyal to Novotny. Normally the 14th Congress would not have been called until 1970, but the Central Committee has the authority to summon an Extraordinary Session at any time it wishes; indeed a Congress should be convoked to ratify

* Discontent was widespread in both forces. On 7 May the Communists of the CID in Prague wrote a letter to the Central Committee complaining of the treatment they were receiving. They disassociated themselves from the illegal methods of the past but went on to complain: 'Today hardly a single action against drunkards or those arrested for disorderly conduct can be carried out without policemen being subjected to physical violence and abuse.' On 18 June Radio Prague reported that attacks upon the police in Bratislava and refusal to carry out their orders had risen enormously. The police blamed it upon the Press.

any major change in Party policy such as Dubcek was about to undertake.

But Dubcek recoiled from breaking his promise to Brezhnev and tried to convince both himself and his friends that he could win the loyalty of even those Committee members (estimated at about one-third) who had opposed his acession. Whether or not he persuaded himself, he failed to convince his colleagues, for it was quite clear to them that until a new Central Committee was elected there was *no guarantee* against a comeback by the conservatives.* Until nationalistic fervour gripped them, great sections of the working class remained extremely suspicious of Dubcek's 'middle-class' revolution which, they feared, would result in a drop in their standard of living. This was a fear which Novotny exploited. So long as he remained President he retained both a seat in the Presidium and an effective public platform; he used both to work up opposition to Dubcek. By the end of February he was successfully rallying support in the lower ranks of the *apparat.* He stomped the country and encouraged trade-union leaders to convince their men that they were about to be betrayed and that Novotny's friends must rush to his aid. By the end of February thousands of them were thinking of doing so.

But during March several scandals involving Novotny and his associates were revealed to an outraged and angry Czechoslovak people. After the defection of Major General Jan Sejna and the revelation of the intrigues in which he and Novotny's son Jan had been involved† any slight public sympathy and support for the President dissolved overnight. The Press took up the stories and gleefully titillated a prurient public with tales of appalling vice and venality in high places of the Party. The Sejna affair had much the same effect on Novotny's leadership as did the Profumo scandal on that of

* Throughout the summer 'guarantees' became the main demand of the supporters of reform.

† Sejna and Jan Novotny had obtained a Government licence to test Western cars. Jaguars, Alfa Romeos and Mercedes were all imported at Government expense, driven by the two until their girl friends were tired of them, and then sold to their friends for their own profit. They lived the luxurious and expensive lives of successful and self-indulgent capitalists and no doubt thoroughly enjoyed themselves. Sejna's defection was announced on 1 March.

Macmillan and on 22 March he resigned 'because of his ill-health'. Dubcek had broken his 6 January assurance to Brezhnev.

On 23 March, just twenty-four hours after Novotny's resignation, the Czechoslovak leaders were summoned to an emergency meeting of Warsaw Pact countries (without Rumania) in Dresden. According to *Pravda* (Moscow, 22 August 1968), 'The Czechoslovak comrades did not deny that . . . the radio, Press, and TV slipped out of the control of the Party and were actually in the hands of anti-socialist elements.'

It is extremely unlikely that Dubcek admitted this, but it is certain that he was very concerned about the activities of the Press. It must be admitted that the fascinating and beautifully vicious attacks upon Novotny and upon the Party's past were often read – if not written – not as cautionary tales or as the denunciations of one man's ways, but for the contempt into which they brought the Party as an instituion. Despite the growing enthusiasm for Dubcek and his policies, this naturally weakened public confidence in his capacity to avoid slipping back into the bad old ways and led to the growth of demands for the formation of 'guarantees', sometimes even seen as opposition parties.

Worse still, from the Russian point of view, was that even more popular than tales of Czechoslovak Party corruption were stories which either ridiculed or denigrated the Soviet Union. Czech papers were not subject to the rapacious demands of capitalist advertisers – they had far more freedom – but every journalist likes to increase his readership and the best way to do so was to reveal the scandal of Moscow's responsibility for the trials of the 'fifties, or the fact that the Kremlin made Czechoslovakia pay more than Italy for Soviet oil. Such accounts inevitably fostered an entirely justified but very dangerous anti-Sovietism.

Dubcek's dilemma was unenviable. After March he came under increasing pressure from his Warsaw Pact partners to slow down the process of reform and to muzzle the Press. At the same time he was being urged by that Press, the mouthpiece of an ever more excited and extremist public, to purge the Party of Novotnyites, to ignore the threats of the Russians and quicken the pace of change.

His necessary attempts at compromise inevitably satisfied neither side; convinced that he was weak and susceptible to threats each increased its pressure.

After Dresden he made concerted efforts to restrain the Press, both by private pleas for self-discipline and public calls for responsibility. In an interview on Radio Prague on 6 April he virtually accused journalists of distorting Party history: ' ... there are ... some extremes which ... cause nervousness and apprehension among our population. This applies in particular to instances where inaccuracies or hasty conclusions occur, or where a thing that has not been sufficiently studied and checked is either broadcast or appears in the papers.'[8] He followed this up with a sharper warning two days later: 'Today we must admit that there is actually a need to restrict various manifestations of anarchy or some tendencies testifying to anarchistic inclinations chiefly where the elementary principles of internal party life or the ethics of our Communist Party are not respected.'[9]

The only reaction the Press gave to these mild and understandable rebukes was to subject him to the first of many attacks for his 'timidity and weakness'.* Indeed, the pressure to induce him to purge the Party was increased through April. The Press – to Moscow's horror – had already managed to secure Novotny's removal from the Presidency, now it insisted also upon his dismissal from the Central Committee and even from the Party. Both because of his promise to Brezhnev and because of his personal scruples, Dubcek had been reluctant to take the first step and to begin with he quite refused to proceed to the next. But he was not able, as is the Prime Minister of England, to ignore public opinion.

* On 11 April a group of Prague journalists wrote to the Central Committee to complain that 'hints' were still being given 'sometimes even as alleged requests by Comrade Alexander Dubcek' that certain news items would be better unpublished. On 21 April a Radio Prague editor, Cestmir Suchy, complained: 'What use is it for journalists and the public if they can quite safely and freely air and condemn the mistakes of Comrades Novotny and Hendrych, if taboos are imposed on all these who are in key positions today?' The fact that by the end of 1969 Suchy was denouncing Dubcek for his 'liberal weakness with the Press' demonstrates the opportunism of so many of Dubcek's 'supporters' and of the so-called 'reformers'.

However spontaneous had been the original unyoking of the Press, by mid-March he needed its support. Faced by the hostility of his allies and unable to rely on a following within the Party, he needed – as well as wanted – to find a mandate in public opinion. Over April-June his attitude towards Novotny and the Congress completely altered.

On 11 April he wrote in *Rude Pravo*: 'In cases where functionaries have lost confidence as a result of serious shortcomings in their work and behaviour towards people, we cannot decide by resolution or command that they should be reallocated that confidence. We should not be surprised if changes are unavoidable in such cases.'[10]

He still did not attack Novotny publicly by name.

By mid-May he had realized that he could no longer resist the call for Novotny's total humiliation and on 30 May his old enemy was dismissed from the Central Committee and from the Party. In a broadcast on 3 June Dubcek explained why:

> We have taken into consideration the fact that Comrade Novotny was not sincere to the Central Committee not only in the past but also at the April Plenum of the Central Committee when he said that during his term of office he had had nothing to do with the deformations which took place in this country in the 'fifties . . . We know the facts and his attitude from the time when he started work as the First Secretary of the Party's Central Committee.[11]

As for the convocation of the Congress: at the Committee meeting on 1 April he declared, 'We want to enforce our Action Programme first and deal with cadre problems afterwards.' And on 5 April, he told the Committee that it was 'fully capable of giving society the proposed Action Programme'. He was worried, he said, that if a 14th Congress were held too soon it might prove more disappointing than satisfying for the people and might result in little more than personnel changes.[12]

But on 26 April he announced that the Congress would meet in October because 'it is necessary to try and reach a preliminary solution regarding those members of the Central Committee who have hampered and are exciting fears for the development of the democratization process'. He was apparently still unhappy about this decision but tried to justify it on the grounds that 'some Party members in recent months have been caught unawares by the tempo of the process that has been taking place and some are particularly disorientated. Many have been shaken by the facts connected with the revelation of violations of democracy and legality in the past years.'[13]

By 3 June he had changed his position once more. He admitted that he had initially been opposed to the calling of an early Congress because he felt that more time was needed for discussion and for drawing up a programme. But, he acknowledged, events had moved much more quickly than he had expected and 'new tendencies have appeared here'. In considering the date for the Congress the Presidium had assumed that: 'It is unconditionally necessary that some comrades who have lost public confidence and will not give a guarantee that they will carry out the policy line presented in the Action Programme should leave the Central Committee without delay'.

He had hoped that the staunchest Novotnyites could be persuaded to leave the Committee of their own accord but, 'as it happened we did not interpret the situation correctly, for many comrades have refused to leave the Central Committee . . . [this] also had to be considered when fixing the date of the Congress,'[14] which he had now decided to convene a month earlier, on 9 September.

He knew the alarm that this would cause in Party Organizations throughout the country and tried to reassure ordinary members they had nothing to fear from the Congress, promising that 'hundreds of thousands of Party men' could not be held responsible for the misdeeds of individuals. His reassurance had little effect, thousands of Party officials knew that they would be sacked and the hastening of the Congress only widened the breach within the Party.

He must also have known the concern that his change of attitude would cause in the Kremlin. His sudden desire to hold as soon as possible a Congress which he had previously refused to convene must have convinced his allies that he had fallen completely into the hands of the strident radicals and obnoxious journalists.

This was not so. Throughout May and June Dubcek was involved in an almost continual argument with journalists. Despite his agreeing to their demands for the Congress he was unable to persuade them to desist in their attacks upon his leadership and upon the Soviet Union, or to cease their varied suggestions that the Party relinquish its leading role. On 26 June he said of an angry meeting at which a group of journalists had explained to him their fears:

> 'We told each other at our meeting what pleased us and what we did not regard as good for the future of our socialist society. We talked not only about pleasant matters but, I would say, about less pleasant matters. During that frank conversation we exchanged views on our work and you know that one sometimes says things which other people don't exactly like. It is not very pleasant, but the most important result of the meeting was that I gained the impression, almost the conviction, that we understood each other.'[15]

He was wrong. They did not understand each other and the next day several Prague papers published the '2,000 Words Manifesto'.

This was a statement of faith written by the writer Ludvik Vaculik and signed by seventy leading writers, artists, sportsmen and other public figures. It pledged full support to the liberalizing regime and it begged the leadership to speed up the process of reform. It was an error.

By Western standards the language used in the Manifesto was mild, but these are not the criteria by which it should be judged. The signatories stated that 'we do not want to cause anarchy and a general state of insecurity', but amongst Party officials insecurity is what it was bound to create. It claimed to reject 'illegitimate, indecent or gross methods' but it called for strikes and boycotts in order to pressure the Government into a thorough purge of the Novotnyites. It asked that disputes with neighbouring countries should be avoided and yet assured the Government that it was prepared to back it, 'if necessary even with weapons'. It offered full support to Dubcek but only just 'so long as the Government does what we mandate'. It claimed to wish not to embarrass or 'prejudice'

Alexander Dubcek, but its publication made his position infinitely more difficult.

The morning the Manifesto was published Dubcek was recording a television interview. He made a good but not outstanding speech, calling upon the young to join the Party and to give it all their energy and support. He had not seen the Manifesto and was in a relaxed and happy mood, betraying none of his usual nervousness at appearing in front of the camera. After he had finished he laughingly autographed a caricature of himself on the front of *Literarni Listy.* He did not look inside to see Vaculik's work, and no one thought to draw his attention to it.

Later that morning he was telephoned at the Central Committee Building by an irate Brezhnev who demanded an immediate explanation of the '2,000 Words' and why its publication had been allowed. Dubcek was in the unfortunate position of having to answer Brezhnev's furious questions without having seen the document in question. His performance was perhaps not such as to convince the Russian that he had the situation entirely under control.

After Brezhnev had rung off, Dubcek summoned the Presidium for an emergency session and rang up Jiri Pelikan, director of television, to ask him if he could insert a denunciation into his recorded speech. Pelikan argued that it would be technically very difficult and that it would be politically more appropriate to say nothing now but to have a separate debate on the subject the next day. Weakly Dubcek agreed, and his speech appeared with no mention of the Manifesto which had immediately become the talking point of the nation. For this reticence he later came under attack from Oldrich Svestka and the Kremlin. He was accused of having refused to take action against the 'counter-revolutionaries'.

In fact Dubcek was extremely vexed by the publication of this provocative document. As he pointed out at a private meeting with some of the signatories, he was forced to denounce them and to side with conservatives. On 29 June he publicly declared that the Presidium had

> '... rejected the conclusions of the statement published under the title '2,000 Words' because they objectively

– I stress regardless of the will and intention of the authors – could lead to the release of forces that could result in such conflicts and clashes as could jeopardize our process of regeneration and further progress of socialist construction.'[16]

The Manifesto, he argued in private, simply made it much more difficult for him to persuade the Kremlin that there was no 'counter-revolution' in Czechoslovakia, Moreover, there was very little that the appeal could persuade him to do that he was not already doing. He was carrying forward all the policies that the signatories had demanded and he had advanced the date of the Congress from October to 9 September – it was technically impossible to summon it any earlier.

But Vaculik was not an irresponsible sensationalist. He wrote and published the Manifesto in order to rally the reformist forces through the country: it did so. The enthusiasm with which it was greeted testified both to the people's support of the reform movement and also to its deep anxiety that the Government was making concessions to the Kremlin.*

Dubcek had made concessions, but only one of them was in principle: on 4 May he had reluctantly agreed in Moscow to allow 'limited staff exercises' in Czechoslovakia, despite his previous public promise that no Warsaw Pact troop manoeuvres would be held until after the 14th Congress. Neither he nor anyone else had been prepared for the enormous invasion of troops that took place.

Nevertheless, despite this threatening encampment, the National Assembly passed, on 26 June, the law abolishing censorship, and Dubcek appeared still utterly committed to the reform movement. On 3 June he had promised: 'One thing is clear. We must not and we will not stop half-way. If we are to be successful, we must consolidate the democratization drive, determine clear goals and the way to realize them and, above all, to set the Party moving in this direction.'[17] Apart from the arrival of the soldiers, little that he had since

* *Vecerni Praha*, the Prague evening paper, published, on 8 July, the results of a poll of its readers which bore out the anxiety of the people. Despite overwhelming support for Dubcek's 'humane socialism' only 53% said that its confidence in the Government had increased since January.

said or done should have caused the radicals to believe that he was choosing another route.

It is impossible to say exactly what effect the '2,000 Words' had upon the Kremlin and its allies, but after 27 June their Press attacks upon Czechoslovakia became even more intense. In denouncing the Manifesto, Moscow's *Pravda* drew ominous comparisons between the situation in Czechoslovakia and that in Hungary in 1956. It is not true that the document was, as *Pravda* claimed, 'an open call to struggle against the Communist Party of Czechoslovakia – but it is easy to understand that to many Russians such a description must have seemed correct.

The Manifesto was a mistake, but it was probably inevitable. It was the product of Dubcek's belief that he could carry through a total transformation of the Party's policy without changing its cadres. His promise to Brezhnev was quite incompatible with the freeing of the Press.

This he later realized and he has since hinted that his greatest mistake was not to prepare for the 14th Congress as soon as he came into office. Whether his enemies in the Presidium would have allowed him to do so is debatable, but had he managed it, a new Central Committee might have been elected and the Action Programme approved by the end of May. Then, with the Party united behind him, he would have had much more chance to resist extremist presssure from both within the country and around its borders.

As it was, the combination of oafish Russian pressure and uninhibited Czechoslovak reporting was fatal. Throughout the summer Soviet threats and Czechoslovak nationalism fed upon each other and escalated in a vicious and inevitable spiral of mutual distrust and alarm. Dubcek was forced to play the part of flustered referee in a savage game between an excited chauvinistic Czechoslovak public and angry frightened Warsaw Pact allies. He performed very subtly but the game was new, neither side knew the rules and the pitch was finally overrun.

9
THE PROBLEMS OF SENILITY

'You will find us only on the very best atlases, because we are the smallest country left in Europe . . . a self-respecting country which deserves and sometimes achieves a colour of its own on the map—usually a dyspeptic mint green, which misses the outline of the frontier by a fraction of an inch, so that one can almost hear the printers saying damn.'
The General, *Romanov and Juliet*, Act I, Peter Ustinov.

'At 11.40 p.m. [on 20 August 1969] Comrade Cernik returned from the telephone for the last time and, after Comrade Dubcek interrupted the debate, announced the following: "The armies of the five Parties have crossed the borders of our Republic and have begun occupying our country."

'The Presidium was in a state of shock – at least some of its members were, particularly Comrade Dubcek who declared: "This is a tragedy, I didn't expect this to happen." '
Rude Pravo, clandestine legal edition: 23 August 1968.

Why didn't Dubcek expect it to happen? He was, after all, under no illusions that the Russians were happy with the state of Czechoslovakia in August 1968. On many, perhaps innumerable occasions over the past three months he had been subject to the most violent abuse and humiliations from the Kremlin. At Cierna-nad-Tisou he had been warned that he must crush the 'counter-revolution' and since that absurd, almost unbelievable encounter little had changed in Czechoslovakia. If 'counter-revolutionary forces' were rampant at the end of July, they had not been routed by mid-August. Surely his surprise must be the most glaring example of what his enemies have called his appalling political naivety? How could he otherwise have pursued so persistently the distant vision of a human face? Did he have no understanding of the international implications of his internal political reforms?

In many ways Dubcek was naive in his dealings with the Russians. Nevertheless throughout the summer he played an extremely delicate and calculated political game – it was a game that he almost won. Many Western commentators, very wise after the event, have suggested that, given the situation described in the last chapter, invasion was inevitable. Dubcek was sure that it was not.

Apart from his personal devotion to the Soviet Union, he had two reasons for believing that the Russians would not occupy his country. The first, and this is perhaps less politically sound, was his intense and unshakeable conviction that he had found the answer to the problems of socialism and that what he was doing was vital to the cause of the international proletariat. The immense popularity of himself and his policies seemed to him to be an irrefutable vindication of his own work.* Never before had the Communist Party of Czechoslovakia had so large a following and therefore, he thought, never before had it been so strong. He knew that the Russians were unhappy at various peripheral aspects, such as journalistic licence, and he shared their concern. But he considered these to be only teething troubles which would vanish after the election of a reformist Central Committee. He may have been right. Apart from these minor problems he was so utterly persuaded of his own rightness that he could not imagine that eventually his allies would not come around and admit that what he was doing was helping socialism.

Secondly, he believed that the Kremlin was hopelessly split upon the question of what to do with Czechoslovakia. He believed that it was undergoing some sort of material or moral crisis that threatened to paralyse it into total inaction. A study of Soviet conduct between March and November 1968 shows some basis for this assessment. As early as 23 March Dubcek was threatened with invasion. The fact that Moscow then dithered for five months before carrying out its threat vindicates Dubcek's conviction that the Russians would not forcibly prevent him from implementing the Action

* On 8 July the Prague evening paper, *Vecerni Praha*, published the results of a questionnaire answered by its readers – 87% were satisfied with the present Government; 7% were unhappy; 89% wanted to continue with the development of 'humane socialism'; only 5% wanted to return to capitalism and 6% had no opinion.

Programme and building Czechoslovakia's own road to Communism. If more evidence were needed that the Kremlin were in an advanced state of schizophrenia then surely none could be better than the remarkable misconduct of the political aspects of the invasion itself; it is arguable that those four days alone were enough to prove Dubcek utterly right. Beside the unpredictable posturing of the Soviet Union Dubcek appears to be the most steadfast and logical politician; but his own calculations were rendered meaningless by the total unreliability of a Kremlin in which the particles of power shifted through 1968 and 1969 in a kaleidoscope of crises that is still quite unresolved.

Not only is it unresolved: its exact nature is not yet clear in the West. It could have been a split within the Politburo and within the Central Committee. It could have been a disagreement between the Politburo and either the KGB or the Red Army. It could have been neither and it could have been a combination of both.*

Whatever it was, the quality of Dubcek's information must have been much better than that of the West: he must have understood the divisions amongst the men who were opposing him and it was upon this knowledge that he based much of his conviction that his reform movement could survive.

With some qualification one can probably employ the terms 'hawks' and 'doves' to factions within the Kremlin. There was almost certainly no dove anywhere near the top of the Moscow cote who unconditionally rejected the use of force to bring Czechoslovakia to heel. The division was not over the virtues of the Prague Spring – there is no evidence of any dispute as to whether or not the experiment should continue – but over how it should best be ended. There were those – apparently Kosygin and Podgorny were the most prominent – who felt that if the Soviet Union were cautious enough Dubcek might himself have to restrict the freedoms he had so rashly granted, and that invasion was therefore unnecessary.

Whether or not Dubcek knew that such was the argument employed by the doves he, like Smrkovsky, probably believed

* It is easy to sympathize with the Soviet dilemma and to understand their crises of confidence. See p. 139; also Windsor and Roberts pp. 62-79.

that the Soviet leaders, on balance, placed unity of the world Communist movement above conformity in the bloc. He was right in that the doves were anxious to avoid the universal obloquy that an invasion would incur and to preserve the possibility of holding the projected World Communist Conference.*

At the beginning of January 1968 Dubcek could quite reasonably imagine that he had the support, if not of the entire Politburo, then at least of Brezhnev and probably also of Kosygin and President Podgorny. But whether or not he had expected Brezhnev's help in December 1967, he must have been surprised by the clear discrepancy between the Russian leader's nonchalant disregard of the problems of Prague and the flustered, incompetent interference of Ambassador Chervonenko. Whoever Chervonenko was acting for, this inconsistency must have been Dubcek's first hint of the schizophrenia in official Soviet attitudes towards him.

His first visit to Moscow was three weeks after his election, on 29–30 January. It has been suggested that this long wait between taking office and presenting his credentials at the Kremlin was a token of Moscow's early displeasure at his election and that he was deliberately kept waiting in order to cow him into subservience.

In his September 1969 indictment of Dubcek's conduct, Vasil Bilak is believed to have offered a completely opposite explanation. Bilak claimed that he 'insisted that Dubcek go at once to Moscow', but that Dubcek replied: 'The Russians must get accustomed to the idea that I am not Novotny and will never be like him.'[1]

Neither of these explanations is plausible. There is little evidence to suggest that the Kremlin was angry at Dubcek's election and even less that Dubcek wanted to treat the Russians with arrogance. He was certainly concerned to

* It is almost impossible to make any proper assessment of the balance of power in the Soviet Politburo, but according to one account in mid-July the division was as follows:

Irreconcilable hawks	*Undecided*	*Doves*
Kirilenko	Brezhnev	Kosygin
Shelepin	Mazurov	Podgorny
Pelshe	Voronov	Polyansky
	Shelest	Suslov

demonstrate to Moscow, Prague, and Bratislava that he was not Novotny, but he had neither reason nor desire to create enemies in the Kremlin. He still regarded the Soviet Union as Mecca and both hoped and expected that he would be able to co-operate with the Russians in every way.

There are two very much more cogent reasons for his not flying at once to Moscow. First of all the Russians were still licking their 1967 wounds and were strikingly uninterested in Czechoslovakia. Secondly he had spoken with Brezhnev by telephone and had nothing new to say. At the beginning of January he was unsure of the exact form his programme would take and he wanted to be able to present at least the outlines of his policy at his first official meeting in Moscow.

He appears to have been treated fairly courteously at the January meeting; despite *Pravda*'s account (Moscow, 22 August) it is unlikely that the Soviet Union already had many complaints to make – the Press had hardly begun to show any independence. But it may well be the case that, as *Pravda* claimed,[2] Dubcek admitted the nation to be very tense; for Czechs and Slovaks had endured three weeks of wondering what their new government would do.

Even after the Dresden threats, Dubcek continued to rely on what he knew of the split within the Kremlin and amongst his allies. It is believed that his most vociferous critic at Dresden was Ulbricht, closely followed by Gomulka who had with difficulty just suppressed the revolt of the Polish students whose main cry had been 'Long Live Czechoslovakia'. It is possible that Dubcek thought that it was mainly from these two men that criticism came and that Brezhnev was still prepared to support him.

Any such illusions must have been shattered by a speech that the Russian made to the Soviet Central Committee on 29 March. In it Brezhnev emphasized the monopoly of the Communist Party's 'guiding and directing influence', called for stricter controls upon the intellectuals and made no mention of inter-party democracy.

But this speech did not mean that the Kremlin had resolved the differences either within itself or within the socialist bloc over what to do with Czechoslovakia. Throughout April, May, June and July the Russians and their allies fell over themselves in an unco-ordinated, undignified and unsuccessful pantomime in which the Happy Prince Dubcek always managed to escape the devious bribes, the bloody threats and the obtrusive traps of his wicked but blundering uncles and emerged not only as a skilful tactician but as an innocent hero cheered and loved by a world-wide audience.

Perhaps nothing – before the invasion itself – illustrates Soviet indecision so well as the débâcle of July. The Warsaw Pact manoeuvres officially ended on 2 July, but the Kremlin refused to withdraw its troops from Czechoslovakia. This was intended to frighten the Czech and Slovak peoples into rejection of their leaders. It had the opposite effect and, when summoned to the Pact tribunal in Warsaw, Dubcek felt strong enough to refuse and to send a politely dismissive reply to to the ultimatum of the 15 July Letter.

The Russians then announced a huge call-up of reserves on the Western borders of the Soviet Union. After thus further increasing nationalistic fervour behind Dubcek they invited the whole Czechoslovak Presidium to Moscow for bilateral talks. The Czechoslovaks demurred and the Russians were compelled to climb down and agree to a meeting on Czechoslovak territory.

It is difficult to understand just what the Kremlin hoped to gain from the encounter at Cierna-nad-Tisou, the Slovak rail-head with the Soviet Union. Dubcek was never so popular in Czechoslovakia as when he left Prague for Cierna. He arrived at the town secure in the knowledge that he was backed by the entire and euphoric people. For the first time in its history Czechoslovakia was a united nation.

But this meant that his mandate was unquestionable – he had not the slightest room for manoeuvre. Before the Czechoslovak delegation left Prague the Central Committee had debated and approved three basic points upon which it was to stand firm:

(1) Czechoslovakia's loyalty to the Warsaw Pact and especially to the Soviet alliance should in no way be changed, or indeed even questioned.

(2) The Russians must withdraw all charges of counter-revolution against Czechoslovakia.

(3) Czechoslovak troops, and they alone, should be used to

guard the borders with Western Germany. Moreover just before he departed for Cierna, Dubcek promised the country that 'Nothing will make us abandon the road we started in January this year ... I am convinced that our friends will understand the rightness of our way. We will not budge an inch.'[3] It was a totally uncompromising position which meant that the talks could suceed only if the Russians were prepared to climb down.

At 9.52 on the morning of Monday 29 July the Soviet delegation – almost the entire Politburo* – arrived in a specially armoured train at Cierna station. They were met by their Czech counterparts and together Dubcek and Brezhnev walked across the dusty road of the little town to the railwaymen's club which had been hastily transformed into a conference room. There, amongst tinted mirrors and long red curtains, the two sides sat opposite each other across a narrow table down the centre of the room. Brezhnev, declaring that he expected a counter-revolutionary attempt upon his life, insisted that the Russians sat facing the windows outside which Czechoslovak and Soviet troops, armed with sub-machine guns and hand grenades, constantly patrolled.

The talks were begun, and practically ended, by Brezhnev. Without allowing for any diplomatic niceties, he launched straightway into a bitter attack upon Dubcek and his colleagues; for four hours he recounted the crimes of the Czechoslovak 'counter-revolutionaries', cited offensive articles in the Press and abused 'bourgeois-revisionists' such as Goldstuecker, Sik and Cisar.

At the end of this tirade the meeting was adjourned for lunch: the two sides did not eat together. During the afternoon Dubcek attempted to answer Brezhnev's angry, shouted insults with calm and reasonable arguments which were thought by his colleagues to be appropriately skilful and soothing but which apparently made no impression upon the Soviets: when the meeting ended that night agreement, and even mere understanding, appeared to be as remote as ever.

* Moscow had insisted that the entire Presidium of each Party come to Cierna, in the hope that the Czechs would split. The Czechs complied, but two Russians, Kirilenko, a 'hardliner', and Polyanski, apparently a moderate, had been left behind.

The next morning the talks were opened by President Svoboda, who had sat fairly silent the day before. The Russians were awaiting his statement with hope; Svoboda, they felt, had been too closely linked with the Red Army and with the Soviet Union throughout his life for him to forsake them now. Were the old President to express his disagreement with Dubcek, as they felt sure he must, then the whole façade of Czechoslovak unity could be expected to crumble, the Presidium would divide and Dubcek be forced to climb down.

It was therefore with considerable dismay that the Russians listened as Svoboda made a long, eloquent and emotional defence of his colleagues and of the post-January movement. The old soldier demonstrated his real feelings for the Soviet position during an incident in which Frantisek Kriegel, a Prague doctor and one of the most liberal of the Czech Presidium, was abused by the Russians for his Jewish blood. He asked, quite reasonably, why he was objected to. Shelest, the Ukrainian, snapped back 'You just *are* – we don't have to explain why!' This attack upon his close friend apparently enraged Dubcek, who banged his fist upon the table and shouted, 'You're not going to treat *us* as your underlings, comrades.'

'You'll get used to it, Alexander,' sighed Svoboda with resignation, 'Marshal Konev treated me as an underling throughout the war.'

That night the Russians withdrew once more across the border to sleep in the safety of the Soviet Union. Dubcek, unable to sleep, wandered unhappily around the town. At 2.45 railroad worker Josef Tarczi was walking home along the tracks when he saw someone coming towards him. It was Dubcek. They both stopped and then went together to the canteen, where they were joined by several other railwaymen. 'He spent an hour with us,' said Tarczi, 'and explained the whole situation. He said that for the last few weeks he had been sleeping only between 3 a.m. and 7 a.m. every night. When he finally said goodnight one of the comrades begged him "Take care of yourself, Comrade Dubcek. We need you."'

Not only does this story illustrate Dubcek's industry and the exhaustion which he must have suffered that long summer; it is also typical of his whole style of unpretentious leadership.

Probably no other leader in the world today is so close to the grassroots and so well aware of the feelings of his people as was Dubcek during the Prague Spring. It never occurred to him that the dignity of his office required him to hold himself aloof. Until pressure of work prevented him, he used to spend every weekend either in the stands watching Slovan Bratislava play football, or at a public swimming bath. Here he revealed a paunch which suggested that, despite his enthusiasm for sport, he now had no time for exercise. This is not to say that he took no care of himself: his fastidiously manicured hands, his beautiful silk shirts and the well cut Italian-style suits – very unusual on an East-European politician – which he has affected since 1967, all testify to a man of considerable personal pride. At the same time he has no false bonhomie and has never had to put on that mask of grim familiarity that poor Novotny needed to assume when slumming it with the workers. Dubcek gained the love and respect of his people as much for his open, unassuming, good-hearted and shy but friendly disposition as for his advocacy of social reform.

The next morning Brezhnev pleaded illness and refused to leave his train. Dubcek went alone to the carriage and begged for some slight measure of understanding. Whatever the effect of his request, after lunch Brezhnev rejoined the two sides in the railwaymen's club and for the first time some sort of constructive conversations were held.

The real reason for the Soviets' sudden desire to co-operate after all probably lay far from Cierna and not in Dubcek's initiative at all.

> 'On 30 July two members of the Spanish Communist Party had flown to Moscow, asked for an immediate audience with Kirilenko and handed him a letter from eighteen European Communist Parties demanding the cessation of Soviet interference in the domestic affairs of the Czechoslovak Socialist Republic. Otherwise the signatories threatened to convene a meeting to examine and possibly condemn the behaviour of the Five. At the same time warning letters also arrived in Moscow from Tito and Ceaucescu – Tito's moderate and factual, Ceaucescu's indignant and in Soviet eyes insulting.'[4]

But, despite the Russian attempt to reach a compromise,

neither side found it possible to work out a final communiqué that was acceptable to the other. This last deadlock was broken only by Brezhnev's insistence that all the Warsaw Pact countries, except Rumania, should meet and sign a new statement of mutual accord and self-congratulation. Dubcek hesitated, but eventually agreed to the idea on the understanding that the meeting should take place in Czechoslovakia and that Czechoslovak affairs should not be on the agenda. Remarkably enough, Brezhnev agreed; the new meeting was organized for 3 August in Bratislava and the Russians undertook finally to withdraw their troops from Czechoslovak soil.

Nothing was decided at either Cierna or Bratislava: there was no common ground for compromise and no possibility of mutual understanding. The two sides spoke the same language but neither could comprehend the other. Their basic assumptions as to what was involved in 'counter-revolutionary forces', the 'leading role of the Party', and 'control of the Press' were so utterly different that no meaningful dialogue was conceivable. This was later illustrated by a remark Dubcek made to the Presidium on the night of August 20–21. As he read out a letter he had received from Brezhnev on the nineteenth, a letter which complained again about 'counter-revolution in Czechoslovakia', Dubcek petulantly exclaimed, "This is what they keep saying, but they do not take into consideration what the real situation is. After all, we are taking measures.'[5] But in Soviet eyes the 'measures' he had taken since Bratislava* were either non-existent or quite meaningless; this he could never understand.

The problems caused by this basic inability to communicate with each other were only aggravated by the fashion in which

* The Bratislava Declaration of 4 August, which was meant to ratify the non-existent Cierna Agreement, was remarkable for the fact that it made not one mention of Czechoslovakia. Nevertheless, the Western Press hailed the two meetings as a triumph for Dubcek, and it did indeed appear at the time that his policy had paid off and that the 'doves' in the Kremlin had won the day. Dubcek himself seemed happy. He told the nation on 2 August that the Soviet comrades had been most co-operative and that all would be well: 'I can say openly that it [our sovereignty] is not being threatened . . . however, it is necessary to stress that the people of our country maintain prudence and a statesman-like wisdom. It is necessary to stress that various essential actions and gatherings be not misused for anti-socialist and anti-Soviet expressions.'[6] His plea had only limited effect.

each side insisted on arguing. Dubcek's tactics for dealing with the Russians were simple but remarkably effective. A colleague of his has described the encounters through the summer months in the following terms:

> It was incredible and moving. There were moments, at Moscow, Cierna and Prague, where the Soviet 'friends' humiliated Dubcek the man, the Communist and the Slovak. They dragged him in the mud and trampled upon him. It made us sick; this is the end, we said to ourselves; let's give up. But after the initial shock, Dubcek always took hold of himself and ignoring the insults, weighed, in what had been shouted, the important against the simple threats. He examined the points of agreement and asserted that after all there was still 'slight room for action', for further negotiations and manoeuvres. He then used to work out how to enlarge this common ground and started to work again. He was capable of holding his own for hours with the Soviet Ambassador in Prague, even if he had to collapse afterwards, absolutely worn out, and even if he had to succumb to despair. But that never lasted very long.[7]

'Enlarging the common ground' appears to have meant for Dubcek making concessions to Soviet concern – but only those from which he also benefited. They involved stressing the dangers of anti-socialism and attacking 'the political and ideological remnants of the defeated bourgeois classes, corrupted pre-February [1948] right-wing politicians who stand in certain opposition to our Party'.[8] The activities of KAN and K231 showed how justified was this concern.*

He also tried to appease the Soviets by condemning the criticism of the People's Militia, the Communist Party's private and very conservative army† which is designed to de-

* Both were potential oppositions to the Communist Party. Klub 231 was a gathering of former political prisoners. KAN claimed to be 'The First Guarantor of Democracy, a kind of prime controlling organization capable of creating a legal vehicle for the political activities of non-Party members'. (*Literarni Listy*, 25 April 1968). According to Arnulf Simon, a member of KAN's preparatory committee 'KAN grew out of a natural reaction to the utter failure of Communist Party policies and was the expression of the people's desire to govern themselves.' (*East Europe*, June 1969).

† On 19 July *Svobodne Slovo* (daily of the Socialist Party) had complained

Alexander Dubcek arriving at Kosice railway station after the talks at Cierna-nad-Tisou with the Soviet leaders, 1 August 1968.

On 4 August 1968 the leaders of the Soviet, East German, Hungarian, Polish and Bulgarian Parties came to Bratislava. Standing on the banks of the Danube Dubcek points out to Brezhnev the way to Moscow.

On 12-13 August Walter Ulbricht came to Karlovy Vary, Bohemia, to inform Dubcek of his continued concern about the Czechoslovak Reform Movement.

fend the gains of the proletariat even, if necessary, against the working class. But in doing so he was also currying for Militia support of his policies. He succeeded; during the invasion the militiamen rallied almost hundred per cent to him; it was they who guarded the clandestine 14th Congress held under Russian noses in Prague's CKD factory.

By his deviousness, humility, patience and perseverance, Dubcek induced the Russian 'hawks' to believe that they could trust him and it took them a long time to realize that they could not. He has himself described to a friend his tactics for those encounters: 'I just try to smile at Brezhnev as he shouts at me. I say Yes, Yes, I agree, and then I come home and do nothing.' *Pravda*'s angry account (22 August) of all the promises that he had made and then wantonly broken suggests that this was indeed his policy. And at the Central Committee meeting of September 1969 Gustav Husak claimed that at a long confrontation between Czechoslovak and Russian leaders in October 1968, Brezhnev traced the whole history of Czechoslovak-Soviet relations before the invasion.

Using the patronymic 'Alexander Stefanovitch', Brezhnev kept asking Dubcek: 'On this occasion we said such and such and you said so and so. Is that not true?' The recital of abandoned pledges apparently continued several hours and, said Husak sarcastically, 'Alexander Stefanovitch could not say a word against it.'[10]

Dubcek's ingenuousness was relatively successful – it played some part in at least delaying the invasion – but it demonstrates an important facet, if not weakness, of his character. He possesses a certain capacity for self-delusion; it may have been this, as much as his rational calculations as to the relative strengths of 'hawks' and 'doves', that persuaded him to persevere.

---

with some reason: 'We consider the existence of the People's Militia in its present form as unsocialist in general . . . .It is intolerable to speak of the equal rights of the political parties if one of them has at its disposal an armed unit.' In a speech to the Militia on 20 July Dubcek went out of his way to contradict this article by saying: 'We are fully aware that you represent an irreplaceable part of the fundamental class nucleus of the Party. . . which has contributed towards the victory and towards the development of socialism in our Czechoslovak homeland.'[9]

A tendency to live in the clouds was obvious in his attitude towards Novotny's associates in January. Another example of it was discovered by one of the secretaries who flew with Dubcek, Cernik, Bilak and Kolder to the Dresden meeting of 23 March. They were all terrified at what the Russians would say. Dubcek was sitting alone at the front of the plane scribbling on a pad. The secretary, imagining that he was making notes for his plea of Not Guilty, went up to speak to him. But to his astonishment Dubcek explained to him that he was reconstructing a football match he had seen on television the night before. He was working out the mistakes his team had made and demonstrated to the horrified secretary how it might have been won.

It was this extraordinary ability to cut himself off from reality that helped him persuade himself that not only was what he was doing right but also that all Socialists must sooner or later realize that it was inevitable. His faculty of regarding the unpleasant and inconvenient only dimly through a mist of wishful thinking enabled him to ignore the Russians' twin fears: either that the Communist Party would lose control of Czechoslovakia and that a new regime would lead to the collapse of the Warsaw Pact, or that, perhaps worse, the experiment might prove successful. Such a success would undoubtedly be contagious and infect all the orthodox and unpopular bureaucracies of Eastern Europe.

Dubcek would never have contemplated withdrawal from the Warsaw Pact and believed he was well in control of the nation. But he probably could not understand at all the Soviet fear of the 'domino'. If it was evident that Socialism with a Human Face was what people wanted, then he believed that that was what they should be given. He was not, however, so consistent as to extend this generosity to any socialist nation that wished to indulge in the delights of capitalism.

If one believes the above accounts of the way in which Dubcek was treated by Brezhnev – and there is no reason to doubt them – then it is possible that Bilak was, for once, telling the truth when he claimed that Dubcek said to him on 19 August, 'Brezhnev is senile. There is no point in discussing anything with him. The Russians are nervous, but I will not retreat for that reason . . .'[11]

10
AS JOSEPH VISSARIONOVICH ONCE SAID

'The Presidium considers this action [the invasion] to be contrary to the fundamental principles of relations between socialist states and a denial of the basic norms of international law.'

The Presidium of the Czechoslovak Communist Party, shortly after 1 a.m., 21 August 1968.

'[This resolution contained] politically incorrect points of view at variance with the Party's present knowledge of facts leading to the entrance of allied armies into our territory.'

The Presidium of the Czechoslovak Communist Party, rescinding its resolution of 21 August 1968, 9 September 1969.

One of the symptoms of Dubcek's divorce from reality, it has been argued, was his failure to warn the Czechoslovak peoples of the terrible punishment they risked from the wrath of the Kremlin. Instead of mouthing, through May, June and July, increasingly meaningless clichés of eternal friendship he should, it is said, have spoken frankly of the fears of their allies and either of what must be done to assuage them or of the calculated dangers of defiance.

The invasion did come as a surprise to Czechs and Slovaks, but it is absurd to blame Dubcek for this. It was a surprise to most of the world. However, it is true that Dubcek was concerned to play down the extent of Soviet displeasure, and a more telling criticism of this policy is that it created an obvious contrast between what he was saying and what was actually happening. It was this that led to the crisis of public confidence that occasioned the '2,000 Words'.* Dubcek's reticence was caused by realizing how very improper was the Kremlin's interference in the internal affairs of his country. He knew the enormous resentment it would create in Czechoslovakia if the truth about Russian behaviour and the extent

* See above pp. 166-8.

of the abuse and humiliation to which he had been subjected were known. He was very alarmed, as early as mid-March, at the 'anti-Sovietism' that was so widespread even before the Russians had started to make public threats, and was perhaps over-anxious to do nothing that might encourage this dangerous and what he initially considered as 'unjustified' emotion. It was this fear more than anything else that compelled him to remain silent about the real threats that the Kremlin and its allies had made to him in March, May and June.*

It is difficult to judge how much difference it would have made had he been franker. Given that this would have inflamed and virtually accorded official encouragement to anti-Sovietism, it is surely the case that there was nothing to be gained by Dubcek's pursuing such a policy unless he was prepared to carry it through to its logical conclusion and – sensible to the will of the people as he was trying to be – prepare for active resistance to Russian threats and the possibility of Warsaw Pact intervention.

Some observers have argued that this is exactly what he should have done. Amongst the most cogent, though from different points of view, are Kamil Winter† and Pavel Tigrid.‡

There were three occasions on which he might have called upon the Czechoslovak army to help resist the Russians; the first, in July, would have been a preventive and deterrent action. The other two, on 21 and 27 August, would have been retributive acts designed to render the Russian occupation more difficult.

General Prchlik, whom Dubcek had appointed Chief of the Party's Eighth Department – responsible for defence and

* According to Vasil Bilak at the meeting of 4-5 May in Moscow Brezhnev warned Dubcek that he would start a third world war rather than allow Czechoslovakia to disrupt or leave the socialist camp. On his return from this encounter Dubcek said: 'It is customary for good friends not to hide behind diplomatic politeness, but to speak openly as equals. In this context our Soviet comrades expressed their anxiety lest the process of democratization be abused in our country against socialism'. See *Le Monde*, 25 October 1969 and *Rude Pravo*, 7 May 1968.

† Ex-editor of News and Current Affairs – Czechoslovak Television. See *The Times*, 6 June 1969.

‡ Editor of *Svedectvi*, Czech political magazine published in Paris. See *Svedectvi*: Nos. 35-36-37, Summer 1969.

security – was one of those who argued that the country should be prepared to defend itself by force of arms. He told Dubcek as early as the second week of June that Czechoslovakia ran a very great risk of intervention from its allies, and tried to persuade him to take some steps to meet the threat. Prchlik realized quite well that with a force of only 175,000 men trained and deployed to resist attack from the west rather than from the north, south or east, it would be impossible to defend the whole country against an army which could, if necessary, muster at least a million men. His point was that troops could nevertheless be used to hold the largest towns and that civilian guerrilla forces should be encouraged to take to the hills and prevent the 'enemy' from gaining control of the countryside.

An excellent opportunity for such a general mobilization occurred in the middle of the next month. The Warsaw Letter of 15 July from five allied socialist countries expressed belligerent concern at the trend of democratization in Czechoslovakia. But it also voiced the fear that the Czechoslovak armed forces were no longer capable of defending the borders of socialism against West German revanchism. Dubcek was urged – this time not only by Prchlik – to take up this point: on the pretext of strengthening his defences against the alleged imperialist threat, he could have put the Czechoslovak army on a general alert and could even have drawn up public plans for defence against a hypothetical (NATO) attack.

He refused the advice. Because, serious though he understood the situation to be, he still could not believe that the Russians would in fact invade his country. He was convinced that the threats were hollow. Mobilization, or indeed any other preventive action, would therefore have been unnecessary and might have disastrously altered the present apparently favourable status quo.

It is easy, with hindsight, to argue that this was mistaken and that the one thing which might have persuaded the Russians not to invade was the knowledge that they would meet with determined Czechoslovak resistance. But in taking this attitude it is necessary to understand just what was being asked of Dubcek. For Dubcek the idea of fighting the

Soviet Union was utterly repulsive and probably almost impossible. He had been suckled as well as weaned by Mother Russia and his whole life had been – at least indirectly – dedicated to her service. To suggest that he should now prepare to fight her on a mere hypothesis in which he did not even believe is expecting too much (or perhaps too little) of him. Dubcek is not a man whose convictions change overnight. His loyalty is not lightly purchased and once gained it is not easily lost. Undoubtedly he was upset by the Kremlin's refusal to perceive in his reforms the brilliant promises that he saw shining there, but that was no reason to order the country to take up arms. To have done that would have been for him flagrantly anti-socialist as well as obviously anti-Soviet. And apart from his personal scruples there was a quite conclusive reason for not accepting Prchlik's counsel: in mid-July the Czechoslovak countryside was already occupied by many thousand Soviet troops. The Russians may well have been considering whether these troops should be withdrawn or whether they should be ordered into the towns. Had Dubcek ordered a general mobilization of reserves he would have given the Kremlin just the excuse it needed: Prague and the military bases would have been occupied by Czechoslovakia's allies hours before his instructions could be carried out. And in such circumstances collaborators would have been much easier to find, world opinion much more quickly satisfied.

But, given that he wanted to convince the waverers in the Kremlin that he should be allowed his head, there was one action that Dubcek might have taken in July. This was not to strike a defensive or militaristic posture, but simply to make use of his friends.

Just after the delivery of the Warsaw Letter it was suggested to him that he should invite Tito and Ceaucescu to Prague to sign some sort of Triple Alliance. He refused to do so for fear of offending Moscow. He also declined to take advantage of the widespread sympathy for his cause amongst Western Communist Parties. By mid-July it was clear that the vast majority of non-ruling Parties – even the Japanese and the one ever pro-Kremlin Indian Communist Party – had enthusiastically embraced Dubcek's portrait of Socialism with a Human Face. And in proportion to their rapture at this inspiring sketch was their concern at the Kremlin's blundering. The most worried was Luigi Longo the Italian Communist leader. He recognized that on the success of the Prague experiment – and on Russian discretion – depended many of his Party's hopes of winning power in a free election. He and Waldeck Rochet, the French Party boss, flew to Moscow on 20 July to warn Brezhnev of the setback that would be inflicted on the cause of the international proletariat were the Russians to invade Czechoslovakia. The French Communists even called for an immediate conference of all European Communist Parties to discuss the crisis, but the idea was abandoned as much because of the opposition from Prague as from Moscow. Perhaps this was Dubcek's greatest mistake. Rochet, who had visited him on 19 July, was offering him the perfect opportunity for exploiting those members of the Politburo who were concerned at the Soviet Union's hawkish attitude and who were counselling moderation. It was on this faction that Dubcek had based his hopes all summer and a conference might have forced the hands of his enemies in the Kremlin. He would not try it.

This failure appears to have been a reflection of his anxiety, even at this late stage of the drama, to avoid embarrassing the Russians in any way at all. It was curiously unstatesmanlike but, considering the abuse to which he and his policies had been subjected, generous compunction, entirely in keeping with his character. Even now – his head perhaps buried in the clouds of popularity – he could not believe that the Soviet Union would fail him: he was sure that a way out of the impasse would be found. This does not necessarily mean that he was willing to compromise, for he was probably far too rigidly committed to his reforms to be able to envisage any concession that would be meaningful to the Soviets. It was simply that he had no wish to expose the Russian leaders to any tribunal or to public obloquy: he was concerned to protect them as much as possible from what was in his mind a terrible mistake which, with a little help, they must soon appreciate and rectify.

Other critics of Dubcek's leadership have maintained that

the Presidium should have called upon the Czechoslovak army to resist the invaders once the Warsaw Pact forces had crossed the borders into Czechoslovakia on the night of 20–21 August. There are three reasons why this did not happen.

It is very doubtful whether a majority of the Presidium would have voted for it. There was enough difficulty in putting out even the statement of 1 a.m. on 21 August that 'The Presidium considers this action to be contrary to the fundamental principles of relations between socialist states and a denial of the basic rights of international law.' Four members, Vasil Bilak, Drahomir Kolder, Emil Rigo and Oldrich Svestka, refused to sign it at all.

An order to resist would have been suicide. The government had made no preparations for military resistance, and any fight that the armed forces and the civilian population had put up would have been ill-conceived, hasty and inadequate. The invading troops did not anticipate military resistance, but they were more than equipped to meet it and there is no reason to suppose they would have shed any less blood than was necessary to its suppression.

The third reason is more remarkable. It is that Dubcek still appears not to have understood the gravity of the situation. There is no reason to believe that he was not telling the truth as he said, weeping: 'I declare on my honour as a Communist that I had no suspicion, no indication that anyone would want to undertake such measures against us.'[1] He was in an advanced state of shock and presumably realized that he would not be able to continue to lead his government as independently as before. But he did not appreciate that the Russians intended to depose and abduct him. He later commented that: 'I thought that someone would come to me on behalf of the allied troops and that we should accordingly convene the Presidium meeting to decide on further actions.' It was not to happen: 'At dawn, however, members of the State Security . . . came to my office and arrested me saying that within two hours it would be decided what was to be done to me.'[2]

What was in fact done to him is not yet clear but it is one of the most hideous and repulsive aspects of the invasion and the most frightening indictment of the Soviet mind. He was dragged off and flown away; reports differ on where he and his colleagues were initially taken – some say Poland, some say the Ukraine – but all are agreed that he was treated more as an animal on the way to slaughter than as the legal head of an allied state. There is not the slightest evidence that the Russians intended ever to return him, Smrkovsky, Cernik or Kriegel to Czechoslovakia. They planned to install a puppet government; the precedent of Imre Nagy suggests that when they succeeded they would probably have murdered Dubcek and his friends.

They were forced to change their plans because of the extraordinary loyalty of the Czech and Slovak peoples to Dubcek, because of the ineptitude of their own political operations, and because of the adamant refusal of President Svoboda* to negotiate without the release and participation of Dubcek and the others. The fact that they had to return Dubcek to office was an unprecedented and almost unbelievable humiliation for the Russians, and not one that they would lightly forget. Dubcek must have known quite well that they regarded his reinstatement as only a temporary and very undesirable expedient. He would be removed as soon as his removal was politically possible; as soon, that is, as he had lost his charisma, as soon as the unity and spirit of the people had been broken and as soon as genuine and effective collaborators had been found. He was sent back from Moscow on 26 August to destroy himself, his reform movement and his following. He was sent back to exterminate his ideals.

Because of this, it has been argued that he should have had nothing to do with the proposition that the Russians put to him. On the grounds that the Russians were negotiating from a position of weakness on 23–5 August, he should have refused to make himself their stooge and to endorse the occupation by signing the Moscow Agreement and by returning to office.

This is easy to propose far from Moscow, but it is necessary

* Svoboda's resistance was forged by a telephone call that Brezhnev ill-advisedly allowed him to make on the night of 23 August to his wife in Prague. The old man, close to despair, was immensely encouraged by her vivid description of the resistance and unity of the people behind him. See Tigrid, *La chute irrésistible*, p. 159.

to try and understand the feeling of Dubcek and his colleagues as they bargained in the Kremlin. They were emotionally and physically exhausted by their thirty-six hours of imprisonment; they had just been miraculously released from almost certain death; the Russians apparently deliberately misinformed them and told them that all resistance to the invasion had collapsed – they certainly did not know the full extent of the Soviet political débâcle in Prague. They must have been convinced that to have refused to negotiate would have resulted in their immediate return to captivity and probably to death and would not, as far as they could see, in the least way benefit their peoples.

Evzen Loebl, who was Deputy Foreign Trade Minister in 1949, imprisoned in the purges, after rehabilitation director of the Bratislava Bank and friend of Dubcek, is convinced that Dubcek acted in an unstatesman-like fashion. He agrees that they could have done nothing in Moscow, but holds that the entire quartet – Dubcek, Svoboda, Cernik and Smrkovsky – should have fled the country on their return from the Soviet Union and should have set up a government-in-exile in Yugoslavia or Sweden.

The most obvious practical argument against their doing this is that flight would probably have been impossible. The KGB must have kept a very close watch upon their unreliable new puppets, for the Russians knew very well that although they held most of the strings, those strings were not yet taut.

In that case, it is argued, Dubcek should have appeared on television on 27 August, denounced the invasion, refused to collaborate with the invaders, thrown himself upon the people and resigned. Some critics have even suggested that he should also have called upon the Czechoslovak army to rise up against the occupying forces. The Russians would then have had to combat far more violent resistance than hitherto.

If there had ever occurred a moment for the use of Czechoslovak troops, it had certainly passed by 27 August, for the Czechoslovak armed units were already well controlled by garrisons of their Allies. But even without the army Dubcek could have resigned and called for total non-co-operation with the invaders. In his moving television address of 29

August Smrkovsky admitted: 'We also considered the fact that at times there is nothing left to do but reject any appeasing settlements, that in the interest of the honour and character of a people it is better to expose one's breast to the bayonets.'[3]

There was one very compelling reason why they did not call upon the nation to do so. They were terrified at the consequences. They believed that as responsible politicians they should exhaust all diplomatic and political channels before they asked the people to die for its freedom. The Kremlin would not have sent Dubcek back to Prague if it had expected him to engender another crisis. The Russian leaders must have impressed upon him very carefully the outcome of any act so provocative as resignation. One account, probably exaggerated, has it that Dubcek was told that if he resigned or gave the slightest encouragement to any 'anti-Sovietism' the Russians would have no hesitation in making Czechoslovakia the 17th Republic of the Soviet Union, imposing military dictatorship and resettling as many Czechs and Slovaks in other parts of their new homeland as was necessary to secure order. According to one story current in the extraordinary atmosphere that was then Prague, Czechoslovaks were either optimists or pessimists. The optimists thought that the Russians would transport at least four million of them to Siberia. The pessimists believed that they would have to walk.

Whether or not the Politburo was in fact prepared to go to such lengths and whether or not the Red Army would have been willing to set up a military regime is irrelevant. Forty-eight hours after their troops had entered Prague the Russians appreciated the blunder they had made and determined to make Dubcek extricate them from it. He had their assurance that if he refused to do so they would carry out their threat. They were offering him the chance of saving his people from that and for a man like Dubcek there was simply no choice. He had to co-operate for he believed that the sanctions upon his good conduct were the lives of perhaps thousands of his countrymen who loved and trusted him. In June 1969 a Yugoslav journalist asked him why he had accepted the Russians' ultimatum and why he had not fled or at least resigned.

Dubcek looked at him and replied: 'Don't you think that would be a terrible thing to do? How could you possibly expect me to do a thing like that?'

In all his despair, he was not without hope. It was such an extraordinary miracle that he had been allowed to resume his work that now nothing seemed quite impossible, and he imagined that he might still be able to salvage something from the reform movement. Despite his exhaustion and disillusion he must have been cheered by the compromise that they had managed to effect in the First Moscow Agreement. It is true that its publication on 27 August was greeted with horror in Czechoslovakia, and the Czechoslovak leaders had certainly had to make immediate concessions, most importantly in the removal of personnel whom the Russians found unacceptable. Nevertheless the Treaty laid down no specific instructions, and it promised that 'the troops that entered temporarily the territory of Czechoslovakia will not interfere in the internal affairs of the Czechoslovak Socialist Republic'.

Perhaps even more encouraging for Dubcek was the statement that 'agreement was reached on the terms of the withdrawal of these troops from its territory as the situation in Czechoslovakia normalizes'. The 'normalization' referred to here could, like the terms of the Bratislava Declaration, be interpreted in very different ways, for there was no public explanation of the meaning of the word. Presumably the Russians had made it plain to the Czechoslovak leaders how much they expected of them. But for Dubcek, Smrkovsky, Svoboda and Cernik, the absence of any particular orders in the Treaty was a remarkable achievement, as extraordinary as the actual signing of the Treaty itself which indeed reaffirmed that Czechoslovakia might 'carry out the mutual decisions adopted in Cierna and Tisou and the provisions and principles formulated by the Bratislava Conference'.[4] If those provisions had been acceptable to Dubcek before 20 August, he must have thankfully embraced them after the invasion. It was very consoling to realize that, at least on paper, the Russians had accepted that part of the reform programme should continue; he could hardly have done anything but try to save something from the wreckage.

This is not to say that he took his decision lightly. He knew that the depressing process of 'normalization', whatever it might mean, would be infinitely harder and more soul-destroying than a dramatic abdication. He knew that he was doing Moscow's dirty work and he knew that this would probably destroy the love that the people had for him. He knew that many would consider that their national hero had turned into a weak and despicable collaborator. But he would have been justified in believing that the invasion itself had done nothing to resolve the crisis that had torn the Kremlin all summer; the indecisiveness of the Russians' actions after the occupation of Prague showed that Moscow was as divided as ever. The decision to release and reinstate him and his colleagues meant a very great defeat for whichever politicans had managed to tip the balance in favour of invasion three days before.* If anything, this climb-down had worsened the crisis in Moscow. Dubcek knew very well that the Politburo, the Red Army and the KGB appeared to be far from united either within or between themselves in their attitude towards the invasion and as to what should now be done.† He had good reason to believe that, the hawks now routed, the doves would prevail.

On 27 August he went on the radio to tell the nation of the agreement he had reached in Moscow. His voice was that of a man in great agony, more unconscious than sentient, who had suffered terribly in the past week and knew that he would suffer more in the months ahead. He wept as he struggled through his speech and as he begged the Czech and Slovak peoples to have faith in him and to respect the Moscow Agreement despite the concessions it embodied. At one stage he broke down completely and was silent for several seconds. It is reported that he was slapped across the face before he was able to continue. He then said: 'Dear listeners,

* According to one excellent source quoted by Robert Littell, the editor of *The Czech Black Book*, voting in the Soviet Party Politburo over to invade or not to invade was seven to four for the use of force. On the side of the doves were still Kosygin, Suslov, Podgorny, and General Voronov.

† One example of this was evident in the Moscow Press; during the first stage of the invasion *Izvestia* concentrated on reporting the ecstatic welcome accorded the Warsaw Pact troops by the Czechoslovak population. *Trud*, however, made it fairly clear that the occupiers had been greeted with hatred. *Trud* is usually thought to represent the views of the KGB. See Windsor and Roberts, pp. 67-8.

I ask you to forgive me if every now and then there is a pause in this largely improvised speech and impromptu appearance. I think you know why it is.' He paid tribute to the fact that without the work done by journalists and broadcasters to forge the will and unity of the nation he would not have returned to office:

> All of us who negotiated in Moscow during the past few days are profoundly grateful to you for your prudent and genuinely Communist work. Without it, it would not have been possible to prevent a worsening of the situation and to maintain circumspection and the true moral and political unity of our people.

At the same time, however, he pleaded for an end to provocative broadcasts and reports, arguing that the time for such manifestations was past. He went on to admit that 'we might be forced to take some temporary measures that limit the extent of democracy and freedom of opinion that we had already achieved and which we would not have undertaken in ordinary circumstances'. But he begged the people to accept these and other aspects of 'normalization' so that there might be a chance of 'realizing in this new situation the programme of our Communist Party which we decided in January, April and all other meetings'. He ended by affirming his belief in the greatness of man and especially his own people and promised them that 'a nation in which everyone will be guided by reason and conscience shall not perish'.* Many people would say that this has been disproved.

He was more frank but no less emotional when he addressed a closed session of the Central Committee two days later; he admitted that:

> In our politics we did not properly assess the force of international factors; we should have paid more attention to the opinion of our neighbours over our internal affairs. [Nevertheless] different classes and social groups in our society see aspects of the invasion in different ways. But the majority is united on one point; they do not understand the military occupation as a help but as a step which has no

* See Appendix.

sense at all and which conflicts with socialist principles.

He was determined to preserve the essentials of the reform movement, for he recognized that 'our Party will keep its leading role only so long as the post-January policies are continued . . . The principal problem on which we should now concentrate is getting the Soviet troops off our territory. This is naturally part and parcel of the process of consolidating the situation here.'* He meant that not only would the troops not depart before 'consolidation' but also that consolidation was impossible without the departure of the troops.

It was this paradox which was to haunt him throughout the next eight months, and twice during his address to the Central Committee he broke into tears. But towards the end he managed to regain some of that unlikely optimism in which he is able so often to find some comfort: 'The question is this – do we have any chance of getting our country out of this situation? The answer is yes. Is it true that there are still deep ties between Party and people? Yes. Well let's get to work.'†

* This part of the speech has not before been published.
† Quoted in Tigrid, *op cit.*, p. 171.

11

A VOICE VALEDICTORY

'La Philosophie triomphe aisément des maux passés et des maux à venir, mais les maux présents triomphent d'elle.'
La Rochefoucauld, *Maximes* No. 22.

Wenceslas Square is a long broad avenue leading up a slight hill in the nineteenth-century quarter of Prague. It is not very beautiful, but it is impressive. At the top of the hill stands the huge and forbidding National Museum of Bohemia, and below it on a tall plinth in the middle of the road is an imposing statue of the patron saint of Bohemia, Prince Vaclav (Wenceslas), astride a great horse.

During the invasion the statue became the focal point of resistance to the Russians and on its steps an eleven-year-old boy was shot dead as he tried to push a Czechoslovak flag down the barrel of a Russian tank. Ever since, the statue has been a national shrine, till January 1969 covered with flowers, bunches of pine, pictures of Dubcek, Svoboda, and Smrkovsky, and before which a small crowd always stood wondering and waiting for the trams which stop there on their way up the hill.

They had much to wonder about, for in many ways the Prague Autumn – the seven and a half months during which Dubcek remained First Secretary after the invasion – was as remarkable a time as the Prague Spring. It was a period of intense contradictions and of increasing disillusion. It had an underlying tension that was savagely punctuated by violent and emotional crises as the Czechoslovak peoples and their leader attempted to come to terms with the conditions that the tanks had imposed upon them. It was a period of great ambiguity – no one in Czechoslovakia knew exactly what were the limits of disobedience, and for a time the Russians appeared not to be any the more certain. They had invaded the country in order to remove Dubcek and to destroy the reform movement and yet six months later Dubcek was still in office and the Czechs and Slovaks still had more personal freedoms than any other peoples in Eastern Europe. At least part of the credit for this untoward achievement must be given to Dubcek himself.

If before the invasion Dubcek was a young and charismatic folk-hero, after August he developed into a much more skilful politician. Before the invasion he had been borne along, mildly protesting but exhilarated, on a tidal wave of popular nationalism. After August his following shrank amongst a despairing nation. Before the invasion his task had been to persuade the Kremlin that his people wanted nothing so much as the development of socialism and eternal friendship with the Soviet Union at the same time as convincing Czechs and Slovaks that he was resisting all Russian pressures. After August half his time was spent in trying to convince the Kremlin that, despite appearances to the contrary, he was in control of the Party and the Party of the nation, the rest in persuading the Czechoslovaks that, despite appearances to the contrary, he was saving the essentials of the reform movement. It was an almost impossible task, but for six months he fulfilled it.

At 3.30 on the drizzling afternoon of 16 January 1969 a battered Skoda drove up Wenceslas Square, past the statue and the trams and stopped for a moment below the museum. A boy of about twenty climbed out of the car and said something to the driver. A young man in the back seat passed him a small can. The boy took it from him and gazed, rather vacantly, at the car as it drove away. He turned round towards the museum above him. Since August the dirty stone had been pockmarked with hundreds of little white scars, for on 22 August a lone marksman in one of the high windows had shot the commander of a Russian tank in the street below. Nine Russian machine guns had at once raked the whole building, sending chips of stone flying, shattering all the windows. The marksman was unhurt. Czechs now point to the pillared façade and say 'A nice bit of work by El Grechko'.

Dubcek probably under-estimated two factors when he

told the Central Committee on 31 August that there was a chance of extricating the nation from its catastrophe. The first was that the Russians had the inestimable advantage of time. By mid-November they appear to have decided to make use of it. Instead of continuing to try and have Dubcek removed, they made him apply salami tactics* to the reforms. Dubcek always reluctantly climbed down, unhappily daring to hope that each compromise he made would be the one that was finally rewarded by the withdrawal of the troops. It never was.

Dubcek's second mistake lay in his too generous judgment of his colleagues. Because no politician of any calibre had agreed to collaborate during the invasion he imagined that none ever would. He reckoned without ambition: during the next six months the rise of 'realists' like Gustav Husak and Lubomir Strougal balanced his own descent. Husak had replaced Vasil Bilak as Slovak First Secretary after the invasion. He immediately began to demonstrate to the Kremlin his reasonableness and his willingness to 'normalize' the situation much more quickly than Dubcek. By January 1969 Bratislava was subject to far greater repression than Prague – the roles of Czechoslovak and Slovak First Secretaries had been reversed since the days when Dubcek worked against Novotny from Bratislava. By splitting the leadership Husak inevitably, and purposely, made Dubcek's job much more difficult: he found it increasingly difficult to argue with the Russians that the Party and the people were united behind him, despite the obvious disgust with which Slovaks viewed Husak's turn of coat.†

Two flights of steps lead up to the museum from Wenceslas Square. The boy looked up them and saw the little group of people who always seem to stand there and gaze down past the statue over the river towards Hradcany Castle on the hill.

There in the red-carpeted, mirrored Spanish Hall the Cen-

* By 'salami tactics' is meant that the Russians decided to make Dubcek slice away at the reforms little by little. They understood that this gradual destruction had a much better chance of peaceful success than a demand for the instant dismantling of all that he had done.

† A poll published by *Pravda* (Bratislava) on 28 December showed Husak to be far less popular than Czech politicians like Smrkovsky and Svoboda.

tral Committee was debating the problem of who should succeed Smrkovsky as Chairman of the new Federal Assembly.

The Smrkovsky affair had dominated Czechoslovak politics for the last six weeks. It is worth studying because it illustrates at one and the same time how much Dubcek managed to extract from his compromises with the Russians in terms of freedom of the Press and Assembly and also his ultimate impotence. The Russians might not enforce total censorship and they might allow him a month in which to plead a case, but the tribute that they really wanted they extracted. They wanted Smrkovsky sacked.

The crisis came into the open at the beginning of December, at the height of an angry Press campaign against the illegal publication of the Russian propaganda paper *Zpravy* and the broadcasts of their occupation radio station 'Vltava'* Dubcek understood the emotions aroused by these media, but in a speech to 12,000 miners in the north-west Bohemian town of Most on 6 December he publicly rebuked the Press for stirring up passions: 'The Central Committee is right to criticize tendencies by which the Press became a force not always guided by principles defined by Party and State leadership. This creates the possibility of publicizing various, subjectivist, one-sided materials, and incorrect, sometimes anti-socialist views'.[1] But he made his real attitude to *Zpravy*-Vltava much more clear in an unscripted and unpublished answer to a question from a worried miner. He admitted that 'we cannot be satisfied with that part of the [Moscow] Agreement which refers to interference in our internal affairs such as the illegal paper *Zpravy* and radio Vltava are now committing ... We do have some complaints against our partners.'

* The Russians began to disseminate propaganda through these media during the invasion. Vltava broadcast from East Germany; its newsreaders spoke bad Czech with heavy Ukrainian accents. Its activities did not arouse the same fury in Czechoslovakia as did those of the paper *Zpravy* (News). This was not registered with the Central Information (Press) Office and was therefore illegal. Few Czechs read it, but it was widely distributed by Soviet troops and its existence was a constant irritating reminder of the presence of the occupiers. The extent and bitterness of the Press campaign against it testified to the remarkable freedom which Czechoslovak journalists still enjoyed, and also to their ultimate lack of power. Despite protest *Zpravy*-Vltava continued their work until summer 1969.

The next day he flew with Svoboda, Husak and Strougal to Kiev for a meeting with Soviet leaders. It was a highly secret encounter and only the barest details of it were released, days after their return to Prague.* Dubcek may have made his complaints about *Zpravy* and Vltava – if so they were not heeded – but the main item on the agenda was undoubtedly the future of Smrkovsky. The Kremlin had insisted that Smrkovsky be excluded from the delegation and, though he is believed to have protested at first, Dubcek agreed. Smrkovsky was furious and on 10 December he publicly attacked him on Radio Prague for the secrecy which had surrounded the Kiev encounter and which had caused great anxiety at home. 'As a functionary and as a Communist,' said Smrkovsky, 'I am and I always have been fully in favour of open politics.' After Dubcek had returned from Kiev Smrkovsky had bearded him with the question of his own future. He demanded to know what the Russians had said of him. Dubcek, very embarrassed, assured Smrkovsky that his work had not been under any discussion, and that he would undoubtedly be appointed Chairman of the Federal Assembly when the country was formally federated on 1 January.† He simply could not bring himself to tell Smrkovsy the truth. This is a weakness of character that he has often displayed; he is terrified of facing up to unpleasant realities and of hurting the feelings of friends. To avoid doing either he will often indulge in either fantasy or half-truths.

Smrkovsky must have known that Dubcek was lying and he had no intention of accepting it. In the same interview on 10 December he volunteered the unsolicited information that he was in very good health and had no intention of re-

* The official communiqué made no mention of 'complete unity of views' that East European cliché which means the Kremlin is content. But it did refer to the 'cordial atmosphere' and 'comradely and friendly spirit' of the talks. This was an improvement upon previous encounters and was most probably a result of Russian pleasure at the performance of the new men, Husak and Strougal, both competing for the approval of Moscow. Husak is thought to have been very eager to help the Russians rid themselves of Smrkovsky. Certainly he did all he could over the next six weeks to stoke the anti-Smrkovsky campaign.

† Federation of the Czech lands and Slovakia was the only aspect of the Action Programme that the Russians allowed to proceed without major modification.

signing his post. The ploy was successful; it was the beginning of a remarkable national campaign to keep him in the Chairmanship.

On 21 December Dubcek made his last major speech of the year. It was his most dispirited and also most threatening yet – he virtually confirmed that Smrkovsky's dismissal had been decided:

> A variety of campaigns against the conclusions of the November Plenum of the Czechoslovak Communist Party's Central Committee are causing the Party and society as a whole immeasurable damage. They contain demands which in the present situation or within the time limit cannot be accomplished by the leadership . . . Their aim is to force [the leadership] to adopt more and more undesirable measures – I should like to stress this – and then to misuse this from a rightist position as proof of their having compromised themselves and deviated from the post-January policy. This pushes the Party and all of society on a road of tragic consequences . . .

Dubcek then made plain what would happen if the Smrkovsky campaign were not abandoned. It would be necessary, he said, to take measures which 'will appear to be undemocratic. But they will be in the interest of democracy; they will be in the interest of preventing anarchist tendencies and their initiators from driving this Republic into a situation not only like the one before January but much further back.'

This was the first time that any politician had threatened the country with a return to the Terror of the Fifties.

That Dubcek was prepared to say it is evidence of the severity of the crisis. But he admitted that he could never bear to do it himself and apologized for his words. 'Naturally this would be done by other politicians. I think this is also sufficiently clear. You might think that these are harsh words, but I am convinced that is the truth, and that it is therefore our duty to say it frankly.'[2]

Dubcek's warning was ignored by the people, so many of whom were utterly disillusioned by what they saw as spineless weakness on his part, and the campaign gathered force over Christmas and the New Year. But it had little chance of success, and it was the knowledge of this that drove many Czechs and Slovaks, and certainly the boy standing in Wenceslas Square, to despair.

On 4 January the one-million-strong Metalworkers Union called for a national strike if Smrkovsky were removed from his job. This provoked a panicked appeal from the Presidium, imploring the nation not to take unconstitutional action and to unite behind the November and December resolutions of the Central Committee which had so castrated the process of reform. 'It is easy to unleash a movement', warned the Presidium, 'but it is much more difficult to bear its consequences . . . Society cannot continue to live buffeted about by conflicts and tensions on the brink of a political crisis . . . these deeds are driving our society into conflicts the consequences of which even those who initiate them cannot probably even imagine.'[3]

This was very emotional language, virtually threatening that if there were a strike the Soviet tanks would return to Prague. That this threat was real was borne out by the fact that Smrkovsky himself finally agreed to appeal for calm. The next night he appeared on television and begged people to listen, to realize that: 'Our foreign policy is based on the close relationship with the Soviet Union without which – please, all from right to left and from left to right understand this – we cannot live in this divided world.'[4]

Despite Smrkovsky's Saturday-night appeal tension continued to rise over the weekend, and on Monday Lubomir Strougal, clearly anxious to keep up with Husak, demanded on behalf of the new Czech Party Bureau set up after Federation that Smrkovsky should give way to a Slovak. The next day the students returned from vacation and this occasioned further panic amongst Prague citizens. On Wednesday *Rude Pravo* reported a bread-shortage in Prague; housewives were stocking up in the fear that the Russians were about to reoccupy the city. The government issued strict instructions of restraint to the Press and for one day at least all photographs of Smrkovsky were removed from the Wenceslas Square statue.

So widespread was the belief that the tanks would come back that a government spokesman appeared on television especially to deny that Soviet troops were ringed around Prague and its largest factories. The very fact that the denial was made at all convinced people that the rumours were true. They reminded themselves of Smrkovsky's own assertion in July that the Russians had no intention of intervening in the affairs of Czechoslovakia.

The area where the boy stood had been destroyed by tanks; no effort had been made to repair it because it was to be the site of the main station in an underground railway that is slowly being built in Prague. Blocks of stone lay untidily in the mud, and flimsy metal barriers surrounded the debris in order to stop people tripping over.

The boy stepped past the barriers and over to a fallen block of stone. He set down the can and took off his coat which he laid carefully on the stone. He picked up the can and poured most of its contents over his head and shoulders. The rest he splashed against his chest and trousers. He then flicked a lighter and set his clothes on fire.

A tram was passing up the hill towards the city cemetery at Olsany. The driver, Jaroslav Spirek, saw the screaming boy run into the road; he was on fire from head to foot. Spirek jammed on the brake and leapt out of his cab: 'I ran towards him, taking my overcoat off. The boy himself cried: "Throw your coat over me." With that he stumbled and fell among the cars in the street where I caught up with him. I threw the coat over him, stifling the flames. I asked the boy what happened: "I did it myself," he replied . . . I could see that he spoke with difficulty and so I did not ask him anything else.'

By 8 January Dubcek seems to have begun to panic. Realizing that neither the warning of the Presidium nor the appeal from Smrkovsky had been successful, he went on television himself to address the nation. He assured his audience that Smrkovsky would remain in the leadership of the Party, but also stressed that the country must be 'guided' by Party decisions, for any other course would prove a 'blind alley'. 'We have done nothing behind your backs and nothing against the ideas of January,' he promised the unconvinced viewers. But he admitted that the Party had been lax in imparting information in the last few weeks; for this he apologized but 'in an extraordinary situation it is sometimes only possible to act in an extraordinary manner'. He tried to excuse himself and claimed, quite justifiably, that, 'I think we have done more than many had regarded at all possible after August. We should realize that what we have achieved since August we have achieved only because we have proceeded in unity and in a disciplined manner, in mutual confidence and with discretion.'[5]

This appeal appears at last to have convinced the country of the need for restraint. The next day the metalworkers withdrew their strike threat and many newspapers issued grave warnings of 'chaos and disruption'.[6] For a moment it seemed that the crisis was over; Dubcek must have been relieved and may have begun to believe that all would be well. If so, he was wrong.

Jan Palach set himself on fire for his people, for the ideals of Prague Spring and for his memory of Dubcek. His death was first of all a unique protest against the savage mindlessness of the Russian invaders. It was also a bitter reproach of Dubcek and of what to many millions, and especially to the students, seemed his total abandonment of the policies of a humane socialism. Palach left in his overcoat a letter:

> 'Seeing that our nations are on the brink of despair we have decided to make our protest and arouse the people of this country in the following way.
>
> Our group consists of volunteers who are resolved to let themselves be burnt alive for our cause.
>
> I have had the honour to draw the first lot and thus obtain the right to draft this first letter and become the first torch.
>
> Our demands are: (1) The immediate abolition of censorship. (2) A ban on the distribution of *Zpravy*.
>
> Unless our demands are met within five days, i.e. by 21 January 1969, and unless the public demonstrate adequate support (i.e. by an indefinite strike), further torches will burst into flames.* Signed: Torch No. 1.

* There were supposed to be thirteen other students in Palach's suicide squad. It is believed that none of them followed his lead. But by the end of 27 February other Czechs and Slovaks had burned themselves to death. Probably only three were genuinely political protests.

P.S. Remember August! Czechoslovakia has obtained room for manoeuvre in international affairs: let us exploit the fact.[7]

Palach suffered third-degree burns on eighty-five per cent of his body and his doctor described his condition as hardly compatible with life. Nevertheless it took him three days to die and he was conscious for some of that time. He continually asked the doctor to describe the reaction of the country to his self-immolation. When told that the whole nation was stunned and horrified, that thousands of flowers had arrived at the hospital, that the switchboard was jammed day and night, that the Central Committee had been inundated with resolutions supporting his demands, he managed occasionally to smile.

Palach's death immediately awakened something great in the Czech spirit, something that since August had accepted continual punishment with a philosophical shrug of the shoulders. Now shoulders were shaken and for a whole week Prague was given over to his glory. He aroused such intense feeling because, having lost their faith in Dubcek, people desperately craved some other idol who could symbolize their national despair and hopes. In the most tragic and heroic possible way Jan Palach provided himself as that symbol. Moreover, by the totally disproportionate nature of his sacrifice he lifted some of the responsibility for action from the rest of his people. For this they were grateful: the need to act decisively was once again postponed – worship of Jan was, for the time being, a great enough spur to national unity and survival.

On the day after his death thousands of students filled Red Army Square which lies on the banks of the River Vltava in front of his own Philosophical Faculty of Charles University.

Speakers harangued the crowd urging it not to allow Palach's demands to go unanswered. They insisted that Dubcek for once take a stand against the Russians and attacked him for being little better than any other collaborator. They tore down the red and white street signs and renamed the square after Palach. Throughout the week the tension and emotion throughout the country rose, and furious secret bargaining took place, with government representatives and student leaders intent on exploiting the feelings of the people. Dubcek did not take part in these negotiations, for he was in the throes of a nervous breakdown. Exhausted by the strains of the last months, Palach's death and its screaming indictment of his leadership had completely shattered him. He went home and spent the week in bed in Bratislava, very ill indeed.*

By Friday night an estimated 120,000 people had come to Prague for Palach's funeral the following day. His body lay in state in the Carolinum, a beautiful old courtyard of the university, and all day long about 350,000 people queued silently in the narrow streets of the Old Town to pass by his coffin where it lay, surrounded by flowers, under the statue of Jan Hus, the Bohemian martyr for truth to whom Palach was already being compared. One old man, who had stood for five hours in the cold, explained: 'I can stand the cold, for five hours is not a lot to give. Jan Palach gave us his lifetime.'

Despite the orderly calm with which the people waited to pay their respects to their new hero, Prague was tense that weekend. There was a very widespread fear that the Russians would attempt to stage some sort of incident in the mourning crowd of some 800,000 at Saturday's funeral.

In fact the burial procession wound through the streets of the university in drizzling rain and stunning dignity. All policing was done by the students themselves; the State forces remained discreetly in the background. So, reportedly, did bus-loads of militiamen ready to take over the vital installations and ministries at the slightest 'anti-socialist' disturbance, which many at the funeral expected to be provoked at any moment.

These fears were aggravated by the speech made on Friday to the militia by Lubomir Strougal. It was not published for four days, but distorted versions of it leaked out almost at once. Strougal directly accused Dubcek of being incapable of exercising any control over the Press: 'Leading officials,

* It is not clear whether he was suffering from anything more serious than exhaustion. Wild but persistent rumours in Prague insisted that he was dying of leukaemia after being subjected to X-ray treatment in Moscow.

from Alexander Dubcek down, held many meetings with journalists, but their entreaties and explanations were not heeded.' He reviewed the dangerous activities that the country was 'witnessing today' and called upon the militia to 'exert all efforts to ensure that the Party and Society can overcome as soon as possible the present tense situation'.[8] When they read this speech many people saw it as a call for an armed putsch, and persistent rumours that Dubcek was not ill but in Moscow pleading for his political life did nothing to ease the tension.

The flaw in the putsch story is simply that it did not happen. A violent demonstration could have been easily provoked in that emotional and defiant city. Had the militia wanted to seize control and invite the Red Army back into Prague they could have staged the necessary conditions. Had either Strougal or Indra wanted to oust Dubcek the only thing that need have stopped them was the disapproval of the Kremlin.

This may in fact have been the deciding factor. The Russians probably appreciated that this was not a suitable moment to rid themselves of the slippery Dubcek. Given the euphoric resolve and unity in Czechoslovakia after the death of Jan Palach, protests against Dubcek's removal might have been immense, violent, and controllable only by bloodshed.

For although Palach's death had been taken up as a protest against Dubcek's leadership, the events of the week had done much to restore his former prestige. The government need not have ordered black flags on all public buildings; it could have asserted that Palach was mentally unstable; and it could have forbidden such huge demonstrations of public sympathy. The fact that it did none of these things reassured many people that Dubcek was after all the man they had thought him to be and that the government was still basically on their side. For a few days the people and their leaders were totally and as positively united as they had been in the most shocking days of August; it seemed as if some great turning point had been reached, and that from now on life would only improve.

Dubcek was infected with this enthusiasm. He had fluctuated all winter between intense depression and the uncertain feeling that he might after all be able to salvage something from the reform movement. His greatest concern had been to convince the Kremlin that he was fully in control of the Party and the nation; there was rarely very much evidence in his favour. At the beginning of January he had been acutely dispirited by his rejection of Smrkovsky and by the nation's rejection of him. But by the beginning of February his health had improved and he was feeling more confident than at perhaps any time since August. Russian resolve had been sadly shaken by Palach's martyrdom, which had had the same effect in Moscow as the Tet offensive had had in Washington. Dubcek believed the Czechs and Slovaks had demonstrated so clearly their loyalty to the leaders and principles of 1968 that the Russians must now admit his obvious authority in the country and make some concessions to it. He felt he was now strong enough to make some demands of Moscow and that he would soon be able to effect what had been since the invasion his main objective – the withdrawal of at least part of the occupation force. It was in this mood of renewed hope that, on 10 February, he made his most provocative and independent public speech since the invasion.

He had gone to speak to a meeting of farmers at his birthplace, the little village of Uhrovec deep in a valley in the West-Slovakian mountains. His speech was fairly informal, but the next day it was reported in the nation's papers and appeared to many people as an open and welcome challenge to the Russians. He said that he was convinced that Czechoslovakia must find its own road to socialism, 'according to our Czechoslovak conditions'. The Party must change its policies to fit the wishes of the people, not the other way around, for 'in a civilized world it is not possible to replace people and nations'. He asserted that it was useless for Czechoslovakia to adopt a merely defensive posture in trying to preserve the reforms that he had introduced a year ago – 'they must be fought for'.[9]

His speech was loudly acclaimed by the villagers, many of whom knew him from the days of the Slovak Revolt if not from 1921, and he was then taken over towards the *château*. There he found that the tiny cottage in which he had been born was now a national shrine and open to the public.

The little whitewashed shack which Stefan had rented on his return from the United States is now a museum to the glory not of Dubcek but of that other great Slovak hero who was born there – Ludovit Stur. Dubcek wandered around, curious, embarrassed and a little melancholy after his provocative speech. He was followed by a group of admiring peasants and a couple of tourists.

He was asked to sign the Visitors Book. He took up a whole page and wrote:

> I am proud of my village. I am proud of its citizens, the peasants, the workers, the teachers, the young ... all of whom continue to develop the traditions of the people of this region.
>
> I am proud of the history of Uhrovec ... which is written into the history of this land by the work of Stur and his friends, by the work of the Communist Party here [which his father Stefan had founded] and also by the battles during the Slovak Revolt [in which his brother Julius had been killed] and in the construction of our socialist state.
>
> I am proud of the fact that our village, lovely Uhrovec, has always been in the vanguard of social progress.
>
> Memories of the great Stur and his friends and of Uhrovec in revolt are always a great comfort to me in my work and also in my misfortunes.

The next visitor to the house was a Frenchman who signed his name under that of Dubcek and wrote ecstatically how overjoyed he was to be able to put his feet in the house where two such great Slovaks were born, especially Monsieur Dubcek. The whole page has now been bound in perspex so that Dubcek's coming home will always be remembered.

12
THEY KILL US FOR THEIR SPORT

Sua confessione hunc jugulo.

Cicero, *In verrem,* Oration II, chapter 5, section 64

'It's over and can't be helped, and that's one consolation, as they always say in Turkey.'

Charles Dickens, *Pickwick Papers.*

At nine o'clock on the evening of 28 March 1969 some six million Czechs and Slovaks saw on their television sets the referee blow the final whistle in a game of ice-hockey taking place in Stockholm. A paroxysm of uncontrolled and furious joy shuddered through the nation and, as the sets were switched off, millions of Czechs and Slovaks burst into song, tears and dance. Their country had just beaten the Soviet Union four–three.

Ice-hockey has been played in Czechoslovakia for sixty years and competes with football as the most popular sport. The excitement which either game engenders is religious, and a match against the Russians is a moment of greatest spiritual crisis. The two countries met twice during the World Ice-hockey Championship of 1969; on both occasions the Russians were beaten. Amongst the spectators in Stockholm were four hundred Czechs who had used up their visas and their tiny hard-currency allowances to travel to see the games. The Soviet Youth newspaper *Komsomolskaya Pravda* denounced them as 'counter-revolutionary scum' for they had around their necks placards with the varied legends: 'It's March Now, Not August', which was true enough, and 'Russians, Your Tanks Won't Help You This Time', which was not so self-evident.

Within minutes of the end of the second game, the dual carriageways leading into Prague from all the suburbs of the city were jammed with cars driving towards the centre. Both sides of the road were taken over by the incoming traffic and no cars were able to leave; all lanes were filled by the apparently endless flow of 'counter-revolutionary scum' whose destination was Wenceslas Square.

There several thousand ecstatic Czechs sang, shouted and clambered all over the Statue of St Wenceslas, uprooting the miniature forest which the police had planted around it to prevent its use as a shrine. It was not an attractive sight, for it was as much a demonstration of general xenophobia as of simple hatred of the Russians. A young Ghanaian engineering student was badly beaten up by a group of Czechs maniacally shouting 'Go home you black Communist bastard!' Open prejudice against the blacks is strong at the best of times in Bohemia (the Moravians are more tolerant and the Slovaks marginally better). On this night, when months of suppressed and impotent anger was spontaneously and violently released, it was unwise for any coloured person to be in Wenceslas Square.

In the lower half of the square the crowd converged on the offices of Aeroflot, the Russian State Airline. Someone threw a brick. And another. The plate-glass windows were smashed and the crowd invaded the office, ripped out all the furnishings, carried them into the street and made a huge bonfire. The police, helpless or sympathetic, stood by and did nothing.*

It was the end of Dubcek's leadership. The Russians seized upon the pillage as clear-cut evidence that he had totally failed to 'normalize' the country and insisted that he be dismissed. The day after the match, Soviet Ambassador Chervonenko handed a very strong protest to Svoboda, and, on 30 March, Soviet Deputy Foreign Minister Semyonov arrived in Prague to deliver Dubcek and Svoboda an ultimatum. Unless the Czechoslovak leadership could maintain order with its own troops, and it appeared that it could not, then the Soviet Army would have to intervene again.

Forty-eight hours later Marshal Grechko flew into Milovice, unexpected and uninvited by the country's leaders. Amongst the soldiers to welcome him at the airport twenty miles south

* Stories that the sacking of Aeroflot was arranged and led by pro-Russian provocateurs (e.g. *Sunday Times*, 27 April 1969) are widespread but unconfirmed.

of Prague was General Rytir, the old Novotnyite, who had come to win the Marshal's support for a Czech army putsch against Dubcek.[1] Grechko gave him no firm answer; his first action was to issue new orders to all occupation troops. In future they were not only allowed to shoot in self-defence but also empowered to impose martial law and take preventive action against any disturbances.

Svoboda and Dubcek were unable to meet their new visitors until 1 April, for the previous day they were visiting barracks in western Bohemia, apparently trying to ensure that the army did not go over to General Rytir. On 1 April, Semyonov, accompanying Grechko, presented Svoboda with a letter in which Brezhnev demanded the dismissal of Dubcek, his replacement by either Strougal or Bilak, and proposed 'as a temporary solution' a military government which might well be headed by the President himself. Grechko filled in some imaginative details of his own in which he assured Svoboda that it would be necessary for the Red Army to reoccupy Prague, Brno and Bratislava. Svoboda refused to consider the idea of military rule, but he realized how serious the Russians were and attempted to persuade Grechko to give him time to work out a compromise. After consulting Moscow, Semyonov and Grechko tentatively agreed.

At a meeting of the Czechoslovak Party Presidium that night there was considerable criticism of Dubcek's allegedly light-hearted handling of the crisis. Instead of sending telegrams of congratulations to the team he should have been busy punishing the demonstrators. It is believed that during this meeting Brezhnev spoke to Dubcek on the telephone and finally agreed to give him time to resign of his own free will before the Russians sent their troops back into Prague. But it was only a very short reprieve for, as Dubcek said, the riots would have to be paid for 'at a great political price'.[2]

He appeared on television on 3 April to make a short sad statement in which his exhaustion and disillusion were very apparent. He admitted that the Russian troops had been on the point of returning to Prague, but added without conviction that: 'the Party is still trying to preserve the *possibility** of continuing the post-January policies ... adventurous, pro-

* My italics. This was the first time he had used this conditional.

Alexander Dubcek, on television after his return from Moscow at the beginning of September 1968, and voting to approve the 'temporary' stationing of Soviet troops in Czechoslovakia, Central Committee, 17 November 1968.

Alexander Dubc
on his forty-seven
birthday, 27 Nc
ember 1968; arrivi
at the Central Co
mittee Building in t
morning, and (le
with his wife, Anı
in the evening.

vocative and anti-socialist actions [are] the main obstacles to the continuation of this policy.' And, he went on, in a voice and in words that seemed to show that he had given up the fight and was too tired to care: 'I would be pleased if you would all understand that the time we have for consolidation is not unlimited. Either we manage to safeguard immediately public order, prevent all extremist manifestations and anti-socialist or anti-Soviet statements, or the growing tension in the international situation and international relations will bring us to where we found ourselves at the end of August.'[3] His words had never before been so curt, so emotionless and so severe. The knowledge that his hopes of retaining the leadership had been utterly destroyed by the demonstrations must have been very hard to bear. He must have been convinced that all his work and the immense strain of the last seven months had been in vain.

On 11 April Brezhnev summoned Vladimir Koucky, the Czechoslovak Ambassador, to the Kremlin. He apparently instructed him to tell Svoboda that the Russians would not be patient for much longer and that if the Czechs did not get rid of Dubcek themselves then the Russians would do it for them. There is in fact no reason to suppose that either Dubcek or Svoboda were trying any longer to resist; they knew that in order to prevent a reoccupation Dubcek would have to go. But they were probably concerned about his successor and anxious that it should not be any of the men the Kremlin would have most liked – Strougal, Indra or Bilak. The only alternative was Gustav Husak.

That same day Husak publicly attacked Dubcek and his colleagues for dithering and for 'half-heartedness and lack of consistency'. He also called for a 'new Party and State leadership which will be able to guarantee peace and security'. It was a direct bid for Dubcek's job and it was successful. On 17 April 1969 Dubcek asked the Central Committee to relieve him of the First Secretaryship of the Communist Party of Czechoslovakia, and recommended that it elect Dr Gustav Husak to take his place. It did so. As Dubcek had done to Novotny so Husak did to Dubcek – once again a Slovak First Secretary had successfully schemed in Bratislava.

Announcing the change on television, Svoboda appealed to

the nation to remain calm, stressing that Husak had been Dubcek's own choice. 'The name of Comrade Dubcek,' said Svoboda, 'remains permanently in all our minds linked with the post-January policy of the Communist Party of Czechoslovakia. During his period in office he enjoyed great popularity and confidence among the people. I am convinced that in future we shall be able to rely on him in his work in highly responsible posts.'[4]

It was not to be. Dubcek kept his seat in the Presidium and on 28 April he was given Smrkovsky's old job – Chairmanship of the Assembly – but no other 'responsible post' was offered him. He lingered on through the sad summer of 1969 in a state of political limbo from which he was forced to watch his successor, Dr Husak, systematically destroy the achievements of Prague Spring.

Husak is complex. A revolutionary once. A humane Marxist intellectual once. Described by Svoboda the night he took over from Dubcek as 'honourable, sagacious, and experienced ... devoted to 'Party and people', and needing support 'in his difficult tasks'.

That his tasks were difficult few would deny. How honourable he has shown himself in fulfilling them is more open to question. Many Czechs and more Slovaks cautiously approved his election in the hope that he would prove both willing and able to stand up to the Russians more effectively than Dubcek. He was elected with the support of the 'progressives' in the Central Committee, but he has done little since to justify their trust. What is not yet certain is how far he has been willing and how far a reluctant agent to the dismantling of the reforms. It may be that his position has been as impossible as that of Dubcek himself. For after April 1969 he seemed to be pushed further and further towards the Russians by the activities of his jealous deputy, Dr Lubimir Strougal. More powerful in Prague than the Slovak Husak, Strougal used his position as Chairman of the Czech Party Bureau to counter Husak's influence over Bohemia and Moravia. Throughout these months Strougal was almost openly coveting Husak's job and was constantly trying to demonstrate to the Kremlin that anything Husak could do, he could do better. In July Husak was even driven to denying publicly that there was any rivalry between the two of them, thereby confirming the rumours of a serious split.

Which of them initially inspired the official campaign of fear leading up to the first anniversary of the invasion is not yet clear, but it is indisputable that the demonstrations of 21 August 1969 and the resultant Emergency Declaration were carefully planned at a high level of the Party.

For two months before the anniversary thousands of leaflets had been surreptitiously copied and passed from hand to secret hand throughout the country. They nearly all suggested that 21 August be regarded as a national day of mourning and that everyone act with the dignity and restraint appropriate to such an occasion.

The Party chose to pretend, however, that these documents called for counter-revolutionary violence against the State, and since the middle of July newspapers, radio and television had been filled with the most aggressive threats against all those 'agents of imperialism' and 'saboteurs of socialism', who were intent on stirring up anti-Soviet feelings on 21 August. The Czechs and Slovaks had been warned over and over again that the severest measures, no quarter given, would be taken against anyone who dared to demonstrate his disaffection on that day.

The purpose of this campaign was to discredit Dubcek, his 1968 reform policies, and those few of his colleagues who still stood by him. The propaganda was expressly designed to allow no one the luxury of forgetting or of ignoring the anniversary. It was intended as a challenge to the national pride and self respect of every Czech and every Slovak. A government which he despised was daring him into the streets. Of course he went.

Dubcek understood very well what was happening, but for several months he said nothing. He had been allowed to make no public speeches since 17 April. Indeed so loud was his silence throughout the summer that the government had to deny the rumours that he was dead.

After the April Plenum I was not entrusted with any Party

or official work. I was even officially excluded from various public functions attended by members of the Presidium, such as Party meetings and organized events. At first I thought that the intention was to keep me, as a former First Secretary, in the background. This I considered both right and natural; frankly I understood. Before the August anniversary I volunteered in the Presidium to voice in my constituency appropriate disapproval of the actions then being planned. I was indeed advised to do this by Dr Husak and later by the Presidium. I made the speech, but I am sorry to say that neither the radio nor the television published my views. Only *Ceteka* and *Rude Pravo* did so.*

That speech was clearly withdrawn very suddenly from circulation, but only after *Rude Pravo* had printed its first edition. It was remarkable for the way in which it contrasted with the hysterical abuse and warnings from Husak, Strougal and official Party agencies. Dubcek made no threats and attempted no intimidation; he merely pointed out how tragic it would be if the people allowed themselves to complicate further an already tense political situation. In other words, he was appealing to his people to resist the provocation offered them.

But the provocation was irresistible.

On 21 August the pleas for passive resistance were observed. The trams were empty of all except pensioners and invalids – everyone had walked to work. In the huge and usually packed Pilsner restaurant in the municipal hall only three tables were occupied – one of them by Poles. But the leaflets had also called for a national five-minute strike at midday, and throughout the country it was observed. In downtown Prague thousands of people left shops and offices and rushed to Wenceslas Square where they cried 'AT ZIJE DUBCEK!' in perhaps the most remarkable and spontaneous demonstration in the last remarkable and spontaneous twenty months.

It was, as planned, brutally broken up by the police, but the fighting continued for over twelve hours.† The entire char-

* To the Central Committee 26 September 1969. See Appendix 4.

† Fighting in the streets of Prague had begun on the 18th. On that day and on the 19th and 20th as well as the 21st the police brutally provoked and dis-

ade was cynical, but perhaps most cynical of all was the use of the tanks. A tank is an ineffective and vulnerable weapon in a city street, unless it uses its cannon. These tanks were not intended to quell the rioters – their purpose was symbolic. A demonstration that is put down by the police is merely hooliganism, but one which calls for the use of tanks clearly endangers the fabric of the State. The threat of counter-revolution had to be established in order to 'justify' merciless purges of the reformists and the imposition of the Emergency Laws which had been long drawn up, were announced the following day and were signed by Assembly Chairman Dubcek.

His signature did nothing to diminish the Press and Party campaign against him. On 23 August *Rude Pravo* triumphantly announced that, after extensive questioning of the prisoners, it was quite clear who was the leader of the counter-revolution. This meant simply that many, perhaps most, of those arrested, admitted that they were supporters of Dubcek. By the end of August the campaign had reached such a level that many people felt it could end in his being brought to trial. The technique was familiar; the publication of letters and resolutions demanding that he be made to accept responsibility for his errors of leadership. When enough such demands have been voiced it is easy to claim that they represent the will of the people.

It appears that there was a moment after 21 August when it was seriously debated whether or not Dubcek should be so fully punished. Husak is believed to have been against such a measure because of Dubcek's continued popularity in the country. In the last two weeks Husak's position had been strengthened by the emergence of Vasil Bilak as another serious contender for the leadership. This meant that the hard-line faction in the Central Committee, though still united in opposition to Husak, the product of the Prague Spring, was divided in its choice of his successor. Furthermore, by the ferocity with which he destroyed the demonstrations, Husak appears to have convinced the Kremlin that there was no need to look for a more ruthless leader.

---

persed the crowds. In Brno the battle continued until the 23rd and four people were killed.

Nevertheless Dubcek was under considerable pressure, both public and private, to recant and was told that if he admitted his mistakes at the next Central Committee meeting he would be guaranteed 'further honourable posts' in the Party or government. One of these was that of Mayor of Bratislava. He is reported to have turned the offer down with the words, 'Thank you very much, but I don't think I know enough about town-planning'.

Certainly the mayoralty – a function even more insignificant in Czechoslovakia than in England – was hardly a sufficient bribe to persuade him to indulge in the self-criticism that the Russians so wanted to hear. Nevertheless, in the week after 21 August, Dubcek is thought to have been quite undecided as to what he should do. Utterly demoralized by the violence of the demonstrations and by the fact that he had been forced to sign the Stalinist Emergency Laws, the temptations to renounce his work and to retire to a sinecure in Slovakia were very great.

But on 26 August he flew to Bratislava on an ordinary commercial flight – apparently he was no longer allowed official transport – and was very moved by the attitude of his fellow-passengers. One of them wrote Dubcek a letter in which he told him how many friends he had, how brilliant his programme had been, and how one day, despite all, Socialism with a Human Face would triumph. Dubcek read the note and began to weep. When the plane landed, tears were again in his eyes as he shook hands with all those passengers who waited to wish him well.

Dubcek then went for a short holiday around Slovakia. On 28 August he was in Banska Bystrica for the twenty-fifth anniversary of the Slovak National Revolt. Sitting silent on the platform he listened while Husak, who had in 1944 so bravely resisted Stalin and fought Hitler, now claimed that 'in no way could the invasion be considered a hostile act ... they came to help us'.[5] After these gloomy celebrations Dubcek continued his little tour which included Uhrovec, Trencin and Bratislava. Everywhere he met with the most moving and enthusiastic reception. He discovered to his delighted surprise that the people understood how much the signing of that decree must have hurt. He was amazed to find that he was still the one man whom they loved and trusted. He realized that, although people would probably also understand his recantation, he owed them something in return for their continued loyalty, and that so great was the disillusion in Czechoslovakia at the end of August that their memory of him was to many all-important. This gave an immense boost to his shattered self-confidence; his doubts and despair apparently dispelled by the faith that people continued to invest in him, he resolved to stand by his beliefs.

The Central Committee was due to meet on 6 September, but the session was delayed whilst further attempts were made to coerce him into recantation. Not only did Dubcek refuse to submit – he counter-attacked. At a meeting of the Presidium in the first week of September he demanded that the abusive Press and Party attacks upon him be ended. According to one eye-witness account:

> Comrade Dubcek entered in great anger, banged on the table and demanded to be allowed to speak. Making use of documents [he] recalled the support that he had received in the past from those comrades who were attacking him today. He recalled that Comrade Indra had warned him in 1968 not to have confidence in Comrade Cernik and had asked that he, rather than Cernik, should be made Prime Minister. He reminded Comrade Bilak of the promises of loyalty that he, Bilak, had given him, and how Bilak had constantly warned him against Comrade Husak, to whom no important Party post should be given. Comrade Dubcek then revealed a conversation he had had in August 1968 with Comrade Husak. According to Comrade Dubcek, Comrade Husak had deplored the slowness of the liberalization process in Slovakia, due he said to the activities of Comrade Bilak, who in Comrade Husak's opinion should be totally barred from any political office.[6]

This account provides a delightful picture of the utter opportunism and insincerity of the men with whom Dubcek was surrounded. One can only hope that Comrades Husak, Bilak and Indra were discomforted by this revelation of their scheming disloyalty to one another; it is unlikely.

The Central Committee session was delayed at least twice

more while increased pressure was brought to bear upon Dubcek. He still refused to recant, and the Plenum finally took place on 25–27 September. The meeting began with the presentation by Husak of a long report upon the problems of 1968 – the new official history which had been especially prepared by Milos Jakes and his Commission of Revision and Control. It was a comprehensive indictment of Dubcek's leadership. After its presentation Dubcek left the hall and for an hour apparently walked around the gardens of Hradcany Castle, still uncertain, and at the last minute wondering whether he should do as the Party asked him. He came back into the Chamber to make use of the fifteen minutes that had been allotted him for his self-defence or self criticism. He spoke for over an hour and it was the most skilful, passionate, moving and yet pathetic speech of his life.*

'As a politician,' said Dubcek, 'I am on the way out. This made me wonder at first whether I should speak out so frankly.' Like a priest accepting the discipline of the church, he continued, 'But I have come to the conclusion that in the present predicament the best I can do is speak sincerely. As a former leading official I think that the better this Central Committee and its leadership performs its tasks, the better for me.'

Referring to Husak's report, Dubcek asked the Central Committee to allow him to put his own point of view because 'I am convinced, and I am sure that the majority of the Central Committee shares my view, that it is necessary to evaluate the political course of the Party up to August [68] in order to defend its essential correctness, because one day, after we have solved the present negative tendencies in the Party and Society we will want to try and work out these principles again.'

He vigorously denied the slanders that were being made of him and the motives imputed him by the Party and Press:

> 'I cannot sanction the attempt that is being made to identify me with adventurers, and even with right-wingers who often complicated our work and made difficulties which I, together with other comrades, tried to overcome in the

* See Appendix 4.

past year. What you should instead do is evaluate objectively whether I fought sufficiently hard against those weaknesses of the Party which I admit existed.'

The most forensically detailed section of his speech dealt with the charge that he had concealed from his colleagues the extent of Soviet displeasure with his reforms.

He claimed that 'biased opinions and even downright lies' were now being published on this subject. 'I wrote to *Rude Pravo* and to *Tribuna* requesting them to publish my reply, but they refused to do so.' So Dubcek now insisted on his right to speak.

'I really cannot accept,' he said, 'the validity of assertions that a number of problems in our international relations arose because I – if I may use the phrase – tried to keep things secret.' In rebutting the charge, Dubcek produced much new and intriguing information on his relations with the Soviet leaders.

Of the Dresden meeting: 'It is neither true nor fair to say that I did not inform the Presidium ... Comrades Cernik, Kolder, Bilak, Lenart and myself agreed on what to pass on.' If there was any fault, Dubcek was saying, it was shared by these fellow-members of the Presidium who were also present at the encounter with the Russians. The point was all the sharper because of Bilak and Kolder's conduct during and after the invasion.

He admitted that, with these Presidium colleagues, he agreed to suppress news of certain demands made by the Russians at Dresden. It would have been 'unwise' according to Dubcek, 'to publicize the fact that there had been talk of changing the President of Czechoslovakia, etc.' He meant, of course, that the news was suppressed in order to avoid inflaming anti-Soviet public opinion.

As for the Warsaw Pact meeting in mid-July, which he had apparently refused to attend:

> Comrade Brezhnev informed me in a telephone conversation that the CPSU felt a meeting should take place on the 10th or 11th of July, 1968 ... As you know and as can be seen from the timing I said [these dates] were impossible because Presidium members were at the time away attend-

ing regional Conferences and because in a matter of such importance I could not decide on my own. The Presidium met on July 8th. We unanimously welcomed the opportunity to meet representatives of the fraternal Parties, but at the same time proposed to hold bilateral meetings in the immediate future rather than a joint meeting after an interval. Late at night on July 11th our Presidium received a letter signed by the five Parties requesting us once more to attend the Warsaw Meeting. We discussed the letter the following day, July 12th. We agreed to appeal to the fraternal Parties to show understanding for the proposed bilateral meetings, especially with the Soviet Presidium ... We had assumed that the definite date [of the joint meeting] would not be fixed until we had discussed the replies of the five Parties to our proposal.

He angrily denied that Chervonenko (the Soviet Ambassador) had informed him of the date of the proposed meeting.

The letter of July 11th which, as you know, was presented at the Plenary Session of July '68 does not give any date. It is now being said that Comrade Chervonenko personally informed me of the date. I am not aware – and there is no other way of putting it – that I had been informed. I had no more reason for secrecy at that time than I have now. What puzzles me is why I should have written to Comrade Brezhnev at Warsaw enquiring about a suitable date, had such a date already been known to me. Why would I have gone with Comrade Cernik to see Comrade Kadar? And why was there no date in the letter presented by Comrade Chervonenko on the day before the meeting of our Presidium? Why is there no trace of this date, supposedly conveyed in a telephone conversation on the day of the meeting, in the transcript made by Comrade Sojak? This really brings me to the end of my tether.

None of us in the Presidium imagined that the proposed bilateral meetings which were to precede the joint conference could be unacceptable to our allies. On the contrary we expected that in view of the complex situation and out of regard for our Party and our country, our request for a preliminary meeting with the CPSU would be given favourable consideration . . . Contrary to numerous abusive assertions we did not break off negotiations, we only proposed a different procedure.

After this minute analysis of the intricacies of his relationship with the Russians he concluded ironically: 'However . . . I do not intend to start a discussion of the problem, it's simply that I cannot make head or tail of it.'

Of his post-invasion attitude towards 'normalization' which he had managed so successfully to retard, he admitted: 'I am open to criticism and it is true that there was much to criticize.' Nevertheless, he argued, Dr Husak's regime would have been unable to act so decisively without the spade-work that he had done himself during the extremely complex period between August and April '69. 'To claim that normalization began only after 17 April is not objective. Please do not think that I do not fully appreciate the decisions of the April and May [69] Plenums [which did much to destroy the remnants of the reforms]. I do, for indeed I was one of their originators.' But it would be unfair to criticize him for not having implemented such resolutions himself – 'it was necessary, because of the violence of anti-Soviet emotions after the invasion, to proceed step by step with the process of retrenchment.'

He then regretted that he had not been allowed to plead for calm before the anniversary; or to condemn the demonstration after the event: 'I deplored such action and . . . had intended to speak out against attacks on the Socialist system and against the misuse of my name for those ends which I had previously condemned. The Presidium, however, informed me that it was not suitable for me to speak [or even to appear] in public. I accepted this, though I must admit that I did not consider the decision quite correct.'

Dubcek even tried to show that he had supported the neo-Stalinist emergency laws imposed on 22 August: 'As you know, I was present when the Presidium of the Federal Assembly discussed the law . . . and I signed the Bill. Please let me remind you of this. I mention the matter hoping that a more correct view of the question will be taken and that my activity since the May Plenary Session will be better understood.' In fact, his signature as Chairman of the Assembly was a constitutional nicety, hardly more significant than that of the Queen on an Act of Parliament.

Dubcek thus paid lip-service to all Dr Husak's most repressive measures. But having done so, he devoted a large part of his speech to condemnation of the inevitable effects of such unpopular authoritarianism. He unhappily pretended not to be aware that a drastic purge of liberals was already taking place in party organizations throughout the country and warned:

> Should an extensive Party purge with all its economic consequences be used as a political tool . . . disruption would ensue in both the Party and society.
>
> I may be seeing things in a different light from others but I have come to the conclusion that in practice the main blow would be directed not against anti-Party forces, as it should be, but in fact against Party members.

Dubcek of course knew that this was exactly what was happening. 'I hope,' he said, apologetically, 'that I will not be accused of protecting right-wing or even anti-socialist forces when I say that the struggle against them must be combined with an attempt to gain the support of true Communists'.

'The Party would not benefit if some functionaries who had proved incompetent long ago – and that means before January, 1968 – were to exploit the present difficult situation for personal revenge or as an opportunity to obtain a better job.' This, too, of course, was exactly what was happening as Dubcek spoke. Since July neo-Stalinists had been climbing back up the *apparat*.

With elaborate understatement, he said that he had been reflecting upon the differences between this approach to the problem and that of the present leadership. He wondered which was the more effective. 'According to information supplied by Comrade Matejka* during the past month Party meetings in Prague have been attended by only about 16% of members.' During 1968, said Dubcek, he had always been convinced that the vast majority of the Party supported the leadership's policies.

* Matejka, head of the Prague City Party, was dismissed in mid-December and replaced by a hard-liner.

Given his years of devotion to the Soviet Union, perhaps his present attitude towards the Russians was the most interesting of all. He admitted that he understood Soviet concern: 'We recognized the right of our allies to criticize our shortcomings and we discussed them. There was no conflict about that .... Discussions centred on the appropriate methods and opportunities for dealing with negative phenomena. I was convinced that it would solve nothing to act rashly [against anti-socialist forces]. I feared that with the bath-water we might also throw out the January baby, born as it was of such labour [*sic*].' He was certain that 'we could ... extend democratic rights and choose a gradual way of overcoming the negative influence which emerged after January precisely because our socialist base was and still is safeguarded by strong internal forces and above all by our alliance with the Soviet Union.'

He even apologized for not having realized that there was a counter-revolution in Czechoslovakia. This mistake had been made 'mainly because by counter-revolution we understand ... an imminent threat to socialism, an imminent attack by anti-socialist forces.'

'I admit that I read the Soviet proclamation [of invasion] with sorrow and regret, because our comrades had not informed any of us four leaders of the Party and Government.' Nevertheless he asserted that nothing could shake his loyalty to the Russians: 'I agree that Soviet troops did not come here to put an end to our socialist development. They came, as comrades have said, out of fear for the fate of socialism in our country.' Considering, however, that Dubcek had devoted so much time to proving that there was no threat, this was roughly equivalent to saying that the Russians were 'honourable men'.

Then follows one of the most ironic, yet also pathetic, passages of the speech. Dubcek demanded an end to purges and victimization – on the grounds that this could only harm the Soviet Union. He could not believe, he maintained, that the Russians came to 'end all such political activity as aims at strengthening and developing socialism in our country .... Let no one try to use the Soviet Union as cover for an effort to revive dogmatism, or to enforce stagnation in our political work. This would discredit the Soviet Union not only in the eyes of our own people but in the eyes of the world.' His tenderness for the Soviet image extends even to his own arrest on the night on the invasion. 'At dawn, members of the State Security, and I stress *our* State Security, came to my office and arrested me saying that within two hours it would be decided what was to be done to me . . . . I am mentioning this only because I do not want all the blame to be put on our allies.'

Dubcek ended by asserting that he accepted the new conclusions that were being drawn from his actions: 'My activities in the past are now producing new consequences and new conclusions are being drawn. As I have said I accept them. But once more I ask you not to put me where I do not belong. Do not ascribe to my personality and character motives which, as you very well know, are alien to me. I have tried to form an opinion of some problems and views and, as you will agree, this is not an easy matter for me. In view of my own involvement, it is difficult to avoid a personal approach, and I have not been able to do so. I am convinced that you will understand this, believe me, I want to be a useful member of our Party and the Central Committee.'

The brilliance of this speech lay in its subtle irony and in the way in which Dubcek managed to keep all of his options open. He was not openly defiant. He did not stand steadfastly by his record and denounce his critics. By turns sardonic, humble and proud, he admitted to personal errors while refusing to renounce his reforms. He made careful obeisance to Gustav Husak, praised him for his hard line and then quietly denigrated everything that Husak had done. He refused to condemn the Russians but would not condone the invasion. His attacks upon his enemies were never open – only implied. The speech was a beautiful blend: it must have delighted most of his supporters in the Central Committee but, were he ever to be brought to trial, he said virtually nothing that could help the prosecution.

Perhaps Dubcek himself summed up Prague Spring better than it could ever be done when he said:

After January we tried to restore the unity of socialist

forces and to find a common factor between the various strata of society interested in developing socialism rather than continuing the old policy of division and disintegration. That was why the post-January policy was so spontaneously accepted by the people . . . (who) came to have increasing trust in socialism and more and more faith that they could be useful members of society and that they would no longer just be ordered about, remonstrated with and abused, as had so often happened in the past.'

He knew that his experiment had failed, but he was still unalterably convinced of its virtues; he realised that there was little hope that Czechoslovak socialism would have a 'Human Face' in the near future, but he still believed that this was the correct answer to the problems of modern communism:

> Do not forget that in January we were not prompted by some individual subjective wish, but forced by the true state of the Party and Society to set out on a new course in search of new and more effective ways of dealing with the problems of society. Let us therefore subject last year's experiences to a thorough analysis (and) let us learn from it.

As he sat down, he asked to be allowed 'to take an active part in socialist development and in the strengthening of our internationalist ties with our socialist allies and the Soviet Union for which, as you well know, I have especially close feelings. . . .'

At the end of the session he was dismissed from the Presidium and removed from the Chairmanship of the National Assembly.

13

THE RAINBOW'S END

'The philosophers have only interpreted the world. Our business is to change it.'

Karl Marx, *Theses on Feuerbach.*

'Our programme is based on the conviction that man and mankind are capable not only of learning about the world but also of changing it.'

Alexander Dubcek, in a speech on Rip Hill, Bohemia, 16 May 1968.

'Dubcekism stood for right-wing opportunism and was characterised by its double-faced policy and a contradiction between words and deeds. [It was] a loss of class approach in solving the vital internal and international problems, a complete failure to understand the international context of Czechoslovak development in the present world divided along class lines.'

Pravda (Bratislava), 8 October 1969.

On 31 May 1969 Stefan Dubcek died; he was seventy-seven. An uneducated carpenter, he had wandered the world in search of the good life. He thought at first that he had found it in Stalin's Russia but was disillusioned by the Terror (more so than Alexander) and angry when all foreigners were virtually thrown out of the Soviet Union. Hating and hated by Novotny and Siroky he had never risen as he deserved in the Slovak Party hierarchy and by the mid-sixties he had begun to feel that his life's search had been in vain. Then in 1968 his own son discovered what Stefan had always sought. The old man was overjoyed but exhausted by those days in August and by the vicarious suffering for his son that he had since endured. He died sad but proud, convinced that Lenin would have agreed with Alexander and that at last the answers to the problems of society had been found.

Whether or not the Czechoslovak experiment was strictly Leninist or Marxist-Leninist is a barren dispute. For, with patience, almost any doctrine can be shown to originate in the writings of either or both of them. More interesting is to ask whether the failure of 'Dubcekism' was simply a function of the Czechoslovak environment or whether the system itself was inherently unstable and impractical. The answer to this question is of significance not only for the light it throws upon Soviet self-justifications but also in a much wider context. If Dubcek's Socialism with a Human Face can be shown to be more than a tantalizing but illusory vision – and clearly Luigi Longo believes it to be more – then the experiment of 1968 holds great promise. For Dubcek was trying to create a Marxist democracy genuinely responsive to the wishes and aspirations of its people. If he was succeeding, he has then provided the world with a real alternative to the blind arrogance of American capitalism, to the apparently endemic marriage of inefficiency and dissatisfaction of the bourgeois-democratic mixed economy, and to the mindless inhumanity of the Soviet dictatorship.

Perhaps the vastness of what Czechoslovakia was trying to achieve in 1968 was best summarized by Eduard Goldstuecker, one of the architects of Prague Spring:

> This transition from necessary revolutionary dictatorship to a system of legal guarantees of democratic rights has so far succeeded nowhere. In the past every revolution has run aground on this problem. We are making the attempt for the first time in history, I believe, to carry through this complicated process. And we have, I believe, grounds to hope that we shall be successful.[1]

During those eight months the Czechoslovak Communist Party unprecedentedly became a genuine mass movement that could claim the support of the vast majority of the nation. To Dubcek this was joy, for he had long considered that the Party should embody and lead a popular crusade rather than represent a narrow political élite. Not surprisingly he invested in his new-found support a significance that it did not perhaps altogether deserve.

At the beginning of April he gave an interview to *L'Humanité,* the paper of the French Communist Party. He was asked his opinion of Western speculation that his reforms might lead to a weakening of the socialist system in Czechoslovakia and might therefore impair his country's relations with the

Soviet Union and its other allies. He replied that this was only a pious wish of the West and that it was quite absurd.

> I do not know why a socialism which is based on the vigorous functioning of all democratic principles and on the people's free right to express their views should be any less solid. On the contrary, I am deeply convinced that the democratic atmosphere in the Party and in public life will result in the strengthening of the unity of our socialist society and we shall win over to active collaboration all the capable and talented citizens of our country.[2]

He went on:

> The freedom of speech, the right of every man to his own opinion, makes socialism stronger. What permits us to make such a judgment? First the fact that for so many years one has never seen as one sees now so many people committing themselves so directly and with such conviction to the cause of socialism.

With touching simplicity he justified his work on the grounds that 'so many people have now lost the feeling of uselessness, a feeling that they had had for a very long time'.

In these statements lies the explanation of Dubcek's single-minded determination to continue along the road on which he had started out. Were it not too derogatory a description, his conviction that his reforms could be the salvation of the socialism both within and without his country might be described as obsessional. He stubbornly refused throughout that summer even to conceive that he could be harming the cause of the international proletariat.

Whether or not he was correct really depends on the quality of the enthusiasm with which those millions of Czechs and Slovaks felt and shouted AT ZIJE DUBCEK! This is difficult to gauge but there is one important point which throws some doubt upon the validity of Dubcek's confidence. It was not only support for the Communist Party which grew through the spring and summer of 1968: interest in the other parties within the National Front also increased and by the end of March membership of the People's Party had grown from 21,328 in January to over 40,000.

It might be argued that this growth was minimal, even that it was proof of electoral content with the Communists and that it was anyway Communist policy to allow the other parties within the Front to expand and achieve some sort of significance. On the other hand it had occurred before the People's Party had really begun to take an independent line. As the summer deepened so did the demands and support of both People's and Socialist Parties, encouraged by the way in which their respective papers, *Lidova Demokracie* and *Svobodne Slovo* used their new-found freedom to demand the establishment of free opposition parties.

These calls began at the end of March. On 22 March *Svobodne Slovo* published an open letter to Dubcek calling for a multi-party system; on 24 March *Lidova Demokracie* issued a challenge to the Communists, asserting that the People's Party 'must rid itself as soon as possible of the complex of subordination and build up the position of a free citizen with equal rights who has unambiguously entered the present revitalizing process and wants by his programme to win more followers'.

By mid-July demands for opposition parties had taken three distinct philosophical forms: some intellectuals like Vaclav Havel and Ivan Svitak argued for full parliamentary democracy in the Western sense.[4] Others – Michal Lakatos and Zora Jesenska – considered that, for the time being at any rate, independent, equal parties could co-operate within the National Front on the same basis as they had before the 1948 revolution.[5] The two politicians Zdenek Mlynar and Josef Spacek had vaguer concepts of the right to dissent from and oppose Party decisions, either within the National Front, or outside it through spontaneous public action.[6] It is useful to examine these demands in the light of Party policy towards the idea of opposition.

One of the most important premisses upon which the Prague reforms were founded was that the old Marxist concept that government should be based only on 'the unity of the interests of the entire people' had little validity for the second half of the twentieth century – if indeed it was ever very useful at all. The Action Programme conceived of more emphasis being placed on the interests of different groups;

it recognized the absurdity of pretending that the interests of all groups were the same. This had implications for the leading role of the Party:

> In the past the leading role of the Party was often conceived of as a monopolistic concentration of power in the hands of Party bodies. This corresponded to the false premiss that the Party is the instrument of the dictatorship of the proletariat. . . . The Party's goal is not to become the universal 'caretaker of society'. . . . Its mission lies primarily in arousing socialist perceptives and in winning over all workers by systematic persuasion, as well as by the personal example of Communists. . . . The Party cannot represent the entire scale of social interests. The political expression of the many-sided interests of society is the whole National Front. . . . The Party policy must not lead to non-Communists getting the impression that their rights and freedom are limited by the role of the Party. On the contrary they must see in the Party a guarantee of their rights, freedom and interests.[7]

Dubcek's ideas on the reform of the Party's leading role are less clearly expressed. Nothing was more important for him than that the Party should remain the guiding light and arbiter of the nation's life. But he did make proposals in the spring that elections should be 'fairer'. These suggestions were as unsatisfactory as they were unclear, for they merely served to increase speculation that the new regime was prepared to allow the growth of Western-type opposition. In an interview with *L'Unita,* the Italian Communist Party paper on 31 March Dubcek said that the Government, as opposed to the Party, must really be allowed to govern and Parliament totally to legislate. Until 1969 both were the creatures of the Communists. 'This means,' he said, 'that it is necessary to restore to elections their true meaning, which is that of a choice between different candidates. From this follows logically much greater freedom of expression . . . much greater, in any case, than that which existed under rigid centralism.' He did not answer the vital question of how elections could provide a genuine choice unless the candidates were representing equal parties, or of how this could be achieved and the Communists yet retain the reins of power. When he was asked at the beginning of April what he thought of the current nation-wide debate on the need for opposition parties he merely said that he could see no reason for the formation of an opposition since the decisions taken at the Committee meetings of January and April opened a wide area of disagreement within the Communist Party itself.[8] This was of course true. The fact that he had not purged the Party of Novotnyites made it perhaps one of the least monolithic ruling Communist Parties in the world. It was split down the middle.

He totally dismissed the idea of a bourgeois two-party democracy to which so many of his countrymen seemed attached. His rejection was largely ideological, but he also genuinely believed that such a system does not really work.

> Our experience from 1945–8 gives sufficient proof that such [parties] in political life [are] detrimental to the interests of the working people. Our democracy must therefore provide also for the right of working people to take a direct interest in the power of the state, to have their representatives in elected bodies: through the trade unions, through an organization of farming people, organizations of youth, women's organizations and the like. The Communist Party is of the opinion that these organizations are equal partners in the National Front.[9]

According to Dubcek socialist democracy differed from social-democracy in two ways:

> First of all it will have to settle the problems which no bourgeois democracy has so far tackled or even formulated: how the working people themselves, workers, and technicians ... can have a say in the management and administration of society. How to make sure that no procedural system can ... carry out State policy without reference to or even against the interests of workers and working people. Socialist democracy cannot develop as a system in which policies are decided by political parties alone.[10]

Secondly that:

> the relations between political parties ... must be a re-

> lation of partnership and co-operation, not one of struggle for redividing power in the State, which is characteristic of a bourgeois political system.

He would never countenance the setting-up of an opposition party outside the National Front, and maintained that within the Front the clash of views and political autonomy necessary for democracy would be genuine but 'based on a common socialist programme'.[11]

It is here that one comes up against the basic and unresolved conflict in Dubcek's political philosophy. On the one hand it was impossible for the Communist Party to lead the country forward 'without the active participation of all strata of society or without the personal feeling of every citizen that he has the inalienable right to express his views without any impediment or restriction in regard to all important questions of management and administration of the country'[12] On the other hand the Party has to maintain its leading role in society and should remain at least *primus inter pares* within the National Front.

How far was Dubcek prepared to allow the expression of opinion? If dissent and the voicing of minority views are permitted, then it is not easy to summon convincing arguments to deny the right of like-minded individuals to organize and lobby for public support. This was happening in Czechoslovakia in July 1968 with the formation and growth of such clubs as K231 and KAN.* Some decision on this problem would have had to have been made, for by the end of the summer demands were rife for an opposition and 'guarantees' more than those the Party had considered providing by a democratization of the National Front.

The Action Programme specified that 'public opinion polls must be systematically used in preparing important decisions'.[13] It is worth taking up this point and applying it to what Dubcek was trying to do.

The *Vecerni Praha* poll of July 1968 has already been quoted. Perhaps more reliable and more relevant was a survey taken in May–June by *Rude Pravo.* On 13 May the paper published an extensive questionnaire prepared by its editors in

* See above, Chapter 9, p. 174.

collaboration with the Institute of Political Sciences. All of the detailed questions related to the current political development, and 38,000 readers took part. The results were revealed on 27 June. This was the same day as the publication of the '2,000 Words Manifesto' and in that furore the poll was largely ignored. But it was perhaps of even greater significance than Vaculik's demand for progress and it must have caused the Russians still more concern than that 'counter-revolutionary' document.

One of its most important and, for Dubcek, most frightening findings was that despite the almost unanimous support within the country for the Party at the time, 90% of the non-Party members who answered wanted the establishment of free opposition parties. 75% of these respondents maintained that the Communist Party was not itself a necessary precondition for the development of the sort of democracy that Dubcek was trying to produce. In other words they thought that the same thing could be done at least as well in a social democracy.

Perhaps even more disturbing to Dubcek, as well as to the Russians, than the obviously superficial nature of the Party's support amongst the public was the turmoil into which the reforms had thrown Party members: the poll showed them to have lost their vital sense of mission. 55% of them thought that there should be other parties on an equal footing with themselves. This was an enormously high proportion in favour of the Party's abandoning what is virtually its *raison d'être* – its leading role. Even worse, a large number of Party members considered that a humane socialism could be achieved without the Communist Party; 27% of Party members with only primary education believed this, and, more alarming, 38% of members with higher education.

All this suggests that not only for the general public but also for a large minority of Party members the most important factor in the synthesis of 'democratic socialism' was the 'democracy'. They saw Dubcek's reforms as extending democracy rather than strengthening the Party. So far as it is valid to make the distinction, one might argue that the Party was popular for what it was doing rather than for itself. It was 'de-Stalinizing'; it was opening up areas of liberty; it was improving the standard of life in the country. Furthermore, it was, for a short time, standing up to a bullying external enemy.

At some stage Dubcek would have had to answer the demands for opposition outside the National Front. He could have either accepted some of them, thus limiting the Party's ultimate monopoly of power and thereby confirming his allies' worst fears of a 'counter-revolution'; or he could have forbidden any further discussion of and demands for opposition, thereby destroying the total freedom of speech which had been so necessary to his maintenance of power and which was so vital and distinguishing a feature of Prague Spring. Given the *Rude Pravo* poll and the nature of his support within the country, this might have meant that his popularity disintegrated over night.

The decision of what to do in this situation was not a personal one – it was collective within the Presidium. But it must have presented Dubcek with a dilemma which illustrates well the contradictions within him. Leaving aside international pressures such as were applied to him by his Warsaw Pact allies, should he abandon the Party or should he abandon the people?

The answer to this question apparently lies in the emotional and unhappy speech that he made to the Central Committee on 31 August 1969. Before 21 August, said Dubcek: 'A new law on the National Front was prepared. This law was intended to make it impossible to form new political parties . . . we had prepared the liquidation of K231 and decided that KAN should not be permitted to become legal'.*

If this is true – and he confirms it in his September 1969 speech to the Committee† – then the 'doves' in the Kremlin were right. Had they been a little more patient, an invasion might well have proved unnecessary – Dubcek was about to do their work for them: the Prague experiment with 'Socialist-Democracy' had failed.

On 15 December 1969 the Czechoslovak News Agency,

* This speech has not been published before.

† See Appendix 4.

Ceteka, announced that Alexander Dubcek was to be appointed his country's ambassador to Turkey. Although rumours of the posting had already been leaked, its confirmation came as a surprise to most Czechs and Slovaks. It was seen as a considerable success for the 'centrists' in the Party who had, since August, sought to protect Dubcek from further punishment and conversely as a defeat for the neo-Stalinists who had demanded his complete humiliation and possibly even trial.

He was given the job for two reasons. First of all, his immense popularity within Czechoslovakia was a source of embarrassment to the regime and presumably also to himself, for it made a normal life quite impossible. At the beginning of December he had driven from Prague to Bratislava and stopped en route for a drink in the town of Caslav. Within ten minutes the café was filled with about 150 people. Despite the protests of Dubcek's security man, the doors were locked and Dubcek was not allowed to leave. For two hours the people made him talk and drink with them.

Because of this and similar incidents he was confined to his house in Bratislava where, guarded by a fierce Alsatian, he kept himself from the devotion of his supporters. But so long as he remained, even idle, within the country, he provided a focus for discontent.

On Sunday 25 January 1970 Dubcek and his wife drove in a black Tatra car up the hill from Prague to the airport. There a small group of people was waiting to see him off to Turkey. As he walked disconsolately towards the customs, a woman rushed forward and thrust a small bouquet of red roses into his hands. Dubcek smiled weakly, brushed the tears from his cheeks and hurried on. Anna, already weeping at the thought of exile and of separation from their sons, cried the harder.

Dubcek flew out from Czechoslovakia exactly one year after Jan Palach was buried. Palach left behind him a nation reunited and exhilarated by his flaming martyrdom, prepared to place some trust in its leaders and able to believe that the future still had some hope. But during the last twelve months all optimism had been dissipated; Dubcek left a Czechoslovakia still remarkably united, but only in its rejection of its present Government, not in hope for the future.

He and Anna were booked on an ordinary Czechoslovak Airlines flight to Istanbul. On the journey they were photographed incessantly by an enterprising West German photographer who had secured himself a ticket. When the plane arrived in Istanbul late that evening, the Turkish police proved quite incapable of controlling the newsmen who had come to record the arrival in Asia of the former First Secretary of the Czechoslovak Communist Party. Dubcek pushed, sweating, through the mob and rushed towards a lavatory. He locked himself in and shouted through the door that he would not come out until the police guaranteed him an unmolested exit.

The next day he and Anna flew on to Ankara. The airport was filled with right-wing student demonstrators shouting their approval and acclaiming him the true leader of his country. The mockery of their welcome for Dubcek himself can easily be understood, and nothing that followed made his position any the more tolerable. Indeed, over the next few weeks he was subjected to humiliations and restrictions that were as unnecessary as they were cruel.

His popularity in Turkey was neither widespread nor long-lasting. Within a week he had insulted and alienated the establishment of Ankara and the editors of Turkey's right-wing newspapers. For he called publicly on the Soviet Ambassador, Vasily Grubyakov, before he formally presented his credentials to the Turkish President. After that diplomatic indiscretion, neatly arranged by Soviet connoisseurs of ambassadorial form, the new Slovak in Ankara became noticeably less attractive to his hosts.

It is unlikely that he was over-concerned by his bad press, and it must have been a relief to be freed from the plaudits of right-wing students, but the incident clearly illustrated his relationship with Grubyakov. From the first the Soviet ambassador, who had been Stalin's consul in Istanbul, established himself as Dubcek's keeper. Almost everywhere that Dubcek went, Grubyakov went also. At diplomatic receptions Dubcek was able to exchange only a few words in his elementary English with other guests before Grubyakov motioned him away. And wherever the Soviet could not accompany him, there was another watchdog, equally severe and equally ubiquitous, within the Czechoslovak Embassy itself. S. Spanily, Third Secretary in name, was a secret policeman in fact: his only job, to keep Dubcek ever under his gaze. He did so.

And so, for Dubcek, life in Ankara sank quickly into a terrible monotony and there must have been many occasions when he wished that he was, after all, Mayor of Bratislava. The Turkish capital is, at the best of times, a depressing and unattractive town – a mongrel Eur-Asian city without mystique, a dirty and displaced light industrial slum set in an Asian dustbowl of unrelieved peasant poverty. The diplomatic colony is little more inspiring than the rest of the town: the Czechoslovak Embassy squats at the bottom of a hill near the Japanese, the Poles and the Swiss. The house is square and khaki-coloured; it is the building that so successfully housed von Pappen, Hitler's emissary during World War Two – how far that particular irony was appreciated by Dubcek must remain a matter of doubtful speculation. Its garden is small and affords little space for exercise. But it was all that Dubcek could take. For on each of the two occasions when he and Anna tried to walk up the hill, tried to escape their dreary prison, they were forced to scuttle back, on Spanily's orders, to avoid the snapping of a Leica hidden in the trees and belonging to a persistent if insensitive Turkish photographer, Mustafa Istemi.

Dubcek and Anna did not have long to wander through their Turkish garden together. On 25 March, just six weeks after they had arrived, Anna returned to Czechoslovakia. Her departure came just two days after Rude Pravo had announced that Dubcek was suspended from membership of the Czechoslovak Communist Party, pending further enquiries into his conduct during 1968–9. It seems reasonable to infer that Anna's departure was merely preparatory to Dubcek's own return to Prague.

For this latest demotion was not only a heartrending humiliation for Dubcek himself, it was also seen as yet another sign that Gustav Husak was losing power to the hardliners and revanchists in his Party. The demands that Dubcek and his reformist colleagues be fully punished for their crimes of revisionism were growing ever more stridently aggressive and confident. Husak's ploy to isolate Dubcek in an Asian wilderness in the hope that he could then be forgotten was apparently to have only a shortlived success. For no East European country has ever had an ambassador who was an expelled or even a suspended member of its Party.

Realising that her husband would probably soon be brought back to Czechoslovakia, Anna spent a month after her return home to Bratislava, visiting all their former friends in the Slovak Party. She pleaded with them to put in a good word for Dubcek whenever his future came under discussion. She implored them not to forget their comradeship with him or his exemplary record of thirty years service to the Party, and asked that in view of all this he should be protected from further indignities. But she found that few of these erstwhile friends were able to remember those qualities of which she spoke.

His suspension only intensified for Dubcek his meaningless life in a diplomatic limbo. Without Anna, he was completely alone amongst an embarrassed, if not hostile staff. For, no longer possessing the rights of an ordinary Party member, he was unable even to attend Party meetings in his own Embassy. While Spanily and the others discussed Prague's orders for his future, Dubcek himself was confined to his room, or reduced to walking round and round the garden. The ambassador now had the rank of office boy.

It appears that he was being offered the choice of three futures. Either he could continue to resist the pressures upon him to recant, or he could submit to those demands and betray his Prague Spring in one of two ways. He could return to Prague, face a Party Commission, admit his 'crimes', deny 1968, and then hope for the tolerable exile of a Slovak village. Alternatively, he could betray his work equally effectively by defecting to the West. Indeed, some observers saw the Ankara appointment and the subsequent pressures upon him in just these terms: Dubcek was being offered the opportunity (if not being actually encouraged) to sell himself to the West. The attractions of this course to the Government of Czechoslovakia were obvious: they would at one and the same time be rid of an extreme embarrassment and the charges that Dubcek was a petty-bourgeois revisionist would automatically be proven. But given what is known of Dubcek's character it seems extremely unlikely that he would be willing thus to oblige his enemies. Quite apart from the fact that to do so would involve total separation from his family, he is simply not defector material. He would find life as the helpmate of the CIA, the pampered poodle of the bourgeoisie and the darling of the Western Press quite intolerable. Perhaps even the risks of returning home to a Party trial (whether or not he decided to recant) would have been less frightening to him.

Unlike most European Communist leaders he has never lived under either feudalism or capitalism. Indeed, he has had only the three years 1945-8 not under dictatorship; and yet he realizes better than most East-European politicians the advantages of some of the 'bourgeois liberties'. His work has been confined to a tiny area (about as big as Norfolk and Suffolk) of a peasant country in the centre of Europe; yet he is not parochial. For the last twenty years he has worked entirely in the narrow and constricting mould of a typical *apparatchik* in one of the most rigid societies of the world; that mould has not formed him as it has formed most of his peers.

His training has been to accept orders from above without question; his curious and largely untrained mind has refused to allow him to do so. His life has been a systematic indoctrination that the Party is always right; he was able to admit that the Party was often wrong. He has lived through Stalin's Terror, through the purges of the 'fifties, through all the illogical twists of de-Stalinization; and yet he has never questioned his devotion to and faith in the Soviet Union. He has fought as a Partisan in the Slovak Revolt, he has watched dozens of friends die or disappear throughout his life; and yet he is a man who weeps with joy when he watches his favourite football team win a match or when someone asks for his autograph, and with real sorrow when he hears a story of individual suffering. His whole career has been dedicated to the pursuit of the material; his beliefs and commitments are often spiritual in their intensity. He has been instructed to live only by the precepts of 'scientific' Marxism-Leninism;

his strongest ties have always been personal and emotional, never theoretical.

His work has always been amidst political opportunists and Party hacks as concerned to exploit the working class as any capitalist; he has retained complete faith in the goodness of human nature and the work of Party workers. He has spent a lifetime in politics; he is prepared to accept anyone at his face value.

His driving force has always been a moral or an emotional commitment, not a mental conviction, and he does not value things so much by Marxist standards as by simpler and more general moral principles. The Communist who was married in church, the *apparatchik* who defended the 'traitor' Karol Smidke, at a time when such deviation could mean death and usually meant dismissal, is a man to whom personal relationships and ideals are much more important than ideological purities.

With all this he is a good political tactician. His scheming against Novotny from Bratislava was subtle and successful. His speech to the Central Committee in September 1969 was brilliantly devious. Indeed it sums up very well his position during the reform movement. It was not the passionate self-defence that some of his supporters would have liked to hear. He stood up for his reforms but admitted that they had sometimes been ill-administered. He accepted criticisms that had been made of him and some of the Party's rewriting of history. In fact he compromised. As he always has done and as any successful politician must.

His spontaneous exclamation on the night of 20–21 August says a lot about him: it *was* the tragedy of his life, and he was for a moment quite unable to understand how it could have happened to him. His devotion to the Soviet Union had never been assumed, and he simply could not envisage receiving such treatment at her hands. As he sadly said to the Central Committee in September 1969:

> Though I was unable by words and deeds to convince some of my colleagues and our allies that we were able unaided to implement and protect our basically correct policy, and even if I may have to bear the consequences of this after

> thirty years' devoted work for the Party. I can say in all honesty that none of this can in any way change my convictions or my feelings towards the Soviet Union.

He does not suspect anyone of lying to him; yet he is prepared to deceive his friends in order to save their feelings and to protect himself. His enemies call him naive; so do his friends. Both are right. Some critics accuse him of indecisiveness, others of stubbornness. Both are true. He often takes a long time to make up his mind; yet once he has decided nothing will induce him to alter his opinion.

He is badly educated and he is not an intellectual; yet he has never been afraid to surround himself with the best minds available and to contradict them if he thought them wrong. He is very shy and self-effacing; yet he was quite convinced that he had discovered in 1968 that for which philosophers and philanthropists have for centuries searched – the just society.

He may have been right.

In emphasizing just one of the more obvious contradictions in Dubcek's plans and in questioning the loyalty of the Czechoslovak people to its Communist Party, I do not wish to call into doubt the validity of his attempt to encourage socialism to emerge from the suffocating chrysalis in which the Soviet Union has for the last forty years compelled it to remain.

Dubcek ended this speech of devious defence by making 'one final request to the Central Committee':

> Do not forget that in January we were not prompted by some individual subjective wish but forced by the true state of the Party and society to search for new and more effective ways of dealing with society's problems. Let us therefore subject last year's experience to a thorough analysis, let us learn from it in order to counter the negative aspects of post-January development.

This should be done, for Dubcek and Dubcekism are one of the more important phenomena of the post-war world. Scepticism about the hypothctical future of his experiment may be misplaced. It is possible that despite his curtailing of fully free expression and his banning of embryo oppositions, he could have persuaded the Czechoslovak people to maintain its allegiance to the Party. It is possible that after the 14th Congress and the election of a reformist Central Committee a united Party might have been able to consolidate public opinion behind it and Dubcek been able to convince the nation that his Party was the best guarantor of its freedoms. It is possible that by allowing the full play of democratic forces within the Party itself, Dubcek might have enabled the Communists to remain both sensitive and responsive to the aspirations of the people.

All this might have happened – we simply cannot know. There is no way of telling whether the Human Face was a seductive wraith or a creature of substance. It is not possible to say whether the failure of the Prague Spring was a function of the subjective Czechoslovak conditions or whether the failure was endemic in such a marriage of Marxism and social democracy. All that one can say is that the Soviet Union was right. There *was* a 'counter-revolution' in Czechoslovakia in the summer of 1968. How it would have ended is unclear; it could have had one of three solutions.

Dubcek might have become a Gomulka and systematically begun to emasculate the freedoms he had so spontaneously and rashly granted. If he was telling the truth to the Central Committee Meetings of 31 August 1968 and 26 September 1969, this tragedy appears quite likely. In that case the invasion was a gross and unnecessary blunder. Alternatively the 'counter-revolution' might have ended either in the overthrow of the Communist Party or in its metamorphosis into a body responsive and responsible to its people. Either would have been a disaster for the bureaucratic, self-perpetuating oligarchy which rules the Soviet Union. The second would have been a great gain for the rest of the world.

Dubcek had many faults, but one glance at the rigid and unoriginal rule of Dr Husak is enough to demonstrate how trifling were those faults beside his remarkable virtues. Dubcek set a completely new style in political leadership.

With his absurd honesty, his unpretentious simplicity, with his emotional sympathy, with his face like a bashful goose, with his words stumbling all by chance, his absolute faith

Jan Palach, 11.8.48 – 19.1.69.

Dubcek with his successor, Dr Gustav Husak, 17 April 1969, the night that he resigned from the First Secretaryship of the Czechoslovak Communist Party.

in his ideals, he was perhaps the only political leader in the world who could say of his programme 'previously the people were not happy with the Party and its policies . . . we cannot change the people so we will change the Party'.[14] With his weeping faith in those people whom he could not and did not want to change, no one but Dubcek could have summed up Prague Spring, as he did in September 1968, as the time when 'We began to trust the people and they began to trust us'.[15]

APPENDIX ONE

(The structure of power in Czechoslovakia is very complex. These diagrams are, of necessity, very simple. The author acknowledges that his interpretation may therefore appear arbitrary.)

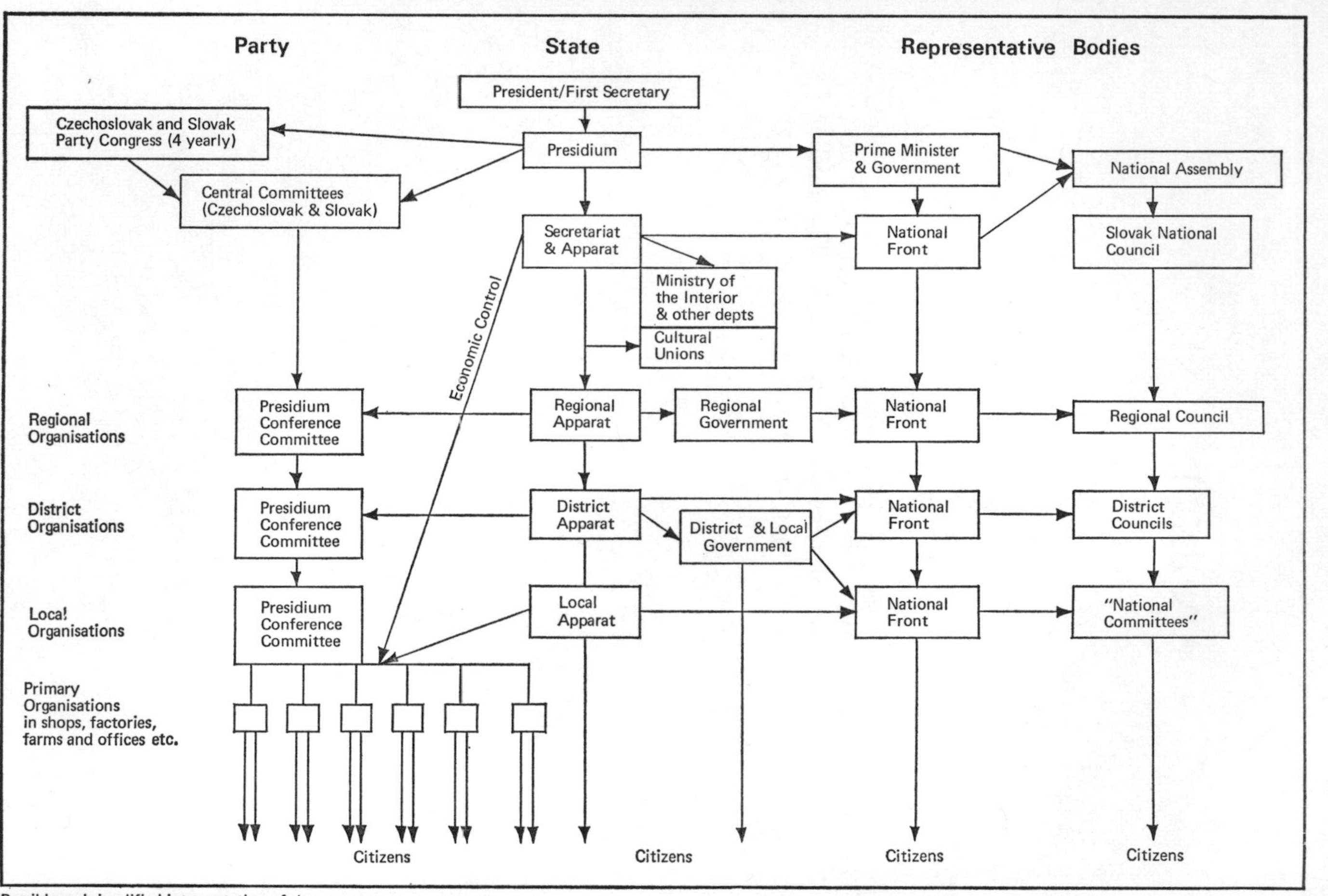

Possible and simplified interpretation of the Czechoslovak power structure under Novotny in 1967.

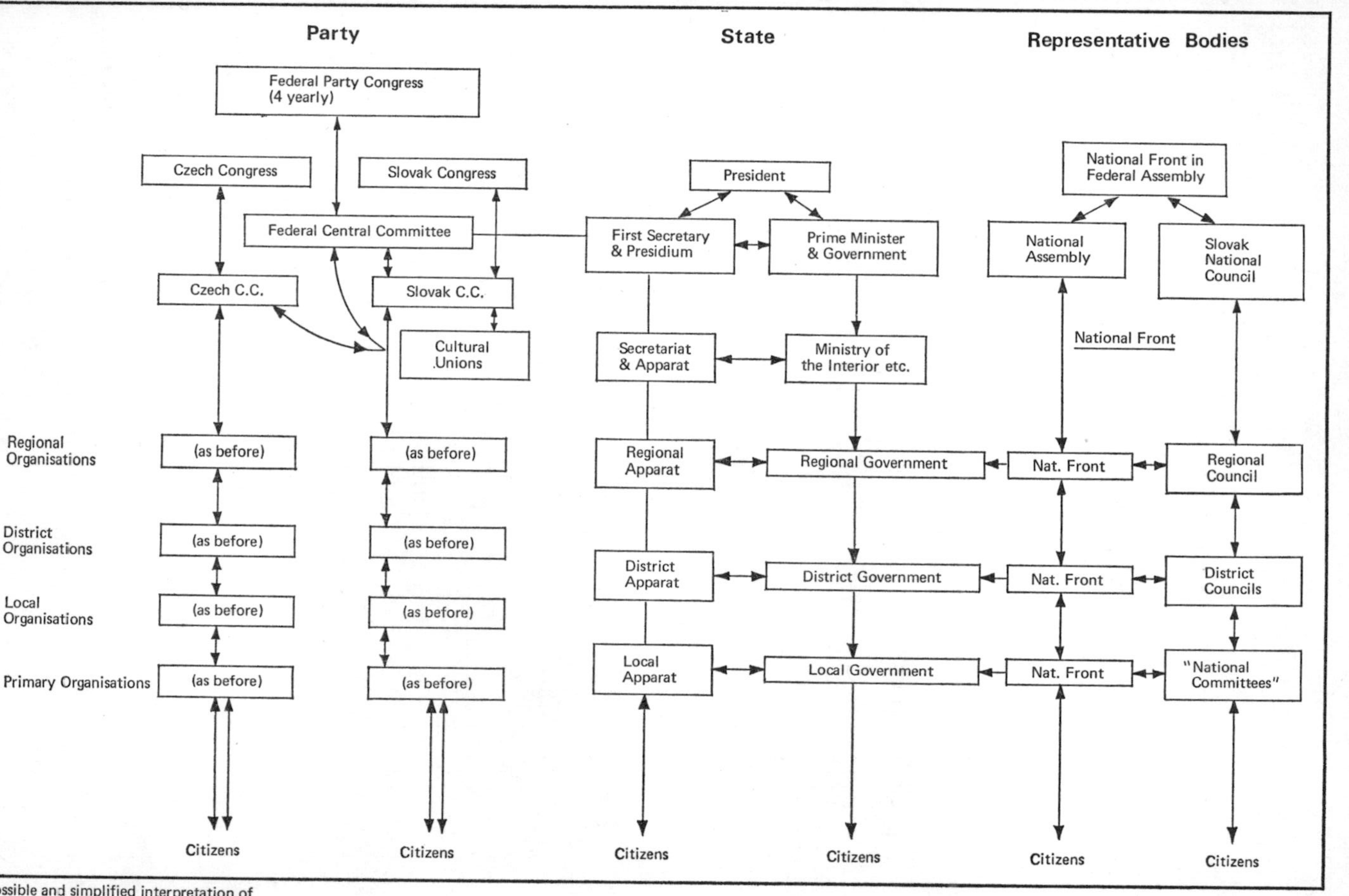

Possible and simplified interpretation of
the power structure that Dubcek envisaged.

APPENDIX TWO

Chronology 1918-1970

1918	28 October	Foundation of the State of Czechoslovakia.
1921	27 November	Alexander Dubcek born in Uhrovec, West Slovakia.
1925		Dubcek family go to Interhelpo, Kirghizia.
1933		They move to Gorkiy: Alexander attends secondary school.
1938	Summer	Alexander Dubcek returns to Slovakia. Chamberlain meets Hitler at Munich.
1939	March	Hitler occupies the Czech lands and Slovakia becomes an autonomous but puppet state. Dubcek joins the new, illegal Communist Party of Slovakia and goes to work as a locksmith in Dubnica-nad-Vahom.
1944	28 August	Beginning of the Slovak National Revolt against the fascists. Alexander Dubcek joins the partisan brigade of 'Jan Zizka'.
	20 November	Dubcek is twice wounded in the thigh.
1945	May	Slovakia and the Czech lands liberated; the Czechoslovak Republic reformed. Dubcek goes to work as a labourer in a yeast factory in Trencin, West Slovakia.

1948 20 February	The Communist Party takes total power in Czechoslovakia; Dubcek later called it 'a great milestone in our history'.
1949	Dubcek enters the Party *apparat*. Works in Trencin.
1951	Dubcek is sent to work in *apparat* in Bratislava.
1950–4	Stalinist trials and purges in Czechoslovakia.
1953	Dubcek appointed Regional Secretary of the Banska Bystrica region of Central Slovakia.
1955–8	Dubcek attends the Higher Party School in Moscow. Graduates with a First.
1958	On return from Moscow promoted to Leading Secretary of the Bratislava Party.
1960	Becomes an Industrial Secretary on the Secretariat of the Czechoslovak Communist Party in Prague.
1962	Elected to the Presidium of the Czechoslovak Communist Party.
1963	Replaces Karol Bacilek as First Secretary of the Slovak Communist Party.
1963–7	Works in Bratislava; most important, but still obscure official in Slovak Party.
1968	
5 January	Alexander Dubcek replaces Antonin Novotny as First Secretary of the Czechoslovak Communist Party.
29–30 January	Flies to Moscow for talks with Soviet leaders. No other Czech or Slovak leaders are present. Communiqué asserts 'full identity of views on all questions discussed.
1 February	Dubcek says of the encounter: 'The

	Soviet comrades have expressed full understanding . . . which corresponds to the character of [our] brotherly relations'.
22 February	Dubcek makes his first major policy speech in Prague and in the presence of Brezhnev. He promises 'the widest possible democratization of the entire socio-political system'. According to Vasil Bilak, 'the Soviet comrades almost stormed out of the meeting'.
13 March	Milan Weiner, Foreign Affairs Commentator says on Radio Prague that a free Press is the only way of controlling the Government. Dubcek, he says, means well 'but I don't know what he will be like in three or four years . . . I am not sure whether . . . there could not be a return to the old methods . . . a free press, free criticism, that is the only possibility'.
19 March	*Rude Pravo,* the Czechoslovak Communist Party daily, calls upon Novotny to resign the Presidency of the Republic.
22 March	Novotny resigns.
23 March	Dubcek, Drahomir Kolder, and Josef Lenart fly to Dresden for consultations with their Soviet, East German, Bulgarian, Hungarian and Polish partners.
27 March	Dubcek addresses off-the-cuff a crowd of a thousand youths who had marched on the Central Committee Building to demand that one of their heroes, Cestmir Cisar, should replace Novotny. Dubcek answers that Cisar is too important to him in the Party. Questioned about the future of Gustav Husak, then a great

hero amongst the young, he answers: 'Perhaps I should not be saying it, so as not to reveal a state secret, but we are counting on him as deputy-premier'. Svoboda chosen President.

4 April — Election of new Presidium of the Czechoslovak Communist Party.

9 April — Publication of the Action Programme.

11 April — Dubcek warns of anarchy: 'It is anarchy to understand democracy as a situation in which everyone interferes with everything and does what he wants. That has nothing in common with real democracy . . . I understand democracy to be a system which not only does not exclude discipline but includes it'.

24 April — Prime Minister Cernik in the National Assembly: 'As long as NATO exists, we shall contribute to the strengthening of the Warsaw Treaty, we shall strive to make the Czechoslovak People's Army a firm link of this alliance'.

Mayday — The Radio Prague announcer: 'At past Mayday parades people were "persuaded" to attend. The parade is being watched by many foreign journalists. We ask them to convey to their own listeners how united the whole nation is this year and how spontaneous are the expressions of joy and confidence. Dubcek's speech was unprepared, stumbling but eloquent: "I am appealing to you workers . . . We are appealing for the co-operation of you, scientists . . . of you, artists . . . your work fills us with pride . . . especially to you, young

	people, knowing that you too, as well as all the others, will continue to help in the solution of all our problems . . . In the work we started a few months ago we are not only pursuing the vital interests of our own country, we are also trying to make socialism more attractive to the whole world".'
4–5 May	Dubcek, Cernik, Smrkovsky and Bilak have what Tass describes as a 'brief, friendly meeting' with the Soviet leaders in Moscow.
24 May	Announcement in Prague that Warsaw Pact 'Signals Exercises' will take place in Czechoslovakia and Poland the following month.
29 May	Dubcek writes in *Rude Pravo*: 'If we criticise deformities that affected socialism in the past we, at the same time, defend its true substance, which certainly comprises socialist ownership, the Marxist programme of social development which is the foundation of the activity of the Communist Party, socialist humanism, the principle of social justice and also the principle of proletarian internationalism on which is based our firm friendship with the Soviet Union and the countries of the Socialist system'.
3 June	Dubcek says that all meetings with the Soviet Union 'have taken and are still taking place on the basis of equality and non-interference in domestic matters'.
4 June	Dubcek: 'Anti-party and anti-communist tendencies do exist . . . what do we mean by the anti-communist danger? The danger arises from

	tendencies to weaken our relations with the Soviet Union. Our whole policy is based on our relations with the Soviet Union – our foreign policy, our economic policy'.
20 June	Warsaw Pact exercises begin.
27 June	Publication of the 'Two Thousand Words Manifesto' in *Prace, Mlada Fronta, Zemedelske Noviny* and *Literarni Listy.*
30 June	Dubcek: 'Nervousness, impatience and imprudence will not help us. Nor will appeals which do not consider realistic facts and possibilities. Democracy for Czechoslovakia means realizing that some words and appeals for strikes or strikes themselves could lead to anarchy and social disruption . . . Success will not be easy – on the contrary the work will be hard and complicated'.
2 July	Announcement in Prague that Warsaw Pact exercises have ended. Soviet troops do not withdraw.
9 July	National Assembly passes bill granting every citizen the unrestricted right to obtain a passport.
14–15 July	Bulgarian, East German, Hungarian, Polish and Soviet leaders meet in Warsaw to discuss Czechoslovakia. Dubcek and his colleagues apparently refuse to attend.
	Meeting sends letter to the Czechoslovak Party Presidium expressing aggressive concern at the course of events in Czechoslovakia.
18 July	Czechoslovak Presidium replies to Warsaw Letter refuting its allegations. Dubcek broadcasts: 'In the previous period the masses, our

	people, were not satisfied with the Party's policy . . . If the people cannot change then the leadership must change . . . To develop socialism into a society which is free on the basis of Marxism-Leninism, with a modern outlook and deep humanism is a great patriotic task and is at the same time our real internationalist duty towards the international communist and workers' movement'.
19 July	Dubcek speaks to Central Committee and reaffirms loyalty to Action Programme.
	Pravda (Moscow) claims that on 12 July the Czechoslovak security forces found a cache of West German and US weapons in Bohemia.
19–20 July	Waldeck Rochet visits Prague.
21 July	President Svoboda reaffirms loyalty to the Warsaw Pact.
22 July	CTK reports the official Czechoslovak view that the finding and indeed the planting of the arms cache was a provocation intended to heighten Czechoslovak-Soviet tension.
	Agreement reached that Soviet and Czechoslovak leaders should hold a bilateral meeting on Czechoslovak soil.
26 July	*Pravda* (Moscow) expresses fear that Czechoslovakia is about to re-establish a 'bourgeois regime'.
27 July	Before departing for Cierna to meet the Soviets Dubcek promises not to retreat: 'Anti-socialist tendencies and some anti-soviet invective and moods are occurring . . . but these are not decisive to our development. The decisive factor is that ever more

people of this country are inclining towards socialism, to the policy of the Communist Party, which will in the end strengthen our alliance with the Socialist countries and especially with the Soviet Union'.

29 July — Cierna talks begin. *Pravda* (Moscow) publishes article stressing Czechoslovak indebtedness to and dependence upon the Soviet Union.

30 July — *Rude Pravo* asserts that 'the idea that relations between Communist Parties can be successfully solved by methods of propagandistic, political or military pressure is a dangerous illusion'.

1 August — *Pravda* (Moscow) ceases to attack Czechoslovakia. Cierna talks end.

2 August — Dubcek broadcasts; thanks the people for their 'wise and circumspect attitude . . . You can be completely satisfied with the results and spirit of the negotiations . . . We kept our promise to you'. Nevertheless 'there must be no misuse of . . . spontaneous meetings for the expression of anti-Soviet and anti-Socialist sentiments'.

4 August — On television Dubcek promises that no secret agreements were reached at Cierna or at Bratislava, where the Five Parties had met with the Czechoslovaks to ratify the Cierna 'agreement'.

6 August — H. Malacek, Secretary of Czechoslovak journalists' association, says that the Press will respond to appeals for 'a calm, matter-of-fact, serious tone in reporting about fraternal countries' only so long as

	Czechoslovakia is not unfairly attacked by them.
9–11 August	Tito visits Prague. Given enthusiastic reception.
12–13 August	Ulbricht visits Dubcek at Karlovy Vary. Reception cool.
15–17 August	Ceaucescu visits Prague. Very warmly welcomed.
16 August	*Pravda* (Moscow) reopens attack upon Czechoslovak Press.
17 August	Dubcek meets Kadar at Komarno. Kadar makes no mention of an imminent invasion.
	On television Dubcek says: 'All these meetings, especially after the Bratislava meeting, went very well. I think that such meetings enable us to understand each other better. I can say quite frankly that we got on very well with our Rumanian colleagues. I am very satisfied'.
19 August	Dubcek receives long and threatening letter from Brezhnev but it was little different from many others he had been sent. It did not warn that Czechoslovakia was about to be invaded.
20 August 11 p.m. approximately	Armies of the Soviet Union, Hungary, Poland, East Germany and Bulgaria cross into the territory of their ally, Czechoslovakia.
21 August 6 a.m. approximately	Dubcek, Cernik, Smrkovsky and Kriegel arrested and flown out of Czechoslovakia.
23 August	President Svoboda flies to Moscow with Husak, Indra, Bilak, Piller, Martin Dzur, and Kucera.
26 August	Moscow Agreement signed between Czechoslovak 'delegation' and Soviet leaders.

27 August	Svoboda and the other Czech and Slovak leaders returned to Prague.
28 August	Dubcek broadcasts to nation. In tears. Extraordinary Congress of the Slovak Party replaces Vasil Bilak as First Secretary by Gustav Husak.
29 August	In brilliantly eloquent radio speech Smrkovsky declares that only the nation's unity has prevented the imposition of even harsher terms in Moscow.
31 August	New Presidium of twenty-one members announced. Dubcek tells Central Committee that he has failed to appreciate the collective interests of the country's allies and that censorship will have to be temporarily imposed.
1 September	Dubcek announces indefinite postponement of 14th Congress.
3 September	Dr Sik resigns as Deputy Prime Minister.
4 September	Tass describes Sik as 'one of the most odious figures among the right-wing revisionist forces'.
5 September	Radio Prague carries Tass statement that the Moscow Agreement is not being implemented fast enough. Interpreted as move to oust Dubcek.
12 September	In a television speech Dubcek promises that there will be no return to pre-January conditions.
13 September	Russians distribute leaflets in Prague accusing Dubcek of a 'personality cult'. Cernik, in speech to National Assembly admits to 'rashness and imbalance' during the preceding eight months.
14 September	Dubcek on TV: 'I know that it is not easy for you to accept our words

openly telling you the facts which faced us all and that it was not easy to accept the only possible solution which we, who represented you in Moscow, reached, after long deliberation, unanimously and to the best of our consciences and abilities. . . . We really understand the Moscow Agreement as a reality which opens up possibilities of further developing the work of our Party, of our country, which offers a chance to escape from the present situation . . . [In January] we said: Let us eliminate deformations, arbitrariness, unlawfulness; to it. This and nothing else is the that human face which is appropriate and give socialism in this country essence of our post-January policy . . . the Party and the people will not tolerate any return to the pre-January conditions in any variation.'

23 September — Smrkovsky speaks of national unity and the unity of the Czechoslovak leaders as 'an arch from which not a single stone must be allowed to fall.' Press full of rumours that Dubcek is to be forced to resign.

29 September — Husak claims on television that the Party had, prior to the invasion, taken steps to re-introduce censorship.

3 October — Dubcek arrives in Moscow with Cernik and Husak. Communique speaks of treaty legalizing the temporary stationing of troops in Czechoslovakia.

4 October — Delegation returns to Prague. let us develop Socialist democracy

	Rumours that they have climbed down completely.
6 October	Spokesman in Prague denies that Dubcek had threatened to resign if the Russians were not more accommodating.
8 October	Presidium approves the measures accepted by Dubcek *et al.* in Moscow. Affirms that there will be no return to pre-January conditions.
11 October	Dubcek, in first public speech since return from Moscow: 'Completely anti-socialist forces also missed the deficiencies of the post-January developments . . . I am aware of everything that happened after 21 August. I am also aware that what happened then was a blow at the feelings of our people. I am aware of the fact that some wounds cannot easily be healed. But I am also aware that this country is and wants to be Socialist and that we can only develop Socialism as internationalists with the Socialist countries.'
15 October	Cernik leads delegation to Moscow to sign Treaty legalising occupation.
16 October	Treaty signed in Prague by Cernik and Kosygin. Approved by Czecho-Slovak National Assembly by 228 votes to four, with ten abstensions; ratified by Svoboda the same day. Cernik speaks of 'new realities' the country must face and promises that the Soviet forces will not interfere in Czechoslovakia's internal affairs.
27 October	National Assembly unanimously passes legislation to federalize the country into the Czech lands and Slovakia, to take effect from 1 Jan-

	uary 1970. National Assembly to be replaced by bicameral Federal Assembly.
28 October	50th anniversary of the foundation of the Czechoslovak Republic; big demonstrations in Prague; police standing by with watercannon do not intervene.
4 November	*Pravda* (Moscow) attacks Dubcek and the critics of the Moscow Agreement in Czechoslovakia. 'Instead of listening to sober voices and using healthy criticism to improve things, certain officials of the Czechoslovak Party are encouraging those forces which used inner party democracy for brazen attacks against party principles.'
7 November	Big anti-Soviet demonstrations in Prague after Dubcek and Cernik are vilified by a pro-Soviet crowd at memorial service for Russians who died in the liberation of Czechoslovakia.
12 November	In speech to Polish Party's 5th Congress, Brezhnev outlines doctrine of limited sovereignty for Socialist states.
14–17 November	Plenary session of the Czechoslovak Communist Party's Central Committee. Formation of eight-man 'Executive Committee': Cernik, Dubcek, Svoboda, Erban, Husak, Sadovsky, Srmkovsky and Strougal. Designed to limit the reformers. Resolution of November 17th condemned right wing opportunistic forces for failure and for causing invasion. This represents greatest

	ideological capitulation since 21 August.
17 November	Some 60,000 students in Bohemia and Moravia start three-day sit-in strike in protest against erosion of Action Programme.
25 November	Severe restrictions on travel to Western Europe announced in Prague.
28 November	*Izvestia* expresses approval of developments in Czechoslovakia and states that there are 'more and more people facing up to the reality of today.'
6–8 December	Czechoslovakia – Soviet meeting in Kiev. Discussion, according to Tass, of 'co-operation' between the two parties. Smrkovsky excluded from Czechoslovak delegation.
11 December	25th anniversary of signing of Soviet – Czechoslovak Friendship Treaty. Commenting, *Rude Pravo* recognizes the 'irrevocability' of the relationship but points out that it is impossible to pretend that 'nothing has happened between us during the last 25 years . . . the dramatic development of events has exposed our mutual relations to a most difficult test'.
12 December	Central Committee opens new session. *Prace* publishes many letters in support of Smrkovsky, questioning his absence from the Kiev talks.
13 December	*Prace* accuses the Russians of 'an exceptional oversight in diplomatic relations between friendly countries, because although Smrkovsky had signed a telegram of greetings to the Soviet leaders on the anniversary of

	11 December, the Soviet reply had not included Smrkovsky's name.
25 December	In a broadcast to Slovakia Gustav Husak declares that Smrkovsky's removal from the Chairmanship of the Assembly has been decided 'in principle'.
27 December	*Prace* publishes an open letter to Husak from Czech writer Pavel Kohout. Accuses Husak of 'trying to thrust from the stage the man who is the most resolute opponent of closed circuit policy'. Kohout even accuses Husak of ignoring the Czechs in the same way as Novotny had ignored the Slovaks: 'You are exploiting the situation in exactly the same way'.
	Konstantin Katushev, Soviet Party Secretary, arrives in Prague. Welcomed at the military airport by a kiss from Vasil Bilak.
1969	
1 January	New Federal Government appointed. Cernik remains Prime Minister.
2 January	*Mlada Fronta,* Czech youth paper, publishes letters from several Slovak readers in support of Smrkovsky. They complain that Husak has forbidden the Slovak Press to campaign for Smrkovsky.
4 January	One million metalworkers threaten to strike if Smrkovsky is removed.
6 January	Smrkovsky pleads with his supporters to do nothing rash.
8 January	Dubcek appeals for calm.
9 January	Metalworkers withdraw strike threat.
11 January	Husak speech: 'Some groups regard themselves as private owners of radio and television magazines. The country must learn that when our

	Party turns into a mere discussion club it cannot solve any problems. It is necessary to discuss things, close the discussion and then act.'
16 January	A Czech philosophy student sets himself on fire in Wenceslas Square. His name is Jan Palach.
19 January	Jan Palach dies.
19–25 January	Enormous demonstrations throughout the Czech lands culminating in Palach's funeral on the 25th. Husak forbids any demonstrations in Slovakia.
26 January	Police, who have been inactive all week, use tear gas to disperse crowds around Wenceslas Square statue.
5 February	Dubcek describes the last three weeks as the greatest crisis the country has endured since August.
28 March	Czech mob sacks Aeroflot office in Wenceslas Square after Czechoslovak ice-hockey victory over Russia in Stockholm, score 4:3.
31 March	Marshall Grechko and Soviet Deputy Foreign Minister Vladimir Semyonov arrive in Prague.
1 April	Extraordinary session of the Presidium condemns the demonstrations and blames Smrkovsky, by name, for certain speeches which conflicted with the November resolutions.
3 April	On television Dubcek declares that the riots are 'acts unworthy of our cultural tradition and of the maturity of our citizens.' Announces reimposition of full preliminary censorship upon the Press.
16 April	Ten Communists, who had been accused of collaborating with the Russians in August, rehabilitated:

	Bilak, Barbirek, Kolder, Piller, Rigo, Svestka, Lenart, Kapek, Indra and Jakes.
17 April	Meeting of the Central Committee. Dubcek replaced by Gustav Husak. Little public reaction; attempt by students to strike largely collapses.
28 April	Dubcek elected Chairman of the Federal Assembly in place of Dr Petr Colotka who had replaced Smrkovsky in January. In the House of the People (basically the old National Assembly) there are 184 votes for Dubcek, 61 against and 6 abstensions. Dubcek makes a short speech: asserts that he has proposed his own resignation, condemns the 'acts of vandalism' and declares that there has never been any place in Czechoslovak policy for anti-Sovietism.
4 May	Stefan Sadovsky replaces Husak as Slovak First Secretary.
27 May	President Svoboda announces amnesty for the thousands of Czechoslovaks who have stayed abroad illegally since the invasion. To remain in force till September 15th.
29 May	Central Committee session opens in Prague. Husak declares that the situation in the Party in 1968 had become little more than 'legalized organizational and ideological anarchy'. Democratic centralism must now be more rigidly enforced but Husak promises that there will be no attempt to 'induce fear' into those who have become 'disoriented'. The session expels Ota Sik from the Committee and Frantisek

Kriegel, one of Dubcek's closest supporters, from the Party. Kriegel defends himself in courageous speech to the Committee in which he repeats his denunciations of the invasion and continued occupation.

11 June — At the World Conference of Communist Parties in Moscow, Dr Husak describes the reformist movement as 'naivety and political romanticism, cheap gestures and slogans not based on a class viewpoint, about democracy, freedom and humanism and the so-called will of the people ... the process of dissolution reached such proportions that even Czechoslovakia's political, economic and military ties with other Communist countries were placed in doubt ... the leaders of the communist parties of the neighbouring allied countries gradually lost confidence that the leadership of our Party was able to stop this critical development. The well-known events of August took place.'

2 August — Husak and Svoboda visit the Black Sea 'for a holiday'. Believed to be discussing with Brezhnev measures to be taken to curb demonstrations on 21 August, the first anniversary of the invasion.

10 August — Radio Prague warns that anti-socialist forces are preparing an 'unprecedented crisis'.

11 August — Ministry of the Interior warns of a plot by 'anti-socialist, anti-Party and anti-Soviet forces' to disrupt the next few days. Warns that strong measures will be taken to preserve

	the peace. The ministry also denies the rumours sweeping Czechoslovakia that Dubcek has died.
13 August	Strougal claims that anti-socialist forces are organizing to endanger the consolidation of State and Party. Such people will be severely punished.
14 August	It is announced that army and militia units will stand by in the streets to try and thwart any demonstrations on the 21st.
17 August	Dubcek is attacked for the first time by name, in a broadcast on Radio Prague. The speech, by Richard Padovy, a veteran Moravian Communist, is later withdrawn.
18 August	Crowds gather around the Wenceslas Square statue. Police disperse them.
19 August	Large crowds gather. The police disperse them more violently, with tear gas and armoured cars.
20 August	Very large demonstrations are very savagely dispersed by the police. Vicious fighting continues in Narodni and Na Prikope Streets, at the bottom of Wenceslas Square, until midnight.
	In an article in *Tribuna*, Oldrich Svestka, Russophile and former editor of *Rude Pravo*, accuses Dubcek of lying. In an article purporting to tell 'the truth of a year ago', Svestka claims that Dubcek knew, from a letter he received from Brezhnev on 19 August, that invasion was imminent. Svestka's allegation is in fact unfounded.
21 August	Midday: Huge demonstration of

loyalty to Dubcek in Wenceslas Square. Dispersed by the police after thirty minutes. Square emptied by tear gas and water cannon. Cordoned off all afternoon by troops. Savage fighting throughout the centre of the town until midnight. At six in the evening tanks are ordered into the city. 1,387 people are arrested in Prague.

22 August — The Presidium publishes 'Emergency Laws' to be put into effect at once, which suspends Habeas Corpus and the rule of law. Supposed to be effective only until 21 December and are allegedly necessary in the face of the previous week's rioting.

27 August — Prime Minister Cernik denounces Dubcek and claims that he misled his colleagues in the summer of 1968.

28 August — The 25th Anniversary of the outbreak of the Slovak Revolt. Dr Husak, in Banska Bystrica, declares that in his view last year's invasion was 'in no way a hostile act towards the Czechoslovak people and State', and that it had been 'motivated by the desire to help the Czechoslovak people and our working-class.'

3 September — Vasil Bilak attacks Dubcek for allowing the leading role of the Party to decay and so causing Czechoslovakia's allies to intervene. Dubcek, he says, was 'not capable of resisting the pressure of the known (counter-revolutionary) forces and that these forces were aided by his indecision'.

5 September — Some 40,000 Czechs shout *At Zije Dubcek* when they realize he is amongst them watching a soccer

	match against Hungary in Prague.
9 September	The Presidium rescinds its 21 August 1968 condemnation of the invasion because it contained 'politically incorrect points of view at variance with the Party's present knowledge of the facts leading to the entrance of the allied armies onto our territory'.
12 September	*Rude Pravo* demands that Dubcek and his colleagues indulge in self-criticism of their 'crimes' and 'mistakes' of 1968.
24 September	Alois Indra says that Dubcek's main faults are his 'lack of determination, his desire to avoid open clashes and his unclear conclusions. . . .'. He was a man of 'wavering opinions who frequently changed his position . . . he frequently attacked the activities of the Press and radio during meetings of the Central Committee Presidium, but later refused to adopt any energetic steps to put an end to these activities.'
25–27 September	Central Committee Meeting: Dubcek dismissed from the Presidium. Twenty-nine of his closer colleagues, including Josef Smrkovsky and former Foreign Minister Jiri Hajek removed from the Central Committee. Central Committee declares: 'The entry of allied troops under the situation which arose in the summer of 1968 was motivated by the interests of the defence of Socialism in Czechoslovakia against right-wing, anti-socialist and counter-revolutionary forces, by common interests in the security of the Socialist camp, by

the class interests of workers and the communist movement.'

Despite pressure upon him Dubcek refuses to recant. (See Appendix 4). Husak criticises him but promises 'We are not butchers and the Party will not become a slaughterhouse . . . I can say honestly there will be no beheadings. There were times when two men behind the front door would drag away the man who had been criticised. We shall never return to this and therefore nobody has anything like this to fear.'

14 October — Husak asserts that he is trying to create a 'political system between the bureaucracy of Antonin Novotny and the anarchy of Alexander Dubcek.'

15 October — Dubcek loses his job as Chairman of the Federal Assembly.

22 October — President Svoboda for the first time attacks Dubcek in public. He calls him 'inconsistent and lacking the principles characteristic of Leninism'. But asserts that Dubcek's had been 'honest efforts' to correct the mistakes of the Novotnyite period, abused by 'various anti-socialist and right-wing elements'.

20 October — Mrs Aase Lionaes, chairman of the Nobel Peace Prize Committee, announces that Alexander Dubcek had been one of the candidates for the prize won by the International Labour Organization.

28 November — General Otakar Rytir, Czechoslovakia's top liaison officer with the Soviet troops writes in *Zivot Strany*, the theoretical Party weekly, that not to take revenge upon rightist forces

	is petty bourgeois, that the Party should be purged 'from top to bottom', and that Husak is in effect hampering the work of the Party by conjuring up an unjustified fear of the left-wing. Dubcek, said Rytir 'should explain to the Party and to the people the motives of his actions, why he procrastinated so long and other questions . . . the facts which are already sufficiently known should be officially published.'
December	The Turkish Foreign Ministry announces that Alexander Dubcek is to be appointed his country's ambassador to Ankara.
1970 20 January	Dubcek described by Alois Indra as 'unstable ideologically, with marked inclinations towards petty-bourgeois ideas and infected with the poison of right-wing opportunism.'
25 January	Dubcek arrives in Istanbul. Mobbed at the airport he hides in a lavatory.
28 January	Plenary Session of Central Committee. Dubcek's resignation from Committee 'accepted'.
22 March	Dubcek suspended from the Czechoslovak Communist Party 'until the completion of Party Investigations'.

APPENDIX THREE

Dubcek's radio address to the nation at approx. 5.30 pm on 27 August 1968.

This translation is reprinted from *The Czech Black Book*, by kind permission of the publishers, Pall Mall, London.

Dear fellow citizens, comrades,

It is difficult for me to find words to express gratitude for the enormous show of confidence with which you have overwhelmed me and the other comrades for whom you have been waiting. Your high morale, your circumspect course and attitude, and the firmly expressed conviction that all properly elected officials of the Party and the central organs would return to their functions was not a vain hope. We are again among you in our work. We thank you. We can again renew the activities of the central organs of our Republic, of the National Assembly, of the Government, and the activity of the National Front.

This activity, like the life of our people, will take place in a situation whose reality does not depend on our will alone. We were fully aware of this fact during the entire time, just as you feel it – and all of you are certainly aware of it. It is the great merit of our circumspection, the circumspection of the people of our Republic, that you abided by the appeal of the Presidium of the Central Committee, of the President of the Republic, Comrade Ludvik Svoboda, and of the Government of the Republic, that no greater open clashes and no additional bloodshed occurred. It is necessary to prevent further suffering and further losses at all costs, because they would not alter the real conditions, and the abnormal situation in our homeland would be prolonged. The fact that we are determined to prevent bloodshed does not mean that we want passively to submit to the situation that has been created. On the contrary, we are doing everything in order that we may find – and we are convinced that we shall find – ways and means of devising and, together with you, implementing the policy that will in the end lead to a normalization of conditions. In this conviction we are being strengthened by the results the representatives of the Soviet Union have achieved in the negotiations we concluded yesterday in Moscow. The Soviet representatives, too, want to contribute to the normalization of our relations.

In today's reality, we are faced with the task of finding a way out of the present situation in Czechoslovakia. First, we have an agreement on the phased departure of troops of the five states from the territory of our Republic. Consequently, any distrust aroused about this matter is groundless and harmful. That agreement, that standpoint, is the fundamental prerequisite for our future activities. We have agreed that troops will be moved immediately from villages and towns to areas reserved for them. This is naturally connected with the ability of our own Czechoslovak organs to ensure order and normal life in individual areas. In this respect, the Government of the Republic has already proceeded today to take appropriate measures in order that our organs may implement steps to regulate our civil life. It would therefore be very imprudent and dangerous to take any actions that would hold up the movements and eventually the departure of the troops of the five states from our country. The final aim of our entire endeavour is to effect the complete withdrawal of these troops as soon as possible. On the basis of the Moscow negotiations, the Government is already taking specific steps in this direction.

Work is going on concerning other measures. We ask you, dear fellow citizens, to help us prevent any provocations by those who are interested in increasing the tension of the situation, which is already very tense indeed, and whose forces are directed against socialism. What we need, above all, in this period is order. We need the conscientious discipline of all our citizens, all inhabitants of our Czechoslovak socialist fatherland, just as we have had up to now. Moreover, in the next period we shall need this conscientiousness even more, for a lot will be at stake, and much will depend on our course, on our work, on how all of you help to perform this work. I want to point out most seriously that the normalization of conditions includes the requirement that each individual should not act on the basis of passions and mass psychosis without knowledge of the facts. In this complicated period, we must not succumb to passions and psychoses. If this happened, we would hardly be able to regulate life in our country, and believe me, we are determined to do everything in this respect that is in our power.

The normalization of conditions is the basic prerequisite for our being able again to concentrate our efforts on proceeding without major mistakes or extended delays along the path in which you have put your trust, along with us, and in which you still believe, in my opinion, even though we now live and work under complicated conditions and in a complicated period. We have interpreted your support in these days as support for the idea of a more successful development of socialism in our country along the path formulated since the January plenary meeting of the Central Committee and during the preparations for the Party's Extraordinary Fourteenth Congress. This support will strengthen us all the more and will be an obligation for us not to abandon, in this complicated time, our striving for the expression of humanist and socialist principles.

It might seem a paradox that I speak about this just now. But we must have faith in our strength and faith in our people, because only in unity, in the unity of our course, in the unity of our deeds, can we assure the success of our future policy. We are returning to work with the determination to create conditions for continuing this policy with as few mistakes as possible. It will not be easy, and it will therefore be necessary to exert much effort. Such is the reality, and from this we must embark on our work. To ignore the real situation could lead in some places only to adventure and to anarchy. That would not be good, and it would not be good for the implementation of the important tasks we now face. You know that the new situation in our country confronts us with new questions and that there are new points of view. The first thing we need is the quickest possible consolidation and normalization of the situation in the country. I know that it will be very complicated, but we must see it as the fundamental condition for further steps. For this very reason, we trust that you will assist us today in the same way you have supported us before – on the basis of a realistic assessment of the situation – with your continued confidence and active participation. We trust you will do this if we must carry out some temporary, exceptional measures restricting the degree of democracy and freedom of expression that we have achieved. I ask you to understand the kind of time we live in. The sooner we are able to achieve a normalization of conditions in the country and the greater the support you give us, the sooner we will be able to take further steps on our post-January course. We do not want to seek the road to the solution of our problems by ourselves. We rely not only on our own strength, but primarily on your strength, on your moral strength, on your character, on your independent thinking based on prudence, circumspection, and proceeding from reality in our country.

This reality must not be ignored. But the broadcasts of some radio transmitters, after the speech of the President of the Republic, Comrade Svoboda, have been spreading mistrust and doubts about the Moscow negotiations and about the measures being prepared for the withdrawal of troops. We warn very emphatically against such a course. Inflammatory words are easily broadcast into the atmosphere. It is necessary to see the link between such speech and responsibility for additional loss of life, and material damage, which even now is far from small.

Your support, calmness, prudence, and the activity of the Party and other mass and social organizations in these days have confirmed again the experience we had already gained since January of this year – that it is necessary to be in close touch with the people, to consult with them systematically, to lean on their good sense and experience, to pay attention to their views and express them in our policy. We wish to continue this way. I know the ideals you fight for. I know that you will never retreat from the idea of socialism, humanism, national independence, and our Czechoslovak sovereignty. I believe, and I say this to you all, that in my life I cannot and will not do anything other than work for the realization of these ideals of my people. With this in mind, I and the other comrades negotiated in the past few days, and with this in mind, I want to work and serve my fatherland in the days to come. There are a great many questions for which we must

Dubcek standing by his brother's grave, Uhrovec, 10 February 1969.

With his family at the funeral of his father Stefan, 4 June 1969.

Alexander Dubcek after his dismissal from the Presidium, 26 September 1969.

seek and find answers. You yourselves know best how many fateful questions have appeared during the last week – from renewing order, to the withdrawal of troops and the solution of many problems in the life of each one of us. All this requires a well-considered answer as soon as possible. I assure you that I intend to consider, along with you, our future steps in the new situation that has arisen and to begin solving the most urgent problems as soon as possible.

Allow me now to address a few words to all Communists, rank-and-file members, as well as functionaries of our Party. Comrades, we all – whether we work in the basic organizations or in the highest organs of the Party – are strong only if we have the confidence of the people. This increases the degree of the responsibility we bear for doing everything in the area of practical politics in the interest of the people and doing it even under today's extraordinary and incredibly difficult conditions. It would be the greatest disaster for the Party if its soundest substance, if all its forces that fought to clear the path to the post-January policy of the Communist Party of Czechoslovakia, were now to disintegrate, if a lack of confidence were to arise within the sound forces of the Party. This would inevitably mean the disintegration of the only force capable of extricating our nation from the present complicated situation.

I want you, members and officials of the Party who have worked at home during these days, to understand those of us who have negotiated away from home. We will jointly and as soon as possible deal with all the questions that have arisen in these truly extraordinary and exceptional circumstances. I ask all functionaries of Regional and District Committees and basic organizations of the Party, all delegates to the Extraordinary Fourteenth Party Congress, that during the next few days they fully respect in their Party work the instructions I shall issue in my capacity as the First Secretary of the Central Committee. I mention this because I and the comrades who have worked in the regions and districts and here at the centre shall have to discuss the additional steps needed to unify the work of all Communists on all levels, to unify the steps of the Communists who have worked here at home, for further implementation of the policy of our Party.

I assume, at the same time, the exercise of my function of Commander of the People's Militia, which is part of the title and function entrusted to me. In the very near future, we shall solve all necessary questions at a plenary meeting of the Central Committee attended by representatives of the delegates to the Extraordinary Fourteenth Party Congress. We must consult with those Communists, with those leading officials of our Party, who worked while I and other comrades were unable to take part in the work of our Party. I want to state quite frankly that we paid dearly for the experience we now have, that we must conduct our policy with determination and consistency. We must also take care to see to it that the present complicated situation is not taken advantage of by elements and tendencies to which socialism is alien. We shall guard decisively and consistently our socialist policy in Czechoslovakia for the future.*

Dear listeners, I ask you to forgive me if every now and then there is a pause in this largely improvised speech and impromptu appearance. I think you know why it is. All of us who negotiated in Moscow during the past few days are profoundly grateful to you for your prudent and genuinely Communistic work. Without it, it would not have been possible to prevent an aggravation of the situation and to maintain circumspection and the true moral and political unity of our people. I would also like to thank the members of the army, the National Security corps, and the People's Militia for showing such high morale, which helped to avoid great conflicts. That has been right, that is the way to proceed according to the order of the President of the Republic. I thank you all, all our people, from the bottom of my heart. Believe me, your confidence constitutes for us all an obligation, and we will never in our lives forget this obligation and will always feel responsible to you for our actions. We understand our work only as service to our people, a service to our Czechoslovak socialist homeland. We all know today that the future course will not be easy, that it will be complicated – that it will be more complicated and also take longer than we thought, especially with regard to the fulfilment of the Action

* Here Dubcek, obviously exhausted, paused – according to some accounts he almost fainted.

Programme. But whichever way life goes today, we must keep in mind that we must think over carefully how to fulfil in this new situation and these new conditions the programme of our Communist Party of Czechoslovakia, the programme we espoused in January and April and in subsequent measures of the Central Committee of the Communist Party of Czechoslovakia. It would not have been possible to do otherwise. Subsequently, too, we stood on this position and stand on it now, and this position of ours will be the point of departure for the next period.

The nation and our people belong to the community of the socialist nations in other countries. We believe that, in spite of everything that has happened and that we are going through today, the relations between our nations and the nations of other socialist countries will be resolved in such a way as to be in harmony with this reality. I cannot put it any other way. For the very reason that our nations, the Czechs and the Slovaks, are people of a profoundly human nature with internationalist feelings, their relations with the nations of other socialist countries – as well as with the nations, the people, the working people of the Soviet Union, and of other countries, too – are relations of international feelings. We must not abandon these relations because we will be working things out not only today but tomorrow, too, and the relations in this respect will certainly be aimed at drawing closer with these nations, resolving the relations in such a way as to be in harmony with, and corresponding to, the reality that our nations and other nations are socialist nations. I beg you not to allow any provocations, not to let panic enter our ranks. In this difficult situation, we cannot do otherwise than to exert all our strength, all our reason, in order to be truly able to pass muster in our future work. A nation in which everyone will be guided by reason and conscience shall not perish. I ask you all, my dear fellow citizens, Czechs and Slovaks, Communists and members of the other political parties of the National Front, I ask all the workers, farmers, I ask our intelligentsia, all our people, let us remain united, calm, and, above all, prudent. Let us realize that only in that and in our loyalty to socialism, in our honour, in our endeavours, in our character, is a guarantee of the road forward.

APPENDIX FOUR

Dubcek's speech to the Central Committee: 26 September 1969.*

Introduction

I must put my case to the Central Committee, and I want you to consider this as my honest, sincere point of view, in spite of everything that has happened, that has been decided and publicly announced. I know of the proposal that I resign from the Presidium of the Central Committee and from the Chairmanship of the National Assembly. I was present at the discussion of this proposal and I accepted it. But I want to talk about something else. I want to state my views on the most essential question – on the political course of the Central Committee after January 1968. I am convinced, and I am sure that the majority of the Central Committee shares my view, that it is necessary to evaluate the political course of the Party up to August† in order to defend its essential correctness, because one day, after we have solved the present negative tendencies in the Party and society we will want to try and work out those principles again.

All of us, and above all the old members of the Central Committee, know that we had agreed at the Plenums of November, and December '67 and January '68, that the Party was going through a very severe crisis. What happened in January was objectively inevitable because serious social problems were coming to the fore. There was an urgent need for a new positive attitude towards not only the principle of democratic centralism in the Party but also towards the relations between the Party and the whole of society. There was a need for citizens, and especially for the younger generation, to participate more fully. There was an urgent need to solve gradually the interminable problems of economic development,

* This is the first publication in English of the full text, smuggled out in December 1969.

† 1968.

and politically that meant again to increase the participation of the people. There was also a more than urgent need to settle nationality questions. This meant to intensify study of the Party's programme, to face complex problems and to try and solve them in a positive way. It was necessary to extend socialist democracy, to do away as much as possible with subjectivism and voluntarism,* and to destroy the political monopoly of a small group of Party functionaries.

There was also an urgent need to replace the old system of personal power with a new system based on *institutional* change.† This was the most difficult, the most important and the most complex task. The pressure of accumulated problems required the removal of dead wood which was impeding our development. But we could create something new only by marching unflinchingly forward – the system of personal power‡ did not allow us to plan ahead in a democratic, gradual and rational way. Nobody can deny that we tried to solve the situation democratically, by discussing it in the Central Committee, by proposing one point of view against another, while keeping strictly to Party rules.§ Nor can it be doubted that basic class questions were involved, such as the problem of how to achieve the revolutionary aims of the working class and how to apply Marxism-Leninism to the building of a socialist society in Czechoslovakia. We referred to the Party's work and to present conditions as well as to the universally valid principles of the building of socialism from the point of view of the international proletariat.

January was inspired by the idea of internationalism, by the brotherhood of Czechs and Slovaks and by efforts to co-operate with the USSR and other socialist parties and countries [...]

On this basis I tried to differentiate between the class policy of the Party and the sectarianism which was so clearly reflected in the Party's loss of influence over the majority of rank and file members, on the working masses and above all on the younger generation. Sectarianism was a defect which has al-

* i.e., Novotny's autocratic rule.
† Emphasis added.
‡ Under Novotny.
§ i.e., no intrigues.

ready proved in the past unable to build and preserve a prosperous socialist state. My opinion was that the socialist state must try to gain the sympathy and support of an ever-increasing mass of people for its policies and thus lead towards both economic and cultural prosperity.

After January we tried to restore the unity of socialist forces and to find a common factor between various strata of society interested in developing socialism rather than continuing the old policy of division and disintegration. That was why the post-January policy was so spontaneously accepted by the people, who believed it to be the result of the collective work of the Central Committee.* As a result of this policy the people came to have increasing trust in socialism and more and more faith that they could be useful members of society and that they would no longer be just ordered about, remonstrated with and abused, as had so often happened in the past.

Before January, during January and still today I am convinced that this is the only way in which we can interpret the leading role of the Party. I am also convinced that this policy still has the greatest appeal to the workers. Because of their socio-economic place in society it is the workers who must carry out the policy. As a class which had borne for many years the main burdens of economic stagnation, the workers are very concerned to co-operate with other classes in order to increase the cultural and economic prosperity of the society as a whole. Nobody can make light of the problems of the post-January development. Like many others, I wonder what it was that prevented us from realizing those excellent ideas. I am especially concerned because, as the report submitted to this Plenum has shown, these problems still remain unsolved. I think a very profound analysis is called for, and I am not the man to supply it. But judging from past experiences I am afraid that many simplified and authoritatively presented explanations can lead us very far from the truth. In my opinion the most dangerous thing would be to avoid deeper social problems and analyse only superficial phenomena.

As for myself I cannot sanction the attempt that is being made to identify me with the adventurists and even with

* i.e., it wasn't just my fault.

right-wingers who often complicated our work and made difficulties which I, together with other comrades, tried to overcome in the past year. What you should instead do is evaluate objectively whether I fought sufficiently hard against negativist tendencies and whether I faced squarely those weaknesses of the Party which I admit existed.

I do not deny that personal problems influenced the development of our programme and as First Secretary I must accept my share of responsibility. But another vital factor was that, from January onwards, the Party leadership was not united.

Communists in the government and in the Party organs had a very difficult task. According to Party policy they had to discard ineffective or obsolete practices and replace them by proper methods of socialist-democracy which would liberate the creative impulses of socialist forces, but which would at the same time clamp down on parasitical and inimical elements which had existed in our society before January, after January and also after August. I sincerely admit that we did not suppress consistently enough everything that went against the political mainstream.

There were, however, a number of objective factors which had been important for many years. Every time you try to move out of stagnation you encounter problems. There were so many accumulated problems that the first wave of participation produced not only justified but also unjustified and harmful criticism. And as I have said before, we were simply unable to make preparations.* Nevertheless, this should not have deterred us from organizing more efficiently the ideological struggle against those who unrestrainedly criticized socialism and our entire political development. Several years of crisis had brought the Party into such a state that it was unable to defend its programme against attack. In the ideological sphere contradictory theories emerged, attacking both Marxist class principles and the Party.

It cannot be denied that the crisis which had built up and the efforts to solve it gave an opportunity to impatient, adventurist forces in our society to attack socialism and to take

* Because of Novotny.

revenge for their defeat.* At the beginning of January, in April, May and at other times we drew attention to this in the Central Committee. The dispute was about their real strength in society and whether or not they could gain the support of the masses to such an extent as to achieve their anti-socialist and anti-Party objectives.

In common with the State and Party leadership I was convinced that the degree of acceptance of Party policy would prove the decisive factor. This was also stated in the resolution of the Central Committee of November.† At the time we had no knowledge of any anti-socialist centre. We were members of the Warsaw Pact and I personally was convinced that in view of this alliance neither West Germany nor the United States would intervene in our affairs, for this would have meant a third world war.

Mistakes

We prepared the May Plenary Session of the Central Committee with this in mind.‡ Considerable time was needed for the political struggle and for the implementation of the principles accepted in January and May. This should have been an important function of the Fourteenth Party Congress. However, one could agree with numerous comrades who have pointed out that the Party and Government leadership should have organized this struggle more quickly and efficiently.§

It was apparent from the mass meetings of Party members after the May Plenary Session – as well as from regional conferences – that, despite differences of opinion, the decisions of the May Session had been taken seriously. In June and July the Party demonstrated its readiness to implement these decisions. There were many who decried the achievements of our twenty years' efforts towards socialism. However, in common with other comrades I acted in the belief that by summer the overwhelming part of our population was already in favour of official Party policy and that the most active

* In February 1948?

† 1968.

‡ May 1968 reaffirmed Action Programme.

§ i.e. held the Congress sooner.

elements in the Party had found their bearings and were strengthening their political influence. As some comrades have pointed out, there was a certain lack of urgency in organizing political and ideological work.

The overwhelming majority of the Central Committee and Presidium set out to implement the decisions of the Plenary Session. Despite its complexity and attendant difficulties this task was steadily tackled. Even the often quoted report on the situation submitted to the Party in August noted a considerable relaxation of tension. It also stressed that parochial tendencies were on the wane, that the firm Party core was gaining ground and that confidence was growing amongst the Party membership.

At the time we were not so much concerned with the existence or non-existence of anti-socialist forces or about all the abuse aimed at the Party. We were chiefly interested in the main influences upon our evolution. Indeed we were feeling our way toward the full recognition of the leading role of the Party by the working masses and toward creating a policy which would ensure close contact between leadership and people within the framework of a truly democratic party and society, based on Marxist theory, revolutionary practice and profound democratic tradition of the CPC. We were aware of the difficulty and complexity of this attempt. We knew that we could not deal with the negative aspects in one single effort but were also convinced that results thus achieved would be more permanent.

That, comrades, was how we saw things. Let me put it frankly: I must stress that we did not wish to rely on the use of force. This is not to say that the state should never assert its power. Indeed, as some comrades have pointed out, in some instances this should have been done more forcefully. And we did fail to implement the decisions of the Presidium consistently enough. However, the problem lay in determining the extent of state interference desirable to the running of society. As for the extreme form of interference – that by armed force – I say quite sincerely that at the time we saw no reason for it because the opposing forces were not sufficiently defined. On this question there were conflicting views leading to different concepts of how to implement Party policy. We agreed, basically at least, in the diagnosis of the ills of our society but our views on the cure began to differ. Compare this year's event in Brno* with the mass anti-Fascist rally we organized last year in Gottwaldov where, in the presence of the Soviet Ambassador, the people spontaneously expressed its confidence in our Party and our allies. Bearing in mind the 'pre-Warsaw'† state of affairs in Prague on one hand and the events of this year on the other, I reflect once more on the relative effectiveness of these two approaches to the solution of our problems. I must once again stress that this view is based on facts available to the Party at the time.‡

I want to explain why in June§ we refused to accept – at least without reservation – the view that we were being threatened by counter-revolution. This was mainly because by counter-revolution we understood – and this is quite clear today – an imminent threat to socialism, an imminent attack by anti-socialist forces. Had it existed, we would have necessarily adopted a different attitude towards the use of armed forces as a means of dealing with internal disputes. But we saw this in a different perspective. I must once more ask you not to overlook, even in the difficulties of today, the January principles regarding the application of state power. It is the duty of the state to protect socialist principles. Without internal discipline based on democratic centralism and unity of views the Party is incapable of action. These principles are of prime importance to strengthening the Party and state.

Believe me, I do not intend to belittle the need to uphold these principles and to suppress all that might obstruct the positive work of the Party. I understand all that. But I am concerned about maintaining close contact between the Party and the people in future. That is why I stress the democratic aspects, the necessity to win over people, to implement in the period ahead – as pointed out in the report – the principles of our post-January policy, as well as the necessity to prepare a positive programme maintaining the salient concrete positive features of Party documents of the

* Anti-Soviet demonstration in August 1969, in which 4 people died.

† i.e., before August 1968.

‡ i.e. I was not concealing anything.

§ 1968.

past, which are still valid today. I hope I will not be accused of protecting right-wing or even anti-socialist forces when I say that the struggle against them must be combined with an effort to gain the support of the majority of true Communists for tackling positive tasks. In this way we can find out who stands where and whether or not any particular member supports the policy of our present leadership and of the CC of the CPC. This is necessary in order to strengthen our Party. A dialogue within the Party must be carried on as the main method conducive to genuine and truthful unity.

According to information supplied – and Comrade Matejka raised these questions in his speech – during the past month, Party meetings in Prague were attended by about sixteen per cent of Communists. I am convinced that this was partly caused by the fact that the positive tasks stipulated by the Thirteenth Congress in the Action Programme and in the November resolutions have either been put aside or forgotten. Of course, I realize that the Party and its Central Committee have to deal with other difficulties in today's complex struggle for control and that there are other causes.* The formulation of new tasks for the Party rank and file as well as for the working masses is being postponed. We should get down to this important programmatic work which is to be judged in the autumn – we cannot afford to postpone it any longer, if we are to remain the leading political force. I reiterate that the Party should prepare in the autumn of this year for its general onslaught on this particular field.

Especially vital is the problem of our approach to young people. We must win them over for our policy; they will judge it on its merits and by whether or not we took sufficient care to understand their controversial thinking and whether we are helping them to find their bearings. The most important thing is to prevent any division of youth into a Party group and an anti-Party group. This would have disastrous consequences and would alienate young people.

The lesson of January is also that more attention should be paid to the various phenomena in the Party and in society, among workers as well as among the intelligentsia. In this respect we must avoid attributing some views expressed in

* For the present state of affairs.

articles to bourgeois propaganda, which, as we all realize, has always been exploiting our weaknesses and mistakes to its own ends. I am aware that my view can be countered by asserting that all this is the legacy of the preceding period, a transient stage which must be overcome. I also realize and agree that the present Party leadership has to work under conditions vastly different from those prevailing during the post-January period. Today conditions are very complex indeed. This I recognized in accepting the decisions of the April and May Plenary Sessions and the Emergency Laws. I take this opportunity to reiterate my agreement with the decisions of the Party organs. I want to say frankly – and I assure you with the best of intentions – that I am not in favour of mass purges, especially not in the present controversial situation. Should an extensive Party purge, with all its economic consequences, be used as a political tool, should the Congress's thesis on non-antagonistic relations in our society be discarded and the purge become the main political directive, disruption would, in my opinion, ensue both in the Party and in society; for such tendencies are bound to run out of control. This would bring about stagnation and later create opposition which would only widen the scope of anti-socialist and anti-Party propaganda.

I may be seeing things in a different light from others, but I have come to the conclusion that in practice the main blow would not be directed against anti-Party forces as it should be – and as is stressed in the report – but in fact against Party members. Under certain circumstances this might involve Communist workers and Communist intelligentsia of all kinds.

I am viewing things, in this complex period, from the standpoint of the ordinary Party member and of a primary Party organization. I am fully aware that it is still necessary to fight right-wing opportunists. But we should not practise catch-as-catch-can, nor should we compete in climbing on the band waggon and discarding as quickly as possible doubts and uncertainties which under some circumstances might briefly have arisen in the minds of our comrades.

To combat opportunism in this manner would not solve any of the outstanding problems, nor would it do anything to strengthen the Party and its ideological basis. It would do nothing toward solving economic problems, it would not assist the work of the state apparatus or of mass organizations and it would not increase Party influence among young people. We should also take note of the sectarian tendencies which are at present so harmful. The Party would not benefit if some functionaries who proved incompetent long ago – and by that I mean before January – were to exploit this difficult situation for personal revenge or as an opportunity of obtaining a better job. This would only harm the great effort of the CC of the CPC and of the Party leadership to implement directives. By taking measures against opportunists we should not at the same time cast doubt upon thousands of rank and file members and particularly not on workers who had for many years been its loyal supporters. I fear, perhaps without sufficient cause, that a landslide might be set in motion – not here in the CC but in primary organizations – a landslide which would go far beyond the intentions and aims of the CC. Far from increasing the influence of the Party, it would in fact diminish it.

These are the matters I am worried about and that is why I raised these questions in the Presidium. I implore you not to doubt my sincerity. As a politician, I am on the way out and this is another reason why at first I was not sure whether I should speak out so openly. But I have come to the conclusion that even in my present predicament, the best I can do is to speak sincerely. You, comrades, will excuse my sincerity, but for me this is also a personal problem. As a former leading functionary I reason that the better this CC and its leadership carries out its task, the better for me. This is simply to say that I am still very much concerned about the work of the leadership, of the CC and about the implementation of its directives.

Another problem I want to talk about is that of our relations with our allies. First of all I must reject all accusations of anti-Sovietism, whether they have been direct or made by implication. These assertions, voiced in some places, are undoubtedly the consequence of the very serious aftermath of the August events in the sphere of our internationalist relations. Admittedly, the consequences are serious, but you have my assurance that my intentions had never been other than good. I was unable, by words or by actions to convince some of my colleagues and our allies that we were able unaided to implement and protect from danger our basically correct policy which had been approved by the CC and Presidium – though admittedly this might have taken longer than envisaged. Even if in this situation I am to face the consequences after thirty years devoted to work for the Party, I can say in all honesty that none of this can in any way change my convictions or my feelings towards the Soviet Union.

In all my Party activities in the past, throughout the [Nazi] occupation, after the liberation and after January – indeed to this day – I have always firmly adhered to the principle of the basic orientation of our Party towards the USSR. I have always expounded this policy and defended it, even if I was unable at times to prevent various attacks on it, especially in the Press. We recognized the right of our allies to criticize our shortcomings and we discussed them. There was no conflict about that. But in view of the complexity of our development, discussions centred on the appropriate methods and moment for dealing with negative phenomena. I was convinced that a rash effort and particularly one aiming at a definite solution in one fell swoop would solve nothing. I feared that with the bath water we might throw out our January baby, born as it was of such labour [*sic*]. It is a fact that Czechoslovakia had no intention of flinching from its alliance with the Soviet Union and other socialist countries. This was the clearly stated position of our CC as expressed in all our Party documents. Equally this was and remains my personal conviction and I intend to continue working for it. As I have said several times during the past year, we could afford a more thorough solution of the problems of our road to socialism, to extend democratic rights and to choose the gradual way of overcoming the negative influences which emerged after January precisely because our socialist base was, and still is, safeguarded by strong internal forces and above all by our internationalist alliance with the Soviet Union and other socialist countries. We supported Soviet efforts steadfastly and in a spirit of unity during all the negotiations which I attended as the First Secretary of the CPC, including such measures as were aimed at improving co-operation within the Warsaw Pact.

Dresden

Truly I cannot accept the validity of assertions that a number of problems in our international relations arose because I had withheld information from Party organs, or if I may use the phrase, tried to keep things secret. I have not kept to myself a single matter discussed with our allies. Naturally, at times matters were discussed outside official meetings of delegations and these I reported to the various groups of colleagues or organs concerned. But on this, biased assertions and even downright lies are even now occasionally being published. I wrote to *Rude Pravo, Tribuna* and *Pravda*, requesting them to publish my reply, for instance, to the accusation that I had failed to inform Party organs about the talks at Dresden and further, that nothing had been done to implement the recommendations.

It is neither true nor fair to say that I had not informed the Presidium. I informed it about Dresden at the meeting held on March 25th. Those present at the meeting, Comrades Cernik, Kolder, Bilak, Lenart and myself, agreed on what to pass on. However, I was not in favour of revealing the fact that in Dresden there had been talk about the change of President in Czechoslovakia, et cetera. I doubted the wisdom of publicizing these and other personal problems at such a time and I think that still holds good. But as for important recommendations – we did indeed take active steps. The Dresden meeting and the discussions in Moscow were followed up by the conference of District and Regional Party Secretaries which was to prepare the Plenary Session. At this conference I explained quite openly what objections had been raised and what fears had been voiced by our Soviet comrades. The decisions reached by the May Plenary Session and its directives were right. We tried to gain the support of the whole Party for their implementation for here we saw the main safeguard against any recurrence of anti-socialist activity and against extremism within the Party itself.

Warsaw Letter

The discussions in Warsaw have recently become the key problem. Various intents are now being imputed and ascribed to me. From the events that followed it is being inferred that I personally decided to disregard our internationalist commitments. This particularly concerns our proposal to hold bilateral talks before the joint meeting in Warsaw, in order to clarify controversial questions.

First some facts which I had mentioned already on July 19th. A letter from the five fraternal Parties meeting in Warsaw reached our Presidium on July 4th–6th. Comrade Brezhnev informed me in a telephone conversation of the opinion of the CPSU that the meeting should take place either on the 10th or the 11th of July 1968. Possibly these dates could have been the cause of doubts about the timing. As you know and as can be seen from the record, I said they were impossible because Presidium members were at the time away attending Regional Conferences and because in a matter of such importance I could not decide on my own. The Presidium met on July 8th. We unanimously welcomed the opportunity to meet representatives of the fraternal Parties, but at the same time proposed to hold bilateral meetings in the immediate future rather than a joint meeting at once.

We proposed to meet the Presidium of the CPSU on July 14th or any other date convenient to them. I informed Comrade Brezhnev about our proposal by telephone as early as July 9th, 8.30 p.m., and the official message was sent through the Soviet Ambassador Comrade Chervonenko on the following day. We submitted similar proposals to the other Parties.

I assure you that we saw in this preliminary meeting with our Soviet comrades, that is in the preliminary meeting of Party organs of both sides, a genuine opportunity to prepare a joint conference.

Late at night on July 11th, our Presidium received the letter signed by the five Parties requesting us once more to attend the Warsaw meeting. The letter was discussed at the meeting of the Presidium on the following day, July 12th. We agreed to appeal to fraternal Parties to show understanding for the proposed bilateral meetings, above all with the Soviet Presidium.

I must now stress one important fact. Opening the meeting of the Presidium I announced that Comrade Chervonenko had been instructed to inform me that the Soviet comrades had repeated their proposal for a joint meeting. It follows that all members of the Presidium knew about the Soviet standpoint – this is borne out by the stenographic record of the meeting.

In this connection I must now go into the question of the timing of the proposed meeting. This matter is mentioned in the report. The letter of July 11th which, as you know, was presented at the Plenary Session of July '68 does not give any date. It is now being said that Comrade Chervonenko personally informed me of the date. I am not aware – and there is no other way of putting it – that I had been informed. I had no more reason for secrecy at that time than I have now. What puzzles me is why I should have written to Comrade Brezhnev at Warsaw enquiring about a suitable date, had such a date already been known to me. Why would I have gone with Comrade Cernik to see Comrade Kadar? And why was there no date in the letter presented by Comrade Chervonenko on the day before the meeting of our Presidium? Why is there no trace of this date, supposedly conveyed in a telephone conversation on the day of the meeting, in the transcript made by Comrade Sojak? This really brings me to the end of my tether.

Surely such matters must be on record in some document or at least in a memorandum? However this came about – and I do not intend to start a discussion about the matter – I simply cannot make head or tail of it. But let me point out that the records of the Presidium meeting and the conclusion reached leave no doubt that the question of timing was not essential during that phase of Presidium business – attention was not focused on it. This can be seen from the stenographic record and also from the fact that no member of the Presidium took the matter up again later during the meeting. This too, proves that the matter was regarded primarily as a question of principle.

The discussion of the Presidium resulted in the formulation

of a common and unanimous standpoint regarding the course of preparations for a joint meeting, despite the fact that during the discussion some comrades had voiced other views. We had assumed that the definite date [of the joint meeting] would not be determined until we had discussed the replies of the Parties concerned to our proposal* and until the Presidium had formulated its attitude to the replies. None of us in the Presidium had considered that the proposed bilateral meetings which were to precede the joint conference could be unacceptable to our allies. On the contrary, we expected that in view of the complex situation and out of regard for our Party and our country, our request for a preliminary meeting with the CPSU would be given favourable consideration.

It would be wrong to overlook now our approach at the time to the question of the preparation of the joint conference. In our common appraisal of the state of affairs we saw no immediate threat of counter-revolution and no threat to the foundations of socialism or of socialist power. Contrary to numerous abusive implications we did not break off negotiations, we only proposed a different procedure.

Cierna

The July '68 Plenary Session instructed us to continue negotiating and to avoid a split. But the directives said we should first negotiate bilaterally, above all with Soviet Comrades, and attempt to strengthen the alliance of socialist states. I immediately suggested that our Presidium should meet with the Presidium of the CPSU. The Soviet comrades gave the matter very careful consideration and they deserve thanks for having taken part in the meeting of both the Presidia then arranged.

This meeting was at Cierna. As the leader of our delegation, I explained our standpoint once more and some issues were clarified at the meeting. We also agreed on a joint communiqué. The main outcome of this meeting was, as you know, the announcement of a further meeting, this time of all six Parties, which took place in Bratislava.

* Which was made on 12 July.

This again provides proof that our leadership was in no way interested in creating a split and that there was no split. On the contrary, a way was found leading to co-operation and to further negotiations about the approach to our internal problems. I never thought our problems could be solved in one single operation – the correct approach surely entails a series of well prepared measures.

I was not deceiving anybody, comrades, when I stated publicly and informed Party organs that there were no additional, secret clauses in the agreement. We did present a report to our Soviet comrades on our proposed methods of control of information media and on those problems of cadres to which we intended to give urgent attention during our pre-Congress Plenary Session. The session was to take place on the 29th, the date was chosen after the Bratislava meeting. We meant business and began to act accordingly. The K231* had in fact ceased to exist before the entry of armies. Its function, the pursuance of rehabilitation, was being taken over by the National Committees† with the approval of the leadership of K231. We were also firm in our determination not to permit the registration of KAN,‡ not to allow the existence of a new social-democratic party or any illegal activity.

We also discussed the internal question of cadres. Now, in the interests of the international movement, I would have never brought this matter into the open but for the present tendency to disclose things in such a manner. It stands to reason that I did not discuss this before a wider forum. If some people now want to censure me for not having submitted this matter for implementation through Party organs immediately after the Cierna meeting, they should think again and realize what would have happened at the time.

These questions were to be settled at the Plenary Session, which as I have said, had been convened for August 29th. On its agenda were the report to the Party Congress and the cadre proposals, so I insisted that the Presidium was to prepare on August 20th its brief for the Congress. Had the international discussion so required – and this I state quite openly – the

* An association of people unjustly prosecuted under par. 231.

† Local authorities.

‡ Club of committed non-party people.

Central Committee could have postponed the Congress by several weeks. This was the line agreed upon by the Presidium, and as First Secretary I tried to adhere to it. I declare once more that the entries of the armies on the night of August 21st came as a surprise to me, that I knew nothing of the decision to cross the border before the event. In fact I had discounted the possibility of such an action, especially after Bratislava, as we were in the course of preparing draft measures to be submitted to the next Plenary Session.

Brezhnev's Letter and the Meeting with Kadar

I wish to clarify another matter, if I may. I received the letter, which I am now accused of having kept secret, on August 19th. I received it, in company with Comrade Cernik, and I believe the time was 11 p.m. I do not know what dateline this letter bore, nor when it was despatched. You will find it in the enclosure. If you read it, you will find no mention of any ultimatum which should have been met by convening the Presidium to consider it the very same night. Naturally, it contained an urgent reminder about the implementation of practical measures and fulfilment of tasks about which we informed the Soviet comrades at Cierna.

A similar explanation applies to the circumstances of my talk with Comrade Kadar on August 17th, which was a Saturday. I informed both these parties about the measures being prepared for the Plenary Session. I read out the letter from our Soviet comrades to the Presidium on the following day – admittedly, the armies had by then entered our country, but there were no ulterior motives behind my timing. I had not known about their entry beforehand and therefore, believe me, saw no need to ponder whether the letter should be discussed as the first or the second point on the agenda. The letter speaks for itself – there is no evidence that I had any cause to discuss it with the Presidium that day.

It was for similar reasons that I was late in informing the Presidium about my talk with Comrade Kadar. As I said, we met on a Saturday. The record was made by Comrade Ujvary of the International Department, who then stayed with his family in Slovakia. The meeting of the Presidium took place on Tuesday, that is two days later. You can acquaint yourselves with the subject matter of our talk from the record which is available to you. I was really unable to inform the Presidium about the meeting otherwise than verbally. I could not submit a written report.

Invasion

In this atmosphere of surprised disbelief the Presidium formulated its declaration stating that the armies had come without the prior knowledge of our Government and Party leaders. We were indeed shocked, but we were not prompted by bad intentions – I just want to make that clear. Imagine yourselves in such a situation. I agree with the criticisms raised with hindsight by some comrades. The question is whether we should have supplemented what was essentially a statement of facts in the first part of the declaration by the passage about international relations* which, as many comrades are saying today, still has a negative effect upon normalization. That was indeed the only sentence of the declaration which was discussed by the Presidium from the points of view of both appraisal and publication. I considered the treaty about the temporary stationing of allied troops as a means of overcoming this as well as of establishing the relationship with the military facts, and I therefore gave it my full support.

The declaration of the Presidium included an appeal to Party members and to members of the armed forces to keep calm and not to offer any resistance to the invading armies. This was accepted by our army and by the public and thus the declaration served its purpose. So far as I could manage I made every effort, with President Svoboda, by telephone and other means, to ensure that this part of the declaration in particular was effected.

Obeying the Party's decisions, I have until now kept silent about questions arising out of the August events. But as by now many people are expressing and publicizing their opinions of that fateful night I hope that I too may make at least a few brief remarks here, at the Plenary session of the CPC Central Committee. I just want to clarify those issues which

* They called the invasion a grave setback, etc.

some people have obscured. It is true that there were two different reports to be dealt with at the Presidium's meeting. One – high time too – concerned preparations for the Party Congress; the other should have been prepared by Comrades Kolder and Indra. At the previous Presidium meeting they had been instructed to produce a draft proposal of measures to implement the conclusions reached at Cierna and Bratislava. But as you can see from the relevant documents, these comrades failed to submit the draft as briefed. Instead they merely submitted a report on the situation. This caused the Presidium great embarrassment and was much disapproved. During the discussion of the agenda I requested them once more in writing to submit a report as instructed. My request produced no direct response other than a demand that their report, though lacking recommendations, be discussed before all other business. I preferred to keep to the agenda and deal with the [first] report. A whole year passed before I read in *Rude Pravo* that Comrade Kolder had at the crucial meeting had the required draft proposals in his pocket and finally decided to publish them. Why comrades, do I take up this matter once more? I want to prevent any impression that I had in any way engineered this dispute over the order of the points on the agenda for that meeting. Please bear in mind that I had not foreseen the events of that fateful night.

It is not true that in the end I left the members of the Presidium to their own devices. Some of the comrades left for their departments with specific instructions to ensure the implementation of our decision to prevent any resistance to the entering armies. We also agreed that everyone should wait at his office and that others would go to a hotel.* I did this because I thought that someone would come to me on behalf of the allied troops and that we should accordingly convene a Presidium Meeting to decide on further action. At dawn, however, members of the State Security, and I stress *our* State Security, came to my office and arrested me, saying that within two hours it would be decided what was to be done to me. True enough it took more than two hours, but I want you to realize in all sincerity – and I implore you to see it this way – that I am mentioning this only because I do

* i.e., his enemies were not to go to their offices.

not want all the blame to be put on our allies. But consider: how could we work efficiently when the top Government and Party leaders were not in a position to tackle all the complex problems that had arisen?

I admit that I read the Soviet proclamation with sorrow and regret, because our comrades had not informed any of us four leaders of the Party and government. That is also why neither the Party nor the people could be prepared for the new situation. I mention this only because the matter is being discussed in public – it is often referred to on the radio and so on. I would not otherwise have come up with it, and I intend never to do so again. I am serious about this – let us leave it alone. Because, what is more, one cannot reach an objective judgment in the whole August affair if viewed only from the single viewpoint of our relations with our allies.

Summer '69

Comrades, this meeting of the CC should help us all – particularly the rank and file – to have done with that extremely complex night which has created such division. But let us beware of revenge and for the sake of Communists and the people of this country, let the division contribute to the positive development of socialism in our country and despite all, to the strengthening of our internationalist commitment as well. I agree that Soviet troops did not come here to put an end to our socialist development. They came, as comrades have said, out of fear for the fate of socialism in our country. I take it however – to put it quite openly – that they did not come here to bring about an end of all such political activity as aims at strengthening and developing socialism in our country. I am convinced that, particularly with regard to the positive attitude of our people, an active approach to the solution of our political and social problems is called for. Let no one try to use the Soviet Union as cover for an effort to revive dogmatism or to enforce stagnation in our political work. This would discredit the Soviet Union, not only in the eyes of our own people, but also in the eyes of the world. It would also hinder the work and the consolidation of the CC and its leadership. These were the principles on which we based our talks on the Moscow protocols and our effort to find a way out of this situation.

To claim that normalization began only after April 17th* is not an objective view. Please do not think that I do not fully appreciate the decisions of the April and May [69] Plenary Sessions. I do, for indeed I was one of their originators. Please bear this in mind when considering what I am about to say. Up to April there was a need to fulfil complex tasks aimed at normalization. That, I am not surprised, is also open to criticism. You too, are aware of the complexity of the problems which we had to overcome since those August days, since the first Plenary Session. At the very first Plenary Session, in August, we prevented the disruption of the Party, and upheld the decisions of the Vysocany Congress.† The stationing of Soviet troops in our country became the subject of a treaty, which required no small effort in our own political work. We made great efforts to work out a comprehensive programme of action under given conditions.

The outcome was the November resolution and the first phase of its implementation. Then followed several months of effort to bring about its acceptance by the Party, the people and the mass organizations.

Post-Invasion Tactics

I am open to criticism and it is true that there was much to criticize after August, where our implementation of the directives was concerned. One must however realize that it was necessary to proceed step by step in the solution of numerous grave problems. It is doubtful whether they could have been solved since then or whether they could be tackled now if the spade-work had not been done in the period under review. The November resolution was to serve as a base from which we could wage our war on both right-wing and sectarian extremists by emphasizing further positive solutions to problems of society. It was the starting point for efforts to renew the active unity of Party and people and to overcome the shortcomings and consequences of the past as well as for

* When he was removed from his First Secretaryship.

† Since declared invalid.

efforts to renew confidence in our allies among our people in general.

I regarded the November resolution as an optimal and balanced basis defining the limits within which the Party should work. I described it as such at the meeting of leaders in Kiev. My view of this was given to you at the January Plenary Session of the CC. It was my conviction that we should try again to establish a political mainstream in the Party and in society, which would undertake the solution of basic problems of our society in a creative way, in accordance with the needs and desires of the people. Having a positive programme enjoying the wide support of the masses, I believed we would be able to enter the inevitable struggle for positive Party activity and against both extremism with its disruptive effect and hostile forces attempting to keep alive anti-Soviet feelings, scepticism and distrust of socialism. I remain convinced that the sooner the Party gets down to such positive action, the more effective and impressive will be its struggle for its own integrity and for the elimination of harmful and hostile forces and tendencies among the people.

Comrades, in conclusion I wish to talk about the apportioning of personal responsibility for problems and shortcomings. I do not wish to, and I cannot, deny responsibility for the shortcomings and for the consequences of the policy of the CC arising from the period during which I held the post of First Secretary, of which I have already spoken. At the April Plenary Session [1969] I came to conclusions concerning my person. Today you will come to further conclusions and agree on further measures which have been dealt with by the Presidium and are today being discussed by the CC. I have accepted them at the Presidium meeting, I accept them here. I do however consider it necessary to comment on some published arguments relative to this matter.

I have already spoken about the accusation that I had kept secret the outcome of international consultation, or withheld information about them. I want to add that I have always acted in accordance with the procedure agreed upon. As a rule I always provide information; verbal and written – this is available. I therefore request that these facts be considered objectively. I am accused of not having actively stood by the

Party leadership in the implementation of agreed policy since April. As you know, immediately after April I made three speeches – all of them were published – in which I declared my support for the decisions of the April Plenum – and these I reiterate now. But after that I was not entrusted with any Party or other official work. I was even officially excluded from various public functions attended by members of the Presidium, such as Party meetings and other organized events. At first I thought that the intention was to keep me as a former First Secretary in the background. This I considered both right and quite natural: frankly I understood. Before the August anniversary I volunteered in the Presidium to voice in my constituency in an appropriate manner my disapproval of actions then being illegally planned. I was indeed advised to do this during a conversation with Dr Husak. I made the speech, but I am sorry to say that neither the Radio nor Television services, beside *Rude Pravo* [*sic*] published my view, though it had been distributed by *Ceteka.* At the time of the anniversary of the Slovak Rising I was instructed to attend as an official delegate, the regional celebrations held on August 23rd and 24th at Jankuv Vrsek, Uhrovec. As this was after the events in Prague and Brno* I had prepared speeches of which I had informed the comrades, in which I deplored such action and once more dissociated myself from such violence and vandalism shown by various elements. I had intended to speak out against attacks on the socialist system and against the misuse of my name for these ends which I had previously condemned. The Presidium however informed me that it was not suitable for me to speak in public or even to attend the celebrations. I accepted this, though I must admit that I did not consider this decision quite correct. I did not make any written declaration against the abuse of my name during the [Prague and Brno] events in place of the intended speeches which were to be made shortly after these events. As you know I was present when the Presidium of the Federal Assembly discussed the law, drafted by the Presidium of the CPC CC and the Government, aimed against such elements and I signed the Bill. Please let me remind you of this. I mention the matter hoping that a more correct view of the

* Anti-Soviet demonstrations.

question will be taken and that my activity since the May Plenary Session will be better understood. You are right to draw your conclusions, I am fully aware of this and I can fully grasp this with my faculty of reason. But I should not be pushed where, as you very well know, I have never belonged and do not belong even now, because in my opinion, this would not help the cause.

This also goes for the non-objective views about the circumstances which led to the choice of date for the Fourteenth Congress and the circumstances of the so-called Dubcek *volte face*. To this and to the assertion that the leadership had succumbed to rightist pressure or even formed an alliance with it – as the report puts it – I must reiterate the known fact – and here I beg your indulgence – that the Secretariat and the Presidium had never ruled out the possibility of convening the Party Congress at a politically suitable time, or even earlier if possible. We simply did not want to fix the date in advance before decisions to cope with the current situation had been taken.

With a view to some of the circumstances mentioned, Comrades Kolder and Indra approached me on their own initiative – they will no doubt confirm this – with a proposal to convene an Extraordinary Congress, and to decide on its date. This view was shared by the Department of Political Organization [of the CC] headed by Comrade Indra, which based its judgment on the positive evaluation of Regional Party Conferences. I listened to their view and, as agreed, immediately arranged, in view of the gravity of such a step, to call a consultative meeting even before the meeting of the Presidium. As arranged, I also invited the Secretary [*sic*] and Comrade Cernik, Comrade Bilak of Bratislava and others to attend this preliminary meeting. Thus was produced the draft for the Presidium and later for the CC. I request that the documents on these matters be brought in line with facts ['objectivized'] before being presented as a report to the Party.

I have one final request to the CC. Do not forget that in January we were not prompted by some individual subjective wish, but forced by the true state of the Party and society to set out on a new course in search of new and more effective ways of dealing with the problems of society. Let us therefore subject last year's experience to a thorough analysis, let us learn from it in order to counter the negative aspects of post-January development, as the present Party leadership is striving to do. This will enable us to make a renewed and more successful effort to fulfil the role bestowed by our times upon the Party. My activities in the past are now producing new consequences, new conclusions are being made. As I have said, I accept them. But once more I ask you not to put me where I do not belong. Do not ascribe to my personality and character motives which, as you very well know, are alien to me. I have tried even now to formulate an opinion of some problems and views, though as you will agree, this is no easy matter for me. In this case it is difficult to avoid a personal approach and in view of my involvement, I have not been able to do so. I am convinced that you will understand this, particularly as some questions are being put and argued in a non-objective way. Believe me, I want to be a useful member of our Party and the CC and wish to take an active part in socialist development and in the strengthening of our internationalist relations with socialist countries, and particularly with the Soviet Union towards which as you well know, I have especially close feelings because of my convictions. Let me end by declaring once more my unqualified support for the conclusions of the April and May Plenary Sessions of the Central Committee of the Czechoslovak Communist Party.

SHORT BIBLIOGRAPHY

Communism in Europe. Vol. II. Czechoslovakia: Zdenek Elias and Jaromir Netek. Ed. by William E. Griffith, Pergamon, Oxford 1966.

Communism National and International: H. Gordon Skilling. Ch 6 and 7, Canadian University Paperbooks, 1964.

Communist Strategy and Tactics in Czechoslovakia: 1918–48: Paul E. Zinner, Pall Mall, London 1963.

Communism in Czechoslovakia 1948–60: Edward Taborsky, Princeton, 1961.

Czechoslovakia 1968: Philip Windsor and Adam Roberts, Chatto and Windus, London 1969.

The Czechoslovak Crisis: Robert Rhodes James ed., Weidenfeld and Nicolson, London 1969.

Prague Spring: Z.A.B. Zeman, Penguin, London 1969.

La chute irrésistible d'Alexandre Dubcek: Pavel Tigrid, Calmann-Lévy, Paris 1969

Le printemps de Prague: Pavel Tigrid, Editions du Seuil, Paris 1968.

La liberté en sursis: Roger Garaudy, Fayard, Paris, 1968.

Dubcek's Blueprint for Freedom: Lunghi and Ello, Kimber, London 1969.

The Czech Black Book: Pall Mall, London 1969.

Prague's 200 Days: Harry Schwartz, Pall Mall, London 1969.

L'Hérésie impossible: Michel Tatu, Grasset, Paris 1968.

Vybrane prejavy prveho Tajomnika UV KSC sudruha Alexandra Dubceka: Bratislava, 1968.

SOURCE NOTES

Chapter One

1 *Guardian*, 31 June 1969. This was the standard wage of the time.
2 T. G. Masaryk, *The Making of a State* (Allen and Unwin, London 1927), p. 21.
3 *Ibid.*, p. 41.
4 Foreign Relations of the US 1918, Supplement I, Vol I, p. 809.
5 Masaryk, *op. cit.*, p. 209.
6 *Ibid.*, p. 208.
7 *Ibid.*, p. 208.
8 *Ibid.*, p. 208.
9 G. A. Macartney and A. W. Palmer, *Independent East Europe* (Macmillan, London 1966), p. 87.
10 For considerable detail on Interhelpo I am grateful to Deryck Viney for permission to use his excellent essay on Dubcek in *Studies of Comparative Communism*, (University of Southern California, July–August 1969). See also Pavel Pollak's definitive work: *Internacionalna pomoc ceskoslovenskeho proletariatu narodom SSSR* (Bratislava, 1961).
11 *The Village Commune*, pamphlet (Petrograd 1917).
12 Lenin, *Works*, 4th Ed., (Moscow 1950), Vol 30, p. 176.
13 CPSU V. Rezoliutskiakh (1953 ed.) Vol. 2, p. 547.
14 Pollak, *op. cit.*, 31 March 1969.
15 *Guardian*, 31 March 1969.
16 Robert Conquest, *The Great Terror* (Macmillan, London 1968), p. 278.
17 Leonhard, *Child of the Revolution* (Collins, London 1959).

Chapter Two

1 G. A. Macartney, *Hungary and her Successors,* (Oxford University Press 1937), p. 130.
2 *Prispevky,* No 2, March 1958.
3 *Prispevky,* No 5, 1961, p. 759.
See also *Communism in Europe,* ed. Griffiths, (Pergamon, Oxford 1966), Vol 2, p. 169.
4 *Rude Pravo,* 6 January 1968.
5 The Kosice Programme. Quoted from 'Programme of the First Home Government of the Republic, a Government of the National Front of Czechs and Slovaks', adopted on 5 April 1945 in Kosice, the regional town of Eastern Slovakia. Published by the Czechoslovak Ministry of Information, April 1945.

Chapter Three

1 Vlastislav Lacina, On the Character and Results of the Agrarian Democratic Transformation in Czechoslovakia, *Casopis Historicky* No 3, June 1962.
2 29 February 1968, speech to the former participants of the 1948 Farmers' Congress, at Hradcany Castle, Prague.
3 *Smer,* 17 July 1953.
4 *Smer,* 12 June 1954.
5 Ladislav Mnacko, *The Seventh Night* (Dent, London 1969), p. 48. And members of the National Front in Banska Bystrica.
6 Griffiths, *op. cit.,* p. 218.
7 *Smer,* 11 July 1953.
8 *Ibid.*
9 *Smer,* 12 June 1954.
10 Evzen Loebl, *Sentenced and Tried,* (Elek, London, 1969), *passim.*
11 *Nova Mysl,* 3 June 1968 and 10 July 1968.
12 *Rude Pravo,* 13 June 1956; Rudolf Barak to Party Conference.
13 *Smer,* 12 June 1954.
14 *Nova Mysl,* ibid.
15 Taborsky, *Communism in Czechoslovakia* 1948–60, (Princeton, 1961), p. 131.

16 *Smer*, 12 June 1954.
17 *Smer*, 24 May 1954.
18 *Smer*, 11 July 1953.

Chapter Four

1 *Hlas Ludu,* Roc 6, c 34, sI a 2, 1959.
2 *Hlas Ludu,* Roc 7, c 13, SI, 1960.
3 *Hlas Ludu,* 6 January 1960.
4 *Hlas Ludu,* 4 May 1960.
5 *Pravda* (Bratislava), 23 February 1961.
6 *Rude Pravo,* 13 February 1962.
7 Simunek, quoted in *Rude Pravo,* 17 November 1960.
8 *Zivot Strany,* 1960, no 12, pp. 727–30.
See also *Hlas Ludu,* 30 March 1960, and 4 May 1960.
9 *Rude Pravo,* 15 May 1962.
10 *Zivot Strany,* 1962, no 11, pp. 627–33.
11 *Rude Pravo,* 18 December 1952.
12 To the Central Committee of the Czechoslovak Communist Party, November 1961, quoted in *Rude Pravo,* 21 November 1961.
13 *Rude Pravo,* 21 April 1962.

Chapter Five

1 *Rude Pravo,* 7 March 1963.
2 Pavel Kohout, *Pravda* (Bratislava), 14 April 1968.
3 *Pravda* (Bratislava), 28 March 1963 and 8 May 1963.
4 *Ibid.*, 3 June 1963.
5 *Rude Pravo,* 13 June 1963.
6 *Ibid.*
7 *Rude Pravo,* 27 June 1963.
8 *Pravda* (Bratislava), 20 September 1963.
9 *Pravda* (Bratislava), 28 June 1963.
10 *Rocnicke Noviny,* 29 August 1963.
11 *Rude Pravo,* 21 September 1963.
12 *Rude Pravo,* 29 January 1964
13 *Rude Pravo,* 17 December 1963.
14 *Rude Pravo,* 13 December 1963.
15 *Problems of Communism,* May–June 1964.

Chapter Six

1 To Slovak Party Congress, May 1966. See *Pravda* (Bratislava), 15 May 1966.
2 Michael Pecho, *Pravda* (Bratislava), 18 July 1967.
3 *Pravda* (Bratislava), 19 June 1964.
4 *Ibid.*
5 *Hlas Ludu*, 17 April 1966.
6 *Kulturni Zivot*, throughout 1963–7: eg: No. 42; 16 November 1963; 7 December 1963.
7 *Pravda* (Bratislava), 14 December 1963.
8 *Ibid.*
9 To Slovak Party Congress, May 1966.
10 *Ibid.*
11 *Ibid.*
12 *Ibid.*
13 *Hlas Ludu*, 17 April 1966.
14 *Pravda* (Bratislava), 12 April 1967.
15 Ota Sik.
16 To Slovak Party Congress, May 1966.
17 *Hlas Ludu*, 17 April 1966.
18 Ota Sik, *ibid.*
19 Quoted by Louis Barcata, *Die Presse*, 5 October 1967.
20 Riveles, *Problems of Communism*, May–June 1968.
21 *Pravda* (Bratislava), 3 June 1964.
22 *Pravda* (Bratislava), 11 June 1964.
23 *Ibid.*
24 *Pravda* (Bratislava), 31 October 1967.
25 *Pravda* (Bratislava), 22 March 1967.

Chapter Seven

1 *Pravda* (Bratislava), 10 June 1967.
2 *Pravda* (Bratislava), 18 November 1967.
3 *Ibid.*
4 See Harry Schwartz, *Prague's 200 Days*, (Pall Mall, London 1969), p. 63
5 Quoted by Pavel Tigrid, 'Czechoslovakia, Agony of a Nation', *Survey*, Autumn 1969.

6 *Pravda* (Bratislava), 14 December 1963.
7 Tigrid, *La Chute Irrésistible d'Alexandre Dubcek*, Calmann-Lévy, Paris 1969, p. 54.

Chapter Eight

1 Quoted by Harry Schwartz in *Prague's 200 Days* (Pall Mall, London, 1969), p. 79.
2 To the Central Committee, 26 September 1969. See Appendix.
3 *New York Times Magazine*, 12 January 1969.
4 To Party Conference, Brno, 16 March. *Rude Pravo*, 17 March 1968.
5 Radio Free Europe monitoring of Radio Prague, 6 April 1968.
6 See H. Schwartz, *ibid.*, p. 77.
7 *Rude Pravo*, 11 April 1968.
8 RFE monitoring, 6 April 1968.
9 To Prague Aktiv, 8 April 1968.
10 *Rude Pravo*, 11 April 1968.
11 Radio Prague and Radio Bratislava, RFE monitoring.
12 For entire speech see *Dubcek Blueprint for Freedom* (Kimber, London 1969).
13 RFE monitoring, 6 April 1968.
14 RFE monitoring, 3 June 1968.
15 RFE monitoring, 26 June 1968.
16 To a Party Meeting in the Ninth District of Prague.
17 RFE monitoring, 3 June 1968.

Chapter Nine

1 *Le Monde*, 25 October 1969.
2 *Pravda* (Moscow), 30 March 1968.
3 Radio Prague, 27 July 1968, RFE monitoring.
4 'Czechoslovakia, Agony of a Nation', by Pavel Tigrid, *Survey*, Autumn 1969. See this article for much of the information on Cierna.
5 *Rude Pravo*, clandestine, legal edition, 23 August 1968.
6 Radio Prague, 2 August 1968, RFE monitoring.

7 Tigrid, *La Chute,* p. 18.
8 Radio Prague, 2 August 1968, RFE monitoring.
9 *Ibid.,* 20 July 1968.
10 *Rude Pravo,* 11 October 1969.
11 *Le Monde, ibid.*

Chapter Ten

1 *Rude Pravo,* clandestine, legal edition, 23 August 1968.
2 To the Central Committee, 26 September 1969. See Appendix 2.
3 Smrkovsky, Radio Prague, 29 August 1968. For full text see *The Czech Black Book.*
4 For full text of The Moscow Protocol see Windsor and Roberts, *ibid.*

Chapter Eleven

1 *Rude Pravo,* 7 December 1968.
2 See *Dubcek Blueprint for Freedom,* (Kimber, London 1968). Appendix. Reprinted by permission of the BBC Monitoring Service.
3 *The Times,* 5 January 1969.
4 Radio Prague, 5 January 1969, RFE monitoring.
5 *Rude Pravo,* 9 January 1969.
6 *Ibid.*
7 *Reporter* (Prague), 30 January 1969.
8 Ceteka, 28 January 1969.
9 *Pravda,* (Bratislava), 11 February 1969.

Chapter Twelve

1 Pavel Tigrid, *op. cit.,* see Chapter 12.
2 *The Times,* 4 April 1969.
3 *Ibid.*
4 *The Times,* 18 April 1969.
5 *The Times,* 29 August 1969.
6 Pavel Tigrid, *op. cit.,* p. 259.

Chapter Thirteen

1 *Der Spiegel*, 18 March 1968.
2 *L'Humanité*, April 1968.
3 *Ibid.*
4 Vaclav Havel, 'On the subject of opposition', *Literarni Listy*, 4 April 1968. Ivan Svitak, 'A Conference marked the sign of the times', *Filmove a Televize Noviny*, 4 April 1968.
5 *Kulturni Zivot*, 5 April 1968, and *Kulturni Noviny*, 5 April 1968.
6 Mlynar, *Rude Pravo*, 26 March 1968.
7 The Action Programme; the entire document may be found in *Dubcek's Blueprint for Freedom* (as above).
8 Radio Prague, 6 April 1968. RFE monitoring.
9 Dubcek's speech to Central Committee, 31 May-1 June, see *Blueprint*.
10 *Ibid.*
11 *Ibid.*
12 *Ibid.*
13 *Dubcek's Blueprint for Freedom* (as above). Entire Action Programme is reproduced.
14 Radio Prague, 18 July 1968, RFE monitoring.
15 Radio Prague, 14 September 1968.

INDEX